THE RESHAPING OF EVERYDAY LIFE

1790–1840

THE EVERYDAY LIFE IN AMERICA SERIES

EDITED BY

RICHARD BALKIN

Detail from the overmantel of the Van Bergen Farm in New York's Catskill Mountains, 1735. Artist unknown. (*N. Y. State Historical Association, Cooperstown, N. Y.*)

The
Reshaping of
Everyday Life
1790-1840

JACK LARKIN

1817
Harper & Row, Publishers, New York
Cambridge, Philadelphia, San Francisco
London, Mexico City, São Paulo, Singapore, Sydney

Designed by: Sidney Feinberg

Library of Congress Cataloging in Publication Data
Larkin, Jack, 1943–
  The reshaping of everyday life, 1790–1840.
  Includes index.
  1. United States—Social life and customs—1783–1865.
1. Title.
E164.L27   1988   973.4   87-46152
ISBN 0-06-015905-7

---

89 90 91 92 CC / HC 10 9 8 7 6 5 4 3 2

To Barbara, and to the memory of my father-in-law

CONTENTS

Illustrations follow page 174.

ACKNOWLEDGMENTS

For seventeen years I have found Old Sturbridge Village, an institution devoted to re-creating a living American past, a rewarding and often inspiring place in which to pursue the historian's craft. I owe my friends and colleagues there a great deal. Alberta Sebolt George, Executive Vice President, and John Worrell, Director of Research, gave me generous and enthusiastic support throughout the writing of this book. Warren Leon, John Worrell, Caroline Fuller Sloat, Myron Stachiw, David Simmons, Andrew Baker and Holly Varden Izard read and commented on various draft chapters of the manuscript and discussed its ideas with me, giving me the benefit of their varied scholarly expertise. Another friend and colleague, Robert A. Gross of Amherst College, gave an earlier draft of the manuscript an illuminating and helpful critique. Theresa Percy and the staff of the Old Sturbridge Village Research Library dealt graciously and helpfully with my heavy demands on their resources. Richard Balkin, editor of the Everyday Life series, and Hugh Van Dusen of Harper & Row were patient with my lengthy labors of research, writing and rewriting. My sons, Timothy and Daniel, were always interested in the strange things I was writing about. But I owe the greatest debt to my wife, Barbara, who encouraged me to begin this project, read and edited innumerable drafts, put up with my preoccupation, and sustained my spirits.

INTRODUCTION

"The life of every community," wrote Francis Underwood, nineteenth-century America's profoundest student of everyday life, "is made up of infinite details." The history of those "infinite details" was once the province only of antiquarians. Everyday life consisted of the curious bits and pieces that remained after the really important subjects—wars, political struggles, economic cataclysms, the biographies of powerful men—had been chronicled. But there is another way to look at this subject, to see it as the history not of the trivial but of the taken-for-granted.

Most Americans—farmers, artisans and laborers, women and children—were enmeshed in the myriad ordinary concerns of their lives: the routines and seasons of work, the chances of sickness and death, times of marriage and childbirth, the familiar spaces and furnishings of their houses, their ways of traveling, singing and dancing, eating and dressing, sex and cleanliness, their visits and social gatherings. Although their lives were deeply affected by the great events and transformations that are rightly the most powerful themes of American history, their concern with them was intermittent. Everyday life should not be exalted above other historical concerns. But it should not be ignored.

To discover what people in the past took for granted in their lives is to give personal, experiential meaning to the bare bones of statistical description and generalization. Limits on the evidence and scope of historical inquiry mean that only a tiny fraction of the lives of past Americans can be recovered and understood in any detail. "Every individual," wrote another enormously perceptive portrayer of ordinary life, Harriet Beecher Stowe, "is part and parcel of a great picture of the society in which he lives and acts, and his life cannot be painted without reproducing the picture of the world he lived in." Capturing the commonplaces of past experience is a route to a fuller human understanding.

The beginning and ending years of this book, between the patrician leadership of George Washington and the democratic hoopla of the "log cabin and hard cider" campaign that elected William Henry Harrison, roughly mark off a time of often startling changes. During these decades the American people created a new national government, and a distinctive party system and culture of democratic politics. Their numbers continued to grow rapidly, as they had in the eighteenth century, nearly quadrupling between 1790 and 1840. They moved westward at an unprecedented speed, vigorously and often violently expanding the territorial limits of their society almost threefold. Americans built a national system of transportation on roads and rivers well before the railroad, and strikingly speeded up travel and the movement of goods and information. A new industrial economy emerged in the North, based on the organization of mass production in cities and rural communities alike and the first stages of mechanization; the calculating ways of the marketplace and the networks of commerce penetrated ever farther into the countryside. Reinvigorated by the increasing importance of cotton to industrial production, the slave-labor economy of the South expanded enormously. Measured by the total output of goods and services, Americans' average income per capita rose significantly. Yet the benefits of economic growth were distributed with increasing inequality. The gap between the richest and the poorest Americans grew ever wider.

Successive waves of religious enthusiasm, the "Second Great Awakening," washed over communities in every region and created a powerful evangelical Protestant piety. What many Americans called a "spirit of reform" prompted them to examine and often to reconstruct their social arrangements and patterns of behavior—most explosively slavery, but also drink, schooling and childrearing, dietary and sexual habits, the role of women and of wage labor, and the care of criminals and the insane. They created an "age of association," covering much of the nation with thousands of voluntary associations from sewing circles to lyceums to Masonic lodges, and establishing new social and economic institutions on a state and national level.

But at the threshold of the nineteenth century, Americans still lived in a world of small scale and scarcity. People, goods and information moved slowly. The tools they used and the routines of their work, their materials and sources of power, would have been immediately recognizable to a man or woman of the seventeenth century.

Their lives continued to be constrained by the weather and the seasons. While assembling their energies to tame a continent they were still profoundly tied to the agricultural calendars of their localities, and each year's jagged alternations of heat and cold, its recurring times of health and sickness, birth, marriage and death.

The physical texture of American life was far closer to that in the villages of many third-world countries today than to anything in the present-day United States. Everywhere the nights were intensely dark and the stars intensely bright. Most houses were small and poorly lit. Americans were usually dirty and often insect-ridden. Smells—of the barnyard and stable, tannery and tavern, house and hearth, privy and chamber pot—

were pungent and profuse. Food was often heavy and coarse; most meat was heavily salted, tastes were harsh. Hard physical exertion was an ordinary and unremarkable part of life for all but a few. Disease and bodily discomfort could rarely be cured, only endured, and death was an early and frequent visitor. Childbirth posed significant risks to health and life. So did many kinds of work. The extremes of cold and heat could not easily be escaped, indoors or out. Courting couples acted with a freedom that would surprise those nostalgic for the "good old days" of sexual restraint. Heavy drinking was part of almost every social gathering, and violent confrontations and blood sports were common in public life.

Many Americans reshaped much of their everyday world in these years. Families changed their patterns of childbearing and their ways of dealing with childbirth, marriage and death. The scale, rhythms and tools of work altered for many. Men and women traveled faster, more frequently and more dangerously. Americans curtailed their drinking and established new standards of propriety in social gatherings and new barriers of self-control in private encounters. They ate, dressed and furnished their houses more abundantly. Ordinary people abandoned old signs of deference and took up objects and customs that had once been the exclusive possessions of the "better sort." Washing, even bathing, became more common.

Still, much remained in the old ways. The poorest Americans —most prominently the one-seventh of the population who were slaves, but also city laborers and the most marginal rural folk—had only a small share in "progress and refinement." The material thresholds and social boundaries of their lives changed very slowly. Cleanliness and sobriety made their way very unevenly through American society. Dirt and disorder remained easy to find. Human muscles and draft animals still did most of the nation's work. For all Americans, despite the struggles of both patients and healers, the risks of disease and death altered very little. Yet looking back, reminiscing Americans knew that they had seen important change in the fundamental arrangements of life, a real if partial "amelioration of society."

The line between everyday life and the wider themes of social transformation is not always easy to draw, but this book tries to maintain its focus on the taken-for-granted, the ordinary aspects of social existence. Aiming principally at an audience of nonspecialists, it avoids historiographical debates and most of the technical details of analysis and evidence. Consequently, it has run the risks of summarizing, synthesizing and sometimes simplifying a great deal of excellent and specialized scholarship.

One of this book's major concerns is descriptive—to evoke the often gritty texture of life as Americans of the early nineteenth century experienced it. The other is interpretive—to find and show underlying patterns of historical change in the "infinite details" of social and material arrangements. It tries to weave the disparate threads of ordinary life into the already rich and complicated tapestry of American history during a period which Stowe long ago recognized as "a transition time of society."

1

"A BUSY, BUSTLING, INDUSTRIOUS POPULATION"

"A Vast Continent"

TRAVELERS often saw the shape and scale of American life more clearly than Americans themselves, who took much about their country for granted. As an experiment in republican government, a new society shaping itself in explicit contrast to the Old World, the young United States was an irresistible magnet for curious Britons and Europeans. Arriving, they were often stunned by the size of the United States, and surprised by the diversity of its people.

The United States was already an enormous country in 1790, particularly when scaled against the slowness and hazards of travel, and over the next five decades it became much larger. After the Revolution the new nation extended twelve hundred miles from north to south, from Maine to Georgia; by 1840 its settled territory stretched a thousand miles west of New York City. It was, wrote the Englishwoman Frances Trollope, "a vast continent, by far the greatest part of which is still in the state in which nature left it." The American people were "a busy, bustling, industrious population, hacking and hewing their way" as they built their society.

Incoming travelers—generally men and a few women of means and education—usually landed in New York, Boston or Philadelphia. They found these commercial cities provincial compared with London or Paris, but much of what they saw seemed comfortably familiar. They did not have to go far into the countryside, however, before they came into much stranger terrain, where there were crops and livestock, faces and speech, landscapes and houses, and ways of greeting and entertaining strangers that they had never encountered before.

"The inhabitants of the cities in the United States," observed another English traveler, Frederick Marryat, in 1835, knew "as little of what is passing in Arkansas and Alabama" as London-bred Cockneys did of the "manners and customs" of the most remote villages of the British Isles. Even for Americans, long-distance travel across their country was sometimes disconcerting. They knew more about each other's lives and conditions than they had in the eighteenth century, but their nation was still a federation of diverse regional cultures and economies. Over their "immense amount of territory," Marryat thought, Americans lived in a great diversity of conditions and manners, "running from a state of refinement," in places like Boston and Philadelphia, "down to one of positive barbarism" in the far stretches of the back country.

When early-nineteenth-century Americans or their visitors talked about the geography of the country, they spoke in terms of four principal regions. Smallest, most densely settled and farthest north was New England, or the "Eastern States": Rhode Island, Connecticut, Massachusetts, New Hampshire, Vermont and, by 1820, Maine. Next came the "Middle States": New York, New Jersey and Pennsylvania. With New England, they sometimes made up "the North." "At the South" were the slave states—originally Maryland, Delaware, Virginia, North and South Carolina and Georgia, then expanding with the annexation and settlement of Louisiana, Mississippi and Alabama. In the years before 1840 "the West" began in the last-settled western sections of New York and Pennsylvania and went on to include Ohio, Indiana, Illinois and just-settled Michigan. Between these states and the deep South were Kentucky, Tennessee, Missouri and frontier Arkansas. They were also slaveholding states, but had smaller black populations and fewer plantations than the states of the deep South. They were sometimes "the upper South" and sometimes referred to as part of the West. Much of the South as well as the West was frontier, or sparsely settled country, throughout the first half of the nineteenth century, with great stretches of uncleared original forest, new fields full of tree stumps and primitive roads.

The growth of the nation's population was as astonishing as that of its territory. Americans had not only abundant land but —due to their habits of relatively early and near-universal marriage—substantially higher birthrates than Europeans did. Their numbers grew from just under four million in 1790 to more than seventeen million in 1840.

Even before the great waves of immigration that began in the mid-1840s, Americans were a heterogeneous people. Scrutiny of the federal census of 1790, classifying the last names of household heads by national origin, has provided a roughly accurate estimate of their diversity. Women and men of English descent, whose ancestors were the seventeenth-century settlers of the Chesapeake, New England, and Quaker Pennsylvania, were the largest single group of Americans, amounting to about half the population. Next in numbers—counted but not named on a separate section of the census—came the involuntary immigrants, the African-born and -descended slaves and free blacks who made up a little over one-sixth of the whole. Many at the turn of the eighteenth century were still fresh from Africa. Totaling almost another one-sixth were Americans whose ancestors were eighteenth-century immigrants from the Celtic regions of the British Isles—the Scotch-Irish from Ulster, the Scottish, the southern Irish and the Welsh. In eastern Pennsylvania and nearby parts of Maryland and New Jersey lived the Germans, whose eighteenth-century origins were in the farming villages of central and southern Germany. Many of them still talked of crops, worshiped, quarreled and courted in their distinctive "Deitsch" dialect. Dutch-Americans, some of them still speaking the language of Nieuw Amsterdam, were unmistakable in New York's Hudson River Valley and northern New Jersey.

New England was America's most homogeneous region, where well over eighty percent of the people were of English ancestry. In Pennsylvania, "the English" were only the third-largest group, outnumbered both by the Germans and the Celtic-Americans as a whole. In the South, Anglo-Americans and Afro-Americans dominated the eastern seaboard, while the Scotch-Irish, Scottish and Irish lived in the newer settlements west of the mountains. In parts of inland North and South Carolina a passerby might even hear Highland Gaelic. In 1803, the Louisiana Purchase added to the American mixture a distinctive population of planters, bayou farmers and fishermen who spoke Cajun French. Starting in the 1820s the beginning of a new Celtic immigration to the North was visible. Pushed by severe rural poverty, Irishmen were coming to the United States as laborers to build the canals and railroads. Their numbers, however, represented only a premonitory trickle compared to the flood that was to begin after 1845.

Not listed on the census returns for 1790 or any other year were the original settlers, the American Indians. They may have numbered half a million, widely and often thinly spread across the American continent. For more than two centuries, devastating European diseases had reduced their numbers and the relentless and usually violent encroachment of European settlement had pushed them west or into shrinking enclaves. With almost two hundred different languages, Indian peoples lived in a dizzying variety of patterns of life. On the United States' western borders there was constant contact, trade, negotiation and conflict between white and red Americans. In the northeastern sections of the United States, relatively few Native Americans remained. Those who stayed on usually lived partially assimilated lives on the margins of the dominant society. In New England, for example, communities remained of a few hundred each of Abnakis, Pequots, Mohegans, Penobscots, Narragansetts, Passamaquoddies and Wampanoags. They preserved their languages and many of their ancient crafts, traveling still in birch-bark canoes and trading intricately woven baskets with their white neighbors, but lived in frame houses and dressed in ways, a New England publisher observed, that "resemble that of the lower orders in our cities." Some of the young Wampanoag men and women of Mashpee, in Massachusetts, had gone further and "forgotten their ancient names and nearly all the Indian language."

Up to the 1830s the largest American Indian concentrations within the states of the Union were the complex agricultural societies of the "Five Civilized Tribes," the Creeks, Cherokees, Choctaws, Chickasaws and Seminoles who lived on tribal territories guaranteed by treaty in parts of Georgia, Mississippi, Alabama and the Carolinas. Responding to governmental pressures and the efforts of missionaries, they had created communities which combined traditional Indian and white American ways of life—with a written language, a formal constitution, "civilized" housing, furniture and clothing, even plantation agriculture and slavery. But this proved no security. Land-hungry white Americans would not leave them in peace. The Indian Removal Act of 1830 legitimized a campaign of economic pressure, political trickery and eventually military force aimed at drawing them off their increasingly valuable land to the "Indian Territory" in what is now Oklahoma. President Andrew Jackson, the old Indian fighter, carried out their removal with unrelenting determination. Their harrowing journeys westward totaling some sixty thousand people, the largest forced migrations in American history, took two years or more. Disease and exposure killed upward of one in ten. In their histories, they remembered it as the "Trail of Tears." After the United States Army forced the last resisting groups of the Creek and Cherokee nations off their land in the late 1830s, the last independent Indian presence disappeared from the states of the Union.

Americans were a predominantly rural people. In 1790, only one American in twenty lived in a place of more than twenty-five hundred people—and some of these were communities whose large areas held a predominantly scattered population. American cities grew rapidly in the next five decades, but as late as 1840, no more than one in nine were urban even in this modest sense.

When she spoke of Americans "hacking and hewing their way," Mrs. Trollope was literally correct. The early-nineteenth-century landscape was the result of an immense labor of land clearing that had begun early in the seventeenth century. Americans on long-occupied farms knew, as a New England farmer's son said, that they were "the result of the labor of generations." Families in the West lived in small clearings next to stands of trees that had been "girdled," their bark cut through so that they would die, fall and rot to clear a new farm field. Americans had spent uncounted, exhausting hours with fire and ax, oxcart and stone drag, "making land," carving farms out of the forest. In the first half of the nineteenth century, as they completed the settlement of the wooded eastern portion of the "vast continent," their labor came to a climax. Shaped by their inheritance of land making, most Americans were deadly enemies of trees and woodlands. They vastly preferred the beauty of "a newly cleared piece of ground," noted the Englishman Godfrey Vigne in 1833, to "the immense forests" or picturesque wooded prospects that remained. Most American farmers, thought the British visitor Margaret Hall, "would scarcely allow a tree to stand" near their houses.

European travelers were accustomed to seeing closely settled agricultural communities, but they soon learned that the majority of American families lived well apart from each other, on their own farmsteads. "We have no villages in America," Albert Gallatin, who had been Jefferson's secretary of the treasury, told the Frenchman Alexis de Tocqueville in 1831, "that is to say none inhabited by people who cultivate the land." American farmers' houses were instead "scattered all over the country."

Most American rural communities were not sharply defined in space. Churches, stores and taverns were often strung along the roads, and families socialized and traded in country neighborhoods with vague boundaries. New Englanders continued to live closer together than other rural Americans, but most of them had long since abandoned their compact agricultural villages of the seventeenth century. As the Massachusetts clergyman Peter Whitney put it in 1796, their houses too "were scattered over the place without much order" on the roads that led to each community's centrally located meetinghouse and common. Families in the more thickly settled and cleared regions of America usually lived in sight of their nearest neighbors' houses, and at night could see the faint gleam of their candles. To the south and west dwellings became dispersed ever more thinly, as an early Western settler recalled, in "little clearings detached from each other by intervening forest, through which foot paths, bridle paths, and narrow wagon roads obstructed with stumps, wound their way."

What European observers might "take for villages," continued Gallatin, "had better be called towns as they are inhabited by shopkeepers, craftsmen, and lawyers." Clustered settlements in America were almost always outposts of commerce or industry. In the Northern countryside small crossroads communities and "center villages" arose by the hundreds after 1800 as places where farmers came to trade and find services; the appearance of these rural commercial places signaled the birth of the American small town.

Another kind of village was emerging alongside them in the rural landscape. Francis Alexander's 1822 painting of *Globe Village* in Southbridge, Massachusetts, shows a small cluster of wooden two- and three-story buildings in a landscape of farm fields and small woodlots. (See frontispiece.) This settlement too was rural, but not agricultural. Its small water-powered factory buildings, two- and four-family houses, and store were part of the first phase of America's Industrial Revolution. "The manufacturing operations of the United States," wrote the Rhode Island industrialist Zachariah Allen in 1829, "are carried on in little hamlets . . . around the water fall which serves to turn the mill wheel." From Pennsylvania to southern New Hampshire, "mill villages" were built near many small and medium-sized streams. Beginning in the 1790s and with accelerated pace after 1820, rural factories harnessed waterwheels to pulleys and belts to drive machinery for spinning and weaving cotton and wool, or turning chair legs and gun barrels. Around the mills clustered the nation's first communities of factory workers.

In 1823 the site of Lowell was only a few farmers' fields being surveyed in an outlying corner of rural Chelmsford, Massachusetts. Less than two decades later, after the great falls of the Merrimack River had been harnessed, it was a true industrial city of twenty thousand, whose factories and boardinghouses reflected the organization of work, and the harnessing of power, on an unprecedented scale.

Gallatin might have admitted one important exception to his observation. There were true agricultural villages in America, and they were in the South. "The quarters of the slaves," noted the Englishman Isaac Weld in 1796, "give the residence of each planter the appearance of a little village," and travelers over the decades echoed him. Slave cabins on larger plantations were built close together along small "streets" in double or single rows, usually under the shadow of the planter family's "great house." Each quarter was a small, dense community of black households, whose adults left every morning for work in the fields.

Five seaport cities—New York, Philadelphia, New Orleans, Baltimore and Boston—each contained 90,000 people or more by 1840. New York City, with 312,000 inhabitants, "the great commercial maelstrom of the western world," as some Americans called it, was the largest. The other urban places of the United States—smaller ports on the coast, towns on inland rivers or major road junctions—ranged from 50,000 people on down.

American cities were important far beyond their size; streams of goods, people, livestock, information and ideas flowed between them and the villages and farms. They were settlements of merchants and artisans, laborers and mariners, teamsters and boatmen, places where goods were bought and sold, moved and made. Early-nineteenth-century urban settlements were "walking cities," crowded and relatively small in area. They had to be compact, because almost all city dwellers walked everywhere and the transportation of goods was slow. Their streets were crowded with men and women afoot, and iron-tired wagons grated noisily over the paving stones. When Zadoc Long of Maine stayed in Boston to purchase goods for his country store, he complained about the noise making it hard to sleep. Cities were noisier, dirtier and more unhealthy than rural communities, but far more exciting, more anonymous, quicker-paced and immersed in cash and trade. They were the focal points of culture as well as commerce. Just as cities took in agricultural produce and rural migrants, they exported not only goods but books and dress fashions, songs and dances, child-rearing ideas and furnishing styles to the countryside.

"In Our Family"

Just after Chloe Peck was married in Rochester, New York, in 1820, she wrote to her sister of "our family, which consists of 7 persons." Living and eating together in the Pecks' establishment were the newly wedded couple and five unrelated men and boys—the journeymen and apprentices of Everard Peck's bookbinding shop. Today "family" denotes people bound together by marriage and kinship, and "household" describes a group residing and taking their meals together, but early-nineteenth-century Americans almost invariably echoed Chloe Peck in describing their domestic groups as their "families," suggesting their sense of the household's functional unity. Assuming the patriarchal authority that traditionally went to the household's male head, Peck a few years later wrote of his strong sense of responsibility for "the welfare of those connected with us, and the harmony and good order of our family."

In the years around 1800, the household's scale and organization still utterly dominated the ordinary business of life. Americans worked as well as lived in families that were tied to farms, artisans' shops and stores. With their sharing meals, sleeping quarters and often beds, households were the primary settings for production as well as consumption. Americans in families also took care of the sick, the orphaned, the widowed and the destitute. Relationships of work or caretaking were not necessarily smoother or more loving than those in later, larger organizations, but they were certainly more intimate.

American families, even in what travelers called "this land of equality" and democratic manners, spanned a vast economic range. In the topmost ranks were the households of the most successful urban merchants, large plantation owners, some "great" farmers in the North and a few professional men. They ranged downward from "middling" farmers, storekeepers and successful artisans to smaller, hard-pressed "common" farmers and "mechanics," landless laborers and slaves.

Because Americans' birthrates were high in the early nineteenth century, children were everywhere. In 1800, the Connecticut clergyman Timothy Dwight observed that the seacoast town of Marblehead, Massachusetts, "abounds in children," and he set himself to taking an informal census as he passed through: "Several times we stopped our carriage to observe and count them. At one door we numbered eleven, differing very little in their stature, and at every door found a new flock." Dwight thought that the families of Marblehead's farmer-fishermen were exceptionally large, even by the standards of his time; but a twentieth-century observer passing through any community of the early Republic would have shared his wonderment. The population of the United States was very young. In 1980 the mythical "average American" was thirty-four years old but his or her counterpart was only sixteen in 1830, the first year for which the census allows an estimate. America's economy of farms and shops was sustained by a relatively small proportion of adults with great numbers of young people working alongside them.

The federal censuses between 1790 and 1840 reveal that the households of free Americans, crammed with children (slaves were not enumerated by family group) averaged close to six persons apiece. They were large not only by today's standards but by those of contemporary Europe; the average size of English households in 1801 was well under five persons.

In the Northern states, household size declined as the birthrate began to fall, but the national average dropped only slowly until 1850. Since that time, reflecting a long and pervasive decline in childbearing and shifts in living arrangements, American households have steadily become much smaller; the 1980 census reported an average household size of 2.7.

But averages only hint at the scale of American domestic life. Up to the middle of the nineteenth century, more than two Americans out of every five lived in households with eight, nine, ten or more members. Fewer than one in twelve does so today. In the contemporary United States, people have come to live alone in rapidly increasing numbers. Perhaps one-fifth of all American households in 1980 contained only one person. Such "families" were rare in the society of the early Republic. In view of the work required to provision and maintain a household it was difficult for a single person to live "decently," but living alone was also socially proscribed; it was customarily seen as a sign of eccentricity or even madness. When the enumerator for the federal census of 1820 passed through Shrewsbury, Massachusetts, he found only two people living singly. One was Mary Garfield, never married and on poor terms with her kinfolk. She "did good work in spinning for her neighbors," town chronicler Elizabeth Ward recalled, but most townspeople "were shy of her," and called her "Old Moll Garfield the witch." The other, Jonas Stone, had become "an insane person," and had driven off his relatives' attempts to help him; the town authorities were petitioning the courts to have him put under their guardianship.

Slaves' households were not recorded in the census or recognized at law, since they could not legally marry. In fact, all slaves were simply listed on the schedules under their masters' names, so that the size of plantation "families," when free and slave were combined, could occasionally reach the figure of several hundred. Household servants, and slaves on small farms, sometimes shared their masters' hearths. But most slaves maintained their own families and hearths and kept them reasonably intact, a significant achievement under the stresses of bondage. The very few surviving population registers that list slave families show a majority with both parents present. Fathers were more frequently missing from black households than from white ones, but this was hardly surprising. The stability of slave families was threatened not simply by the chances of parental death, but by enforced separations. Masters could and sometimes did permanently sever slave marriages by selling one of the partners off the plantation, but this was not usual. More often, slave husbands and wives could not live together continuously, because they belonged to different owners and lived on different estates; men living away could travel to see their families only on Sundays and holidays. Slave families held together with a web of kin connections, grandparents, aunts and uncles, brothers and sisters, which were often vital to rearing and nurturing children.

Although American households were large, it was rare for three full generations—parents, children and children's children—to live around the same hearth. Two or more married couples—whether of the same or different generations—seldom shared the same living quarters, although in rural New

England a father and son or two brothers sometimes partitioned off the ancestral house and lived separately in the two sections. Far more frequently, households contained kinfolk, lodgers and workers who were neither parents nor children. Most Americans, at some point in their lives, lived in families that contained "extra" people.

In the North, prosperous households usually had domestic "helps" living with them—often young women from poorer families. In the country, they were dairymaids and spinning girls as well as strictly domestic workers. British travelers found American helps strikingly unwilling to be subservient and, by the standards of well-run aristocratic households, inefficient. They entered domestic service to vary the routines of life at home, to earn a little money, or to escape a difficult domestic situation. They were strikingly mobile. Few stayed in one household as long as a year. Prosperous American farmers employed and housed farm laborers—often young men trying to accumulate enough to begin farming on their own. They too were movers, rarely remaining more than a year or two with the same employer. On ordinary Northern and Western farms, full-time hired men were rare.

The chances of early death made for many widows and widowers who frequently found places in the households of their children or of their married brothers and sisters. Kinfolk came into their relatives' families as paid or unpaid domestic help, apprentices and employees, even paying lodgers. As they reached marriageable age, young women from prosperous families often spent long periods of time visiting kinfolk and enlarging their circles of acquaintance. At more "middling" levels, they were also invited to help with children and housework; "my married sisters," the New Englander Lucy Larcom remembered, "had families growing up about them, and they like to have us younger ones come and help take care of their babies." Younger brothers arrived as extra farmhands, business partners, store clerks or journeymen.

"Sixteen in family," Caroline Ward wrote in 1827 about the household headed by her father Thomas, a highly prosperous Massachusetts farmer. During the 1820s Ward had living under his roof himself and his wife, unmarried sons and daughters, a grandchild whose mother had died, farm laborers and domestic helps for household and dairy. For over three decades, the household's size never dropped below eleven people. The largest and most complex households of all were those of people like the Wards, those whom Americans called "great" farmers and planters as distinct from "common" ones. They had the room and economic resources to employ and house domestic workers and laborers, black or white, to support dependent kinfolk and to entertain long-staying visitors.

Unable to take members in, the households of the poor sent them out. The old, infirm or insane whose kin could not help them were often auctioned off by town or county authorities "at public vendue," to be taken into the households of the lowest bidder. Orphans and children from destitute families were "bound out" to farm and household service in wealthier ones, usually until they reached adulthood. Young people from families "with more children than money," as the American saying went, sometimes left at early ages to live in other households. Asa Sheldon's parents in Wilmington, Massachusetts, were not totally impoverished, but they had virtually no land, and he remembered how they sent him out at age eight to work on a farm in the next town.

Fathers had powerful claims, both legal and customary, on their children's labor until they reached maturity. But in the early nineteenth century these traditional claims were often balanced by shifting economic opportunities and expanding mobility. From their midteens into early adulthood, many American farmers' sons lived in fluctuating partial independence from their fathers' households. They "worked out" in farms or shops in nearby communities, but often returned home to labor with their fathers again, balancing their families' needs and their own aspirations. Young women working as domestics or dairymaids also moved in and out of their families, but usually over shorter distances and with less freedom.

"I Have Followed That Plow"

"I have followed that plow," wrote Horace Clarke in his journal on May 8, 1837, "more miles than any one man ever did or ever will any plow whatever in my *opinion.*" He had just discovered that it had been "completely worn out" after many years of service. Clarke's comments, like those of almost all diary-keeping farmers, were usually spare notations of weather and work. But in this rare aside, he voiced a sense of the endless recurrence of the agricultural cycle on his Connecticut farm that generations of American men would have shared, who felt an urgency rising—as spring began and went out, in the Carolina warmth or the New Hampshire chill—to prepare for planting the fields.

Work with the plow followed a laborious pattern which went back to the European Middle Ages. Hitching their plows to yokes of oxen or teams of horses, farmers guided them up and down their fields, preparing seedbeds for corn, wheat, rye, oats and sometimes cotton. The part that failed on Clarke's plow was a crucial one—the moldboard, the curved surface that turned over the earth and made the plowman's furrow. How it worked would have needed little explaining to any man or woman in rural America, or even to most city dwellers—who, after all, had grown up in the countryside. The most common currency of American conversation was talk of the agricultural year, with its anxious scanning of the weather and concern for crops, livestock and new or worn-out tools.

At the opening of the nineteenth century the United States was far from a landscape of subsistence agriculture. Merchants and artisans, fisherman and country traders, were important parts of the economy. Yet those years were a time "when farming absorbed society," as Samuel Goodrich of Connecticut wrote. The great majority—four-fifths in 1800—of American families farmed the land, for themselves or others. Although with the expansion of commerce, transportation and manufacturing that proportion declined, it was still around two-thirds in 1840, and the total number of farms and acres cleared for tillage increased enormously. Agriculture was still the largest single sector of the economy even in the highly commercial and industrial states of Massachusetts and Connecticut.

In the agricultural world of 1800, centuries-old limits on the tools and motive power of work held fast. Muscle power, with some assistance from falling water, determined what could and could not be done. On American farms and plantations, horses and oxen hauled loads, pulled plows and harrows and turned cider mills and cotton gins. New Englanders worked their land with oxen—sure-footed on rocky slopes, cheaper to feed and eventually consumable as meat. Farmers in the Middle States and the West preferred horses, whose superior speed and maneuverability made them preferable for working larger fields. Southerners used oxen, horses and a few mules, as well as the "flocks of slaves passing over the land with hoes" that observers noted on plantation fields.

Waterwheels drove small-scale mills for grinding grain, sawing timber and fulling handwoven woolen cloth. Almost everything else fell to human effort—felling trees, hauling wood and water, digging stones, hoeing weeds, picking cotton, mowing hay, harvesting grain, husking corn, churning butter, pressing cheese. Where streams were too sluggish, or mills had not yet been built, women and children pounded corn in "hominy blocks" or ground grain in hand mills, and teams of men pit sawed lumber by hand. The only important machine in American agriculture was the cotton gin, first developed in 1793, which mechanized the picking of seeds from "short staple" cotton and made the vast expansion of American cotton cultivation possible. But it still supported an agriculture based on labor with the hoe.

Men's and women's tasks on American farms were intertwined and almost totally interdependent. But in space, time,
tools and authority they were distinct. Farmyard, garden,
house, kitchen and hearth, in diminishing concentric circles,
enclosed and bounded women's daily realm. The world of
men's work circled outward. It began with farmyard, barn and
workshop, and went on through gates and across fences to
fields, pastures, woodlands and then to the roads leading off the
farm. Women minded poultry, men cared for horses, sheep and
cattle. Men stabled the cows and mucked out the stalls, women
milked and made butter and cheese. Some "domestic events,"
such as dairying, gardening and textile production, "circled
with the seasons," as Goodrich put it, but much of what women
did was what the Vermonter Sally Brown called the "same dull
round of chores," cooking, clearing away, washing, sewing,
mending—a daily sequence of time-consuming, physically demanding, constantly repeating tasks. Men's work included daily
chores, but it was more strongly seasonal, and more varied from
day to day. Women's "everyday work of the household," as a
Massachusetts man remembered of his mother, was always liable to be interrupted by "the care of half-a-score more or less
of children," and the needs of their husbands and neighbors.
Women were expert at laying down one task to pick up another.

Men occupied the realm of major physical force. Most edge
tools—plows, axes, saws, scythes—and other heavy implements
and vehicles were marked off as their territory. Cooking pots,
crockery, washtubs and baskets, butter churns, spinning
wheels, needles and thread were counted as distinctively female. Men and boys usually handled the raw materials of farm
production and undertook the first steps in processing them—
after which they handed them over to women and girls to finish.
Finally, and probably most important, American families
worked as patriarchal units, governed by their male heads.
Men's work, and men's decisions about work, were primary.

Much of the work on American farms followed the centuries-
old patterns of European agriculture, with gradual adaptations

that settlers had made to new crops and to local soils and climates. The interweaving rhythms of crops and livestock, the timing of work on the land, the handling of animals, the choice of tools, were governed by the accumulated experience of farming communities and passed from one generation to the next. Encountering different soils and conditions as they moved west, American families retained their farming practices when they could and changed them when they had to.

The best-selling publications in early-nineteenth-century America were almanacs, the small pamphlets that came off the presses in many thousands of copies each year. Farmers read them much less for their predictions of the weather, jocular stories or solemn advice than for the traditional lore of astrology. For men and women who worked daily with plants and animals, the natural cycles of growth and procreation were still powerful mysteries, governed at least in part by the phases of the moon and the great celestial wheel of the zodiac. Rural folk "believed that many things must be done, or left undone, during the reign of each constellation," recalled the Cincinnati physician Daniel Drake of his Kentucky boyhood, and that "the moon had a powerful influence on vegetation and animal life." Women planted radishes in their gardens "downward at the decrease of the moon, for they tapered downwards." Some crops had to be planted at the dark of the moon and still others while it was waxing toward full. The annual hog slaughtering in December had to avoid a waning moon as well; otherwise "the pork would shrink and wither away in the barrel." Choosing the time to wean a baby or a calf, or to begin making butter, sometimes awaited the arrival of a more auspicious sign in the heavens.

The most insistent and visible rhythms of Americans' work were those of plowing, planting, cultivation and harvest. They ranged from the long and intricate patterns of tobacco and rice cultivation to the sharp, comparatively short struggles to bring in the hay or harvest the wheat fields. In southern Louisiana the harvest season for the two great crops, cotton and corn, ended only a few weeks before planting began again: "ploughing, planting, picking cotton, gathering the corn, and pulling and burning stalks took up the whole of the four seasons of the year." In Vermont and New Hampshire the time between plowing and harvest was startlingly brief. The most widely familiar routine of work was that of growing corn, America's virtually universal crop.

Across the United States, families North, West and South, white and black, shared the routines of growing corn, a staple in the diets of both people and livestock. Most often they planted it in "hills" three or four feet apart. Men plowed and cross-plowed their fields to start the hills, then dropped and covered the seeds. Corn did not require an all-out, intensive effort at harvest time; instead, it needed steady cultivation from late spring through the end of summer to kill the weeds and build the soil around each cornstalk. Often there were three hoeings—a "weeding," a "half-hilling," and a complete "hilling." Men went into the field to cut the ripened ears off the stalks and carted them back to the barn. They cut the stalks down for livestock fodder or allowed them to stand in the field for browsing. Husking and shelling corn were later fall and winter work, which often became the occasion for neighborhood "frolics," to share the work and celebrate the end of the harvest.

In New York State and New England, the five or six weeks of the haying season, between late June and early August, were the time of most concentrated effort, "the hardest part of the labor required to be performed on a farm," as the *Maine Farmer* noted in 1832. Throughout the countryside, most other work ceased as craftsmen, merchants and their clerks left shops and stores to go into the field. While he was supervising a force of teamsters hauling stone to repair Boston pavements in the 1820s, Asa Sheldon found it difficult to keep them at work during haying time. Farmers came right into the city to recruit his men on the street.

Haying, wrote John Burroughs of New York, had "the urge,

the hurry, the excitement of a battle." Men assembled early in the morning, at daybreak or even before, "to cut the grass while the dew is on," when it was easiest to mow. One after the other they moved across the field, the blades of their long-handled scythes flashing as they swung them "in a gentle sweep from right to left," leaving broad swaths or windrows of cut grass. Many young men welcomed haying as a time of physical challenge and competition. To be the best mower in a neighborhood, the one customarily chosen to lead "a gang of hands in hay" across the field, was a distinction they eagerly sought. A slow hand with the scythe might suffer friendly derision, or risk having his ankles nicked by the blade of the man coming next after him. Mowers stopped only for brief rests, to gulp rum or brandy and whet their scythe blades on grindstones brought into the field.

The day's mowing was finished by noon, and after a dinner in the field men were raking, spreading and turning over the cut grass so that it would cure into hay, or hauling hay that had been "made" into the barn. Rainstorms brought a frantic struggle to get hay under cover or rolled into "cocks" to protect it from rot. Working through the long summer hours of daylight —often fourteen to sixteen hours a day—hayers battled "against the heat and the rain and the legions of timothy and clover" until all the hay was in. In the months to come men faced more work to do—harvests of oats, rye or wheat, bringing in corn and digging potatoes, threshing grain on the barn floor with wooden flails—but they knew that the year's most difficult task was done.

"There are few sights more pleasant to the eye," wrote Solomon Northup of his twelve years as a slave, "than a wide cotton field when it is in the bloom. It presents an appearance of purity, like an immaculate expanse of light, new-fallen snow." Cotton was also hard work, as slaves, and many white Southerners, had reason to know. Common farmers grew cotton as well as great planters, and many small slaveowners worked alongside their bondsmen in the fields. They grew the crop to feed the clock-regulated textile machinery of England and New England, but they worked it with intensive hand labor. Southern workers in the field, black and white, planted it in long hilled rows. They cultivated cotton, like corn, with hoes. Stooping over the hills placed a couple of feet apart, they killed the weeds and grass to protect the single cotton stalk. In the deep South, there were four separate hoeings through the growing year; they continued "from April until July, a field having no sooner been finished once, than it commences again."

When the steady, repetitious labor of the hoeing had finished came the time of harvest. Cotton hands then gave up their hoes for large sacks, fastened "breast high" from the neck and reaching "nearly to the ground." Walking and stooping up and down the rows, they pulled the ripe cotton bolls off the branches and filled their sacks. All but the most dexterous pickers risked ripped and bleeding hands from the sharp edges of the fibrous calyxes that held the cotton bolls. The most skillful picked with "great rapidity, using both hands"; others struggled to produce half as much during a day's work. To bring the crop in, workers toiled almost unceasingly from "light in the morning" until it was "too dark to see," or well into the night when the moon was full. Anxious to bring in the harvest, masters on the large plantations that produced most of the South's cotton offered special incentives to labor. Some of them fostered competitions, encouraged an air of driving excitement and held out the prospect of a great feast. There was also the whip. Some plantations were terrible places during the cotton harvest, where workers were driven relentlessly by white overseers or black drivers. Sometimes slaves approached the "gin house," where their daily production was weighed, "with fear and trembling" for what might happen if they fell short of their expected weight.

Americans' schedules of work on the land were driven not by the clock, but by the task to be done. Men, especially, labored in rhythms that quickened and slowed with the changing seasons. The Northern agricultural calendar was most sharply seasonal; in the cold months there was livestock to tend, timber to cut and repairs to be made, but little that could be done in the fields. Some men practiced part-time crafts. The most "progressive" mended harness, cleaned and oiled their tools and totaled up their accounts. Winter was the time for long visits, dances and neighborhood socializing. Many men spent dark winter evenings drinking in their communities' taverns.

Seasonal leisure meant something very different for men than for women. Women could sometimes combine their work with sociability, in quiltings and sewing visits. But the daily nature of so much of their work, and the spinning and weaving that filled up so much time in the winter, meant that they had fewer respites from toil. Even holidays that men found times of liberation and celebration often meant a great deal of work—in preparation, cooking and clearing away—for their wives.

Southerners, white and black, worked through a longer growing season and faced a punishingly hot summer climate. At peak harvest times, they worked as hard as any Americans, but during the rest of the agricultural year probably worked fewer hours a day than Northern farmers.

The work regimes on Southern plantations varied greatly. There were masters who "wore out" their slaves, driving them to chronic exhaustion, collapse in the fields or—rarely—death. Most owners made more moderate demands. But the clearest reality of the slaves' work was not the time schedule but the whip. "Six or seven feet in length, made of cowhide, with a platted wire on the end of it," as the former bondsman William Wells Brown recalled, the "negro-whip" was the South's most distinctive tool of agriculture. Slaves were not usually beaten every day, but the whip was always present. Watching slaves at their work near the Combahee River in South Carolina, Margaret Hall noted the "drivers, each with his wand of office in his hand." The field hands "seemed to work on mechanically, aware that the slightest relaxation was watched by the driver and would be followed by the infliction of his cart whip."

The large planters disdained the manual labor that most great Northern farmers—and often their own wives—put in as a matter of course. But they were not indolent. They exerted themselves vigorously in hunting and riding, and many worked hard, though intermittently, at managing their plantations, keeping accounts and supervising their overseers.

The farmers who worked to the most leisurely rhythms were probably some of the Scotch-Irish farmers of the mountain South. They hunted abundant game, cleared and planted enough land to grow a single big field of corn, rarely raised much else, and caught and slaughtered free-ranging hogs that did not need to be penned or fed. Content to remain in log cabins rather than to build frame houses, uninterested in changing their standards of domestic comfort, they were able to work more episodically than other American men— although their wives, with children, domestic chores and no slaves, could not.

The urgency of getting in the crops sometimes blurred the divisions between the sexes, as they traditionally had in Great Britain and Europe. During the critical time of the wheat harvest in eighteenth-century Pennsylvania, Maryland and Virginia, women worked alongside men in the fields, reaping with sickles—small curved blades with short handles—then gathering and binding the sheaves. The German-American women of eastern Pennsylvania, wrote the physician Benjamin Rush of Philadelphia in 1789, would temporarily give up "their dairy and spinning wheel and join their husbands and brothers" in the harvest field. Some American women continued to do so into the nineteenth century, but there were far fewer of them in the fields. Men in the wheat-growing regions had begun to reap with the "grain cradle," a heavy scythe with long wooden fingers attached which caught the fragile stalks without shattering them. It allowed fewer workers to harvest the same acreage, and was too heavy for women to use easily. In the wheat fields of western New York and Ohio, men exclusively "did the work of the harvest."

"Women in New England," Timothy Dwight thought, were "employed only in and about the house and in the proper business of their sex." Grain harvests there were not large enough to bring women into the field. Yet rather than let the crucial hay crop be lost, there were New England farm women who would "go into the field . . . before it rains," as Robert B. Thomas's *Farmer's Almanack* urged them, and help rake and cock the hay. Returning from teaching school one evening in early August of 1837, Pamela Brown of Plymouth, Vermont, "found Mother very tired by raking hay."

Much of the labor of American slaves was less strictly divided according to sex. Men and women alike performed field work with hands and hoe—planting, cultivating and harvesting cotton and corn, rice and tobacco. The hoe was a tool which both men and women used widely in America, although free women rarely used it outside the garden. Women often excelled at these tasks, as "lead hoes" or top cotton pickers. On some Louisiana plantations, women plowed "as frequently as the men," Northup wrote, "in all respects doing the field and stable work." But away from the fields, and particularly on large plantations with their array of specialized tasks, the sexual division of labor returned in its traditional white European form. Only slave men worked in the woods. Slave women worked as general household help, cooks, nurses and midwives, laundresses and dairymaids; and men performed the tasks of carpenters, blacksmiths, coopers and teamsters.

"Domestic Events"

Looking "back at the useful arts" his mother was "accustomed to practice," an Ohio man was "almost surprised at their number and variety." Women's arts clothed and fed American families. Everywhere, their work was essential, since households needed a great deal of domestic labor to function at all, and even more to be "decent" or "genteel." But American men paid it comparatively little regard. This was evident in relative wages. A young woman coming to work as a domestic help on a farm would be paid one-third to one-fourth as much as her brother would receive for agricultural labor. Men depended nonetheless on the "domestic events" of their households.

"Garments, in days gone by," reminisced Amasa Walker from the changed vantage point of the later nineteenth century, ". . . were made by the very persons that wore them, or by those connected to the families to which they belonged." Fabrics produced in the household—woolens, linen and "towcloth" made from flax, and their combinations—clothed the great majority of Americans in 1800. Men took primary responsibility for the farm's sheep, washed them, and sheared their wool. In New England and the Western states, men and boys pulled the flax plants, and spread them outdoors to rot the hard outer casing; eastern Pennsylvania women undertook these tasks themselves. Males usually took over the next steps. They broke the fibers with repeated pounding on heavy wooden "flax-brakes," which grown-up Americans like Horace Greeley and Daniel Drake remembered as some of the hardest boys' work they had ever done, "performed through many a tedious day." Finally they swingled the fibers clean using a board and a wooden "swingling knife" until they were "soft and pliable."

German-American women sometimes undertook the heaviest tasks of "dressing flax" themselves, which amazed New Englanders like Timothy Dwight, who was "struck by the strangeness" of white women performing heavy outdoor labor.

Women and girls then took the flax and wool fibers for finer, more intricate processing. They "hetchelled" the flax over spikes set in wooden frames to sort out the longer fibers for linen and the shorter ones for coarser tow. They sorted and picked the wool clean of twigs and stones, then carded it, combing out the fibers between "hand cards" set with fine wire teeth.

Then they began to spin, a task not only important but power-fully emblematic of all women's work. Spinning was often a young woman's task that mothers preferred to delegate to their daughters, or to domestic "helps." Older unmarried women living in a household—hence the traditional English "spinster" —might do it as well. In most farm households the "buzz of the foot wheel," the smaller foot-powered spinning wheel that pro-duced tow and linen thread, and the lower-pitched hum of the "great wheel" or "walking wheel" used for spinning wool were a persistent background music, which Walker remembered he "could sometimes hear at some distance from the house."

Spinning well was a skill of hand and eye which girls learned with long practice, carefully feeding fibers to be twisted into thread by the swiftly turning spindle. But it was also long, drawn-out, tedious work. The sound of his mother's flax wheel was "soothing music" to Lyndon Freeman of Sturbridge, Massa-chusetts, lulling him to sleep as a little boy. For Francis Under-wood, a young woman "in the management of the great spinning wheel" was a figure of almost balletic grace, as she walked back and forth "with a long gliding step, advancing and retreating . . . the left hand controlling the yarn while the right governed the wheel." But neither Freeman nor Underwood spent endless hours in spinning. For New Hampshire–born Ellen Rollins, on the other hand, "the moaning of the big wheel was the saddest sound of my childhood. It was like a low wail from out of the lengthened monotony of the spinner's life."

The thread was then readied for weaving, and in some households, Freeman said, "the music of the loom," a rhythmic thumping, "succeeded to that of the wheel." Handloom weav-ers mastered the intricate rhythms of throwing the shuttle, pulling the weft through the multiple harnesses that held the threads of the warp in their preset patterns. Weaving, although reasonably widespread, was a less common art than spinning; looms were rarer than wheels in household inventories. Many households exchanged goods or labor with a neighboring family for weaving work. In longer-settled rural areas, there were households that depended completely on exchange for their cloth.

After cloth was woven came the tasks of cutting out and sewing clothes. "I have about two months sewing to do," wrote a North Carolina planter's wife in 1837. "I never was so tired of sewing in my life. My fingers are worn out." Skill with a needle, and a lifetime of sewing, were virtually synonymous with womanhood. American women remembered the "long and varied sewing lessons" or tasks their mothers, so often "busily plying a needle" themselves, set for them—sewing endless straight seams, "darning stockings and stitching wristbands" until they could move on to more complicated stitches and ornamental needlework. All but the wealthiest American women cut and sewed their own clothes, and many made their husbands' and sons' garments as well. Others had the somewhat more difficult work of "man-tailoring" done by more specialized country "tailoresses." Only the most affluent went to tailors in the city. "I somehow or somewhere got the idea," wrote Lucy Larcom, "when I was a small child, that the chief end of woman was to make clothing for mankind."

In the dairy—a corner of the kitchen, an adjoining room, a shed or even a separate springhouse—American farm women practiced the arts of transformation, handed down from mother to daughter. Under their hands, milk took on solid shape, powerful flavors and far longer life in the form of butter and cheese. Nowhere else in the agricultural world did change occur so quickly, even mysteriously. After milking and putting the milk into shallow pans to separate the cream, dairywomen would churn it vigorously—usually for an hour or so for each churnful —to "bring the butter." They then "worked" the butter, kneading and pressing it into a solid consistency; some used their hands, wetting them to keep the butter cool and clean, while others worked with wooden paddles. To perform these tasks well required women's skills of a high order, "dexterity as well

as strength." A skilled dairywoman, who produced clean, fla-
vorful, long-lasting butter, provided well for her family's table.
She was often a powerful economic asset as well, since good
butter, packed in tubs or crocks and marked with a distinctive
butter print, was a valued item in exchange. Each major American city was the center of a flourishing butter trade, but the
dairywomen in the countryside around Philadelphia were
widely known as the most skillful of all. Passed along from one
generation of women to the next, the skills and traditions of
making cheese and butter were a source of pride in many farming families. His family's dairy, wrote Thomas Ward II of
Shrewsbury, Massachusetts, to his sister, "with 75 to 80 pans
of milk looks rather imposing. We make more than 80 lbs. of
butter a week, and you know my wife makes good butter."

Most American families made butter, but "the art and mys-
tery of cheese making," as a New Jersey man called it, was far
more widespread north of Pennsylvania. For New Englanders,
cheese was a major source of protein in the diet, and a significant item of exchange. Much of the skill of the process resided
in the proper preservation and use of "the rennet," a piece of
the lining of a young calf's stomach, which contained the di-
gestive enzyme that solidified the milk into curds. "Squeezing
the whey from the curds" in cheesecloth and compressing
them into a dense and compact wheel by "managing the
heavy lever" on a wooden cheese press were the next steps in
every cheesemaker's routine. She then set the rounds of
cheese onto her dairy's shelves to age, waxing the rinds to protect them, and turning them frequently. Cheeses were often
classified by the quality of the milk they contained; the best
were "fresh milk," and those with increasingly smaller frac-
tions of whole milk were called "one-meal," "two-meal," or
"four-meal" cheeses.

Earlier in American history, in seventeenth-century New
England, trouble with cattle and milk had often been the occasion of serious accusations of witchcraft. In some communities,

cows and dairying still had a faint aura of magic about them. So mysteriously did the butter either "come," or fail to appear, that there was a sense of unseen forces at work. Lewis Miller kept an illustrated journal of daily events in his predominantly German-American community of York, Pennsylvania, and described how in 1810 Mrs. Weiser, discovering that "no butter I can make," called in Claus Hufschmidt "to see what is the matter in the butter churn." He reported that "it is bewitcht," threw a silver coin into the churn, and "made Butter" successfully. Just after Hufschmidt had finished, he paid for his interference with a painful inflammation of the face—"witchcraft in full and in earnest," Lewis half-jokingly commented.

For most American housewives, cooking stood at the center of every day's work. During the later eighteenth century, in fact, it had become increasingly important. As variety in the American diet increased, many housewives were spending more time than their mothers and grandmothers had in preparing attractive and "well-cooked" meals. Yet in 1800, most American women shared a technology of cooking that had changed little in the preceding century. The domestic utensils used in American homes had gradually increased in number on the average over the eighteenth century, but there was little change in their size and weight. When women went to "cook over a fireplace," they used heavy iron pots and kettles that sat directly on "the coals on the hearth," or "hung on a crane, which swung over the fire when the things were cooked," as Susan Blunt of Merrimack, New Hampshire, described it. Cooks did an enormous amount of back-wrenching stooping and lifting. The blazing fire itself might become "a terror to the cook," recalled Lyndon Freeman, and the preparation of meals "a firey trial." The quantity of kitchen equipment varied greatly with the wealth of the household. Affluent ones had large fireplace ovens and an abundance of cookware—pots and kettles, gridirons and toasting forks. In poorer houses "the bread was baked in the ashes," or as in the family Asa Sheldon visited in

Marlborough, Massachusetts, around 1810, "there was only one article to cook with, a dish-kettle."

In all these American kitchens, Harriet Beecher Stowe recalled, "everything came in the rough, and had to be reduced to a usable form in the household." Women needed to know the crafts of salting, pickling and smoking meat to preserve it, of making wheat or "rye and Indian" bread, johnnycake or hominy, of stewing, roasting and frying. Salt, sugar, spices and coffee had to be taken in bulk form, ground and pounded. Housewives hauled water, killed chickens, set their children to search for eggs in the barnyard and harvested vegetables from the garden or the root cellar.

On washing days—Monday in some American households, Fridays in others, no more than once a month in some, women woke up "long before sunrise," as Ellen Rollins remembered, to scrub and pound clothes, plunging their arms up to the elbows in tubs of near-boiling water and homemade soft soap. After repeated washing and rinsing, they emerged in the afternoon with "bleached, par-boiled fingers" to spread their laundry out to dry. It was a day of unpleasant work and special urgency, a good day for children to stay away from the house. And "sevenfold worse in its way even than washing day," Stowe thought, was that annually recurring winter's day when women worked from "day-dawn" to late at night dipping strings into melted beef tallow to make the year's supply of candles.

The wives of urban artisans made contributions to the maintenance of their families as vital as those of farm wives. In addition to the regular domestic round of food preparation, cooking, laundering and child care, they did the extra hours of work needed to keep apprentices, journeymen or paying lodgers in their homes, tended small garden plots and kept pigs or cows, did the daily marketing for food and helped out in the shop. Poor laborers' wives struggled even harder to scratch out a living. They spent hours each day searching for firewood, scavenging clothing and domestic goods cast off by wealthier families and hunting for cheaper provisions.

The most leisured women in America were the wives who presided over wealthy city households. "A Philadelphia lady of the first class," as Frances Trollope described her in 1832, the wife of a leading lawyer, spent the first hour of her day "in the scrupulously nice arrangement of her dress." She ate breakfast with her family, cooked and served by the family domestics; after breakfast, she washed the delicate and fragile china cups and saucers herself. She then put on an apron and made some fine pastries. Later her carriage took her visiting where she would sew or embroider and talk with her friends. On returning, she walked "into the kitchen to see that all is right," and then "cast a careful glance over the table prepared for dinner." Following the midafternoon dinner which brought her husband home from his offices, she read, sewed and prepared to receive company at tea. "And so," wrote Trollope, "ends her day." In reality she also surely spent much time with her children, closely supervised the routine of her household and dealt with the problems of frequently changing domestic help. But the routine of her days was far different, and far less wearing, than that of the vast majority of her American sisters.

The mistresses of plantation households were spared much heavy drudgery by the work of household slaves, but most of them worked nearly as hard as farm women in the free states. Their work combined the management of slaves with many traditional—and physically demanding—women's tasks. They bore the chief responsibility for allotting food and clothing from plantation storehouses, and for gardening, dairying and food preservation. All supervised and directed; the majority toiled themselves, salting meat, feeding chickens, making butter, dipping candles. Sarah Gayle of North Carolina had been salting pork so long, she wrote in her diary in December 1829, that "all the skin was nearly off my hands." Clothing their households and their field slaves was usually their responsibility, and often their heaviest burden. "We have nearly a hundred shirts to make, besides other parts of dress," wrote Anne Cocke from her large Virginia plantation in 1811, adding that her household would be "a perfect workshop all the next month, and part of the month after."

"The principal hardships" of plantation life, thought Frances Kemble Butler after her stay on the Georgia plantation owned by her husband's family, fell "to the lot of the women" who worked in the fields. They were compelled to attend to the needs of their own households and children last. "After a long day's toil," slaves returned, said Solomon Northup, to have a "fire . . . kindled in the cabin," deal with children, mend clothes and make "supper, and dinner for the next day in the field." Slave women were given some time off both before and after pregnancy, but they often had to leave their infants completely in the care of girls and boys who were themselves very young. The most ill-treated slave women were sent back into the field too soon after pregnancy. They and their children both suffered.

"Early Made Acquainted with Labor"

In the years around 1800 in Mayslick, Kentucky, when Daniel Drake and his sister Lizy were both very young, they were "employed in common rocking the cradle, carrying about, 'tending' and taking care of the younger children, while mother was at work" in the house. Girls and boys were reared in a matter-of-fact involvement with farm and household tasks; as the New York editor Horace Greeley recalled of his own rural childhood, they were "early made acquainted with labor." As they grew a little older Daniel began to work with his father and Lizy with her mother on the Drakes' pioneer farm, helping and learning. Because he had no older sisters, Daniel "occasionally assisted mother in milking," but he recalled that "Sister Lizy was taught that accomplishment as early as possible, seeing that it was held by the whole neighborhood to be quite too 'gaalish' for a boy to milk, and mother, quite as much as myself, would have been mortified if any neighboring boy or man had caught me at it."

Daniel Drake recalled mastering an impressive array of tasks, taking on more work and responsibility every year. Starting at age eight, he rode on the horse to steady it while his father plowed, planted the corn seeds in their hills as his father covered them, spent endless hours weeding—"we returned from the fields at night, black with needles" from the prickly burrs —and guarded the young crops by throwing rocks at crows and squirrels. During the wheat harvest, he would "bind the handfuls of cut wheat" that his father had sickled and "carry the sheaves." Young Daniel "had much care of our stock—for boys can do that kind of work." In winter, his father felled trees, split rails and built fences; Daniel hauled wood and chopped it "four or five feet long for the fireplace," and carried the rails to the fields.

As he became stronger and more skillful, Drake took on more adult tasks. At age eleven, he was given an old gun to scare the pests away from the fields. At twelve, he "was able to hold the plough and guide the horse," and at thirteen he began to split rails and build fences himself. He was also allowed to "wield the sickle" at harvest time. "The maxim of the harvest field" in Kentucky "was that no boy becomes a good reaper until he cuts his left hand," from the force of the sickle's right-handed sweep against the wheat stalks gathered in his left. "I cut mine several times," Drake recalled, and realized "my greatest ambition," which was, like his father, "to sweat so as to wet my shirt." By sixteen, he was doing a full man's work in the fields.

"Sister Lizy" wrote no corresponding account of her increasing mastery of a woman's skills. Susan Blunt, however, left a description of what she was able to do "when I was about ten" in the 1830s. Her mother, she recalled, "let me go and keep house . . . for a week" for a family living a mile away, with "twin little girls and an aged father to leave in my care." Young Susan had complete charge of the household; her mother had told her "to work like a little spider." She got up at five o'clock to begin her day's work, going to "a well quite a distance from the house" to get water. She "boiled potatoes, fried pork and made coffee" for breakfast, got the girls ready for school, tended to the elderly invalid, then "cleered away . . . put on some beans to stew for dinner," and "made some biscuits and baked them in a tin baker before the fire." For this impressive display of youthful female competence, cooking, cleaning, mending and caring for young and old, Susan received about fifteen cents, which she used to buy a new calico apron.

Instruction in the context of the household, or apprenticeship in its broadest sense, was the way in which Americans learned the most important things in their lives. Most sons and daughters learned to work, and what it meant to be a man or a woman, by "following on" after their parents and imitating them. Not only craftsmen but merchants, lawyers, doctors and clergymen acquired their occupational skills by apprenticing in the workplace—clerking in a store, reading law or divinity, or "studying physic" with an established practitioner.

Formal schooling was important to most American families, but they had relatively limited expectations for it. They wanted their sons, and usually their daughters as well, to acquire the rudiments of reading, writing and calculating—enough to read an almanac or the Bible, understand a property deed or reckon an account. New England, often called the "land of schools," had schoolhouses, paid for by local taxes, spread across its countryside. Elsewhere schooling was thinner, supported by varying mixtures of private, local government and church arrangements. Far to the South and to the West they became comparatively scarce. Nowhere was school attendance compulsory.

In all rural communities children old enough to do serious work took whatever schooling they might get in the winter months between the end of harvest and the start of planting. They were often kept at home whenever their parents needed their labor, so that those from hard-pressed families attended very irregularly, and some were still struggling through elementary reading and arithmetic in their late teens. Children as young as two or three went along to school with their older brothers and sisters, less to learn than to get them out from underfoot in busy households. Schoolmasters—usually young unmarried men who took the job on before settling on a trade or taking over a farm—faced a heterogeneous mixture of ages, from "infants just out of their cradles," as the Massachusetts educational reformer Horace Mann observed, to "men . . . enrolled in the militia." Schoolhouses were small, poorly kept structures, usually built near roadsides on barren, unwanted corners of land. In most of them, pedagogy stressed memorization before understanding, and the custom of reciting aloud often made their interiors a constant buzz of discordant voices.

In 1800, most white American children between five and fifteen spent a few weeks, up to a couple of months, in school every year. Some never went at all, and in some back-country communities illiteracy was common, with many who "could neither read nor write, did not send their children to school."

The substantial majority of white American men—perhaps as many as three-quarters—had acquired enough schooling, sometimes with instruction at home, to be able to read. A slightly smaller number could write, the result of traditional practices that taught reading and writing as separate skills. American women lagged behind men in literacy; girls were more often kept from school. Slaves were kept unschooled and illiterate by conscious policy and in many Southern states by law. To be found reading, or trying to learn, could be positively dangerous for Southern blacks.

For a rural people, by the standards of their time, Americans were strikingly literate, surpassing most of the nations of Western Europe. But this did not mean that they were a country of great readers. Some of them, due to their meager instruction, read slowly and haltingly. Most Americans did not read very much; their cramped houses, scantily illuminated by a candle or two, made reading at night difficult. Books were relatively expensive, and usually bought to fill only pressing needs. Bibles, hymn books, primers, spelling books, arithmetics and almanacs —books which guided worship, elementary instruction and the planting of crops—made up almost all of what country store-keepers stocked on their shelves and inventory takers recorded of household libraries. In Kentucky, "newspapers . . . was almost as scarce among the country people around us as the Sibylline leaves." New Englanders read more than Southerners and Westerners, but even in the countryside of Massachusetts, no more than one household in ten or twelve received a newspa-per, and most families owned only a few volumes and "the year's almanack." Middling and prosperous city people, and some of the great farmers and professional men in the country-side, often read much more. The gulf was less profound than in societies with mass illiteracy, but it was real enough—in some communities almost a "matter of centuries," Francis Under-wood thought.

"Changing"

Even with their myriad productive activities, American rural households were almost never completely self-sufficient. Few families had all the resources—land, livestock, labor, skills and tools—to produce all of what they needed. The largest farms and plantations actually came far closer to this ideal than mid-dling and common ones. Almost all rural Americans traded within their communities. Most, in varying degrees, sought wider markets for some part of what they produced.

Webs of rural exchange linked neighborhoods together along with "frolics" and habits of visiting. There was not very much cash in circulation in the country; what there was tended to flow quickly back to the cities. Families built up credit or debit balances with each other as they "changed" an enormous variety of labor and commodities—a few days' help at harvest, a young woman to spin, cheese, woven cloth, firewood, meat, the loan of a horse and wagon, a few weeks' pasturing of a cow. Economic life was deeply, inextricably entangled in social life. Visits and economic transactions were usually indistinguishable.

In Western and Southern settlements, "changing," or the "borrowing system," as the people of Illinois called it, often worked with oral accounting held in the memory. "I expect I shall have to do a turn of work for this," said her new Ohio neighbors to the uncomprehending Frances Trollope when she loaned utensils or gave foodstuffs; "you may send for me when you want me." She thought it an attempt to avoid saying "thank you" for neighborly kindness. But they were trying to involve her in their economic web, in which kindness was far less important than maintaining patterns of reciprocal obligation.

Many American families tried to keep their exchanges straight with informal accounts, using "a shingle or oven lid, with marks or scratches upon it," Robert Thomas noted, or even "a few chalk marks upon the buttery door" of a farmhouse to keep records for future payment. In the rural North, where pupils were most apt to learn arithmetic in school, some farmers and most artisans kept account books that gave each of their transactions a precise monetary value. They settled accounts most often in March or April, at the beginning of the agricultural year, but often let them run for two years or even more. The world of account-book exchange was still one of neighborhood relationships, but its careful measuring and valuing of labor and commodities brought daily life far closer to the world of commerce.

In parts of the West where New Englanders and Southerners mixed in new settlements, ways of exchanging sometimes produced conflict. Southerners found the Yankee preference for written accounts between neighbors unfamiliar, even insulting; it suggested to them that an individual's word and memory about economic obligations were not trusted.

Settling up accounts and making monetary payments was a complicated matter. "The perplexities of the currency," as Underwood put it, "were manifold." Although the United States had established a decimal currency in 1793, many rural Americans into the 1820s continued to think in terms of the disused English pounds, shillings and pence when they figured prices and wages. They then translated from the traditional "currency of reckoning" into American dollars and cents when it was time to total up and pay.

There was no national or state paper money, and in the years around 1800, money primarily meant specie—gold and silver coin. The actual coins which Americans used were usually not their own country's currency at all. Before gold was discovered in California in 1849, the federal mint did not coin enough precious metal. A bewildering variety of foreign coins circulated: Dutch rix-dollars, Russian kopecks, as well as French and English specie. Most of the coins Americans used were the silver dollars, halves, quarters, eighths and sixteenths minted in Mexico and in the South American republics where silver was abundant. With the variegated coinage, the need to state final amounts in U.S. currency, and "the traditional but imaginary shillings," as Underwood noted, "there was a rare confusion."

Some farm families brought their produce directly to city or village markets, but for most, country stores were the primary points of contact with the larger economy. Storekeepers were economic intermediaries who funneled country produce to markets and stocked the imported and manufactured goods— "assortments for the country trade," city merchants often called them—that their communities needed or wanted. Most store exchange was part of the account-book world, precisely recorded but expressed in the trading of commodities and labor. Every household's accounts were kept in the husband and father's name, but a great deal of what farm families offered in exchange was produced by women and girls. In many com-

munities men and women brought their own commodities separately to the store; "women . . . brought butter, eggs, beeswax
and feathers to exchange for dry goods," a country merchant
recalled, while "men . . . wanted to trade oats, corn, buckwheat,
axe halves [handles], hats and other commodities for ten penny
nails, molasses or New England rum." American storekeepers
were not only neighbors but men whose livings depended on
their success in thousands of small transactions, on their mastery of mental arithmetic and shrewdness in allocating credit to
their customers.

Americans loved the games of swapping and bargaining,
claimed scores of foreign observers. Exchanging sometimes became a competitive test, a trial of wits. The great purveyor of
American hokum, Phineas T. Barnum, worked as a boy and
young man in Connecticut country stores. For him, they were
theaters of practical joking and sharp trading, where storekeepers and purchasers, although members of the same community,
were not necessarily bound by mutual trust. "I cut open bun-
dles of rags," he recalled, "brought to the store by country
women in exchange for goods, and declared to be all linen and
cotton, that contained quantities of worthless woolen trash in
the interior, and sometimes stones, gravel, ashes. . . . Of course,
the astonished woman would impute the rag-swindle to a ser-
vant or neighbor who had made it up without her knowledge."

The Artisan's World

Hervey Brooks was a potter who began working in the "South
End" settlement of Goshen, Connecticut, in 1802. His farm,
"pot shop," and bottle-shaped brick pottery kiln were familiar
sights in the neighborhood for over sixty years. Like all potters,
Brooks had learned the skills of shaping clay through his fingers'
ends. A lump of fired pottery found near the foundation of his
kiln, used to prop up pieces while they were being fired, still
preserves the clear impress of his hand. Over the course of

every year, Brooks dug and carted his clay, ground it in a horse-drawn pugging mill, mixed and kneaded it to a proper consistency, and "turned ware" or shaped it into vessels on his foot-powered wheel. In addition he ground lead to prepare his glazes, glazed and occasionally decorated his pots, stacked them in his kiln and cut several cords of wood to fuel the firing. During the virtually sleepless two- or three-day vigil of "burning a kiln of ware" he judged the temperature and condition of the glowing kiln with all his senses—the color of the flames, the sounds of expanding brick and clay, even the smell of the super-heated air.

Brooks made redware, the ordinary, utilitarian earthenware containers used in eighteenth- and early nineteenth-century American households—stewpots and bean pots, chamber pots, pitchers, "pudding pans," mixing bowls, butter churns and milk pans for the dairy. He exchanged his pots in small quantities with his neighbors in Goshen, his account books show, but traded larger quantities with country merchants who stocked them on their shelves. Against all this was set the regular daily and seasonal routines of a Connecticut farmer, for Brooks intertwined the raising of crops and livestock with the making of pottery. Synchronizing the rhythms of his trade with those of his farm was actually a considerable challenge for him, because unlike a woodworker or metalworker a potter could not concentrate his activity in the winter months. Clay was only workable in warm weather, when the fields demanded his attention as well. Brooks interwove other work with his two principal occupations; at various times he undertook brickmaking, blacksmithing, carpentry and running a sawmill.

Hervey Brooks was an American craftsman, or "mechanic" as his countrymen and women usually called them. The United States at the beginning of the nineteenth century was still predominantly a handmade world, where the production of goods was as yet small-scale, unmechanized and unstandardized. Artisans did not work with blueprints and technical specifications but with the memory of their hands and three-dimensional, visual thinking. Without measurements, but through innumerable repetitions of a single action—forcing a block of wood against the sharp blade of a drawshave—coopers learned to judge the angle and taper of wooden staves precisely enough to create watertight barrels. Housewrights laid out and squared off the frames of their buildings with only minimal measurements. Blacksmiths determined the temperature of their forges, and the right times for working or welding iron and steel, by minute gradations of the metal's color.

Mechanics' work was often a severe physical test. Blacksmiths clearly needed great strength and endurance, but less obviously strenuous trades had their own hardships. "Printing, as you know," wrote a Massachusetts apprentice, Edwin Fobes, to his sister in 1831, "is very tiring to the eyes." Within a year, in fact, Fobes had to leave the trade to take up employment less taxing to his vision. "The cases of type" for printers, the novelist William Dean Howells recalled of the printing offices of his boyhood in northern Ohio, "had to be placed very near the windows so as to get all the light there was," for men setting type by hand were usually straining hard to see clearly. An inventory for the Merriam printing office in Brookfield, Massachusetts, in 1824 listed eight candlesticks; this was more than in most households, which usually had fewer than three. Yet on dark winter afternoons, and when the office worked late into the evening, those flickering candles had to illuminate the demanding work of ten men and boys.

Typesetting was also painful when the weather turned cold. As printers moved close to the windows in winter for light, Howells continued, "they got all the cold there was, too. From time to time, the compositor's fingers became so stiff that blowing on them would not avail; he passed the time in excursions between his stand and the stove; in very cold weather, he practised the device of warming his whole case of type by the fire, and when it lost heat, warming it again." Once type was set, turning out books and newspapers on hand presses was even more arduous. "My hands were blistered and my back lamed," remembered Horace Greeley of his early printing years in Vermont, "working off the very considerable edition of this paper on an old-fashioned . . . press."

Although there were some craftsmen—silversmiths, clockmakers, cabinetmakers—of extraordinary skill who created objects of still-enduring beauty, for the most part American artisans were not conscious artists. In city and countryside, they worked like Hervey Brooks to produce goods and see them sold.

Mechanics, like farmers, still worked according to the task, not the hour. In many shops, there were times of comparative relaxation, when men worked at a leisurely pace. They were punctuated by "periodical fits of desperate industry," as Harriet Beecher Stowe called them, as craftsmen drove themselves to complete their tasks to fill an order or satisfy a customer. Printing his first book in 1798, Ebenezer Merriam remembered, he "worked twenty four tokens at press without stopping (eight tokens was accounted a day's work) to sleep, and the next day . . . entered the holy bonds of matrimony." When streams ran high and produced abundant water power, sawmills ran night and day to cut the logs that had accumulated during times of low water. Many sawyers worked in pairs, "twelve hours on, twelve hours off," for weeks on end until the backlog or the water ran out. From the clear evidence of his accounts, Brooks worked in similar rhythms, sometimes producing pots at a rate that astonishes modern-day artisans trying to replicate his craft.

American mechanics had always lived in a far more loosely organized world of work than their counterparts in Europe. Americans retained the language of "master," "journeyman" and "apprentice," but the statuses did not have the binding power that they had in England. The powerful system of the English craft guilds had not been successfully transplanted, so that American artisans had never been able to limit entry into their trades or to regulate how they were practiced. Still, the traditional ladder of succession in a craft embodied the ideal pattern of the mechanic's life: first was an extended period in youth spent learning the trade; second, a time of competence in young adulthood, sometimes of moving between shops— hence "journeyman"; and finally, the eventual achievement of independence as a master mechanic, with his own shop and household. Some American artisans learned their trades by serving lengthy apprenticeships, up to seven years, sealed with an "indenture," a legally binding agreement between the master and the youth's father. "Indented apprentices" were commonest in highly skilled trades like silversmithing and printing, but some might be found in almost every craft. Many acquired their work skills under more informal, oral apprenticeship agreements. Some of them tried two or even three trades in succession before settling on an occupation. In the small shops of the countryside, most artisans learned their craft from their kinsmen—fathers, uncles or brothers.

On large plantations slaves worked as carpenters, blacksmiths, coopers, tanners, shoemakers and harness makers, passing their skills down from one black artisan to another. Slaves could not become independent mechanics, but their skills brought them higher status and better treatment than field hands.

Mechanics' wives and sometimes their daughters often helped in their shops with retail trade and keeping accounts. In some trades, usually those working with "soft" materials, the sexes worked together. Customarily their work still maintained clear lines of sexual division. In city butchers' shops, men slaughtered and hung the carcasses while women cleaned and processed the meat. Men sometimes worked as handloom weavers, but never spun. Male tailors made only men's clothing, never women's. In the making of shoes, both men and women stitched. However, men did the "bottoming", using awls, punches, heavy needles and coarse thread to attach the soles, while women worked with finer needles and thread to sew the thinner uppers. And shoemakers, tailors and weavers never had quite the status or the wages of men working with harder, more overtly masculine materials.

Virtually all the tools and skills of working with metal or with wood were implicitly reserved for men. It was unknown, or at least extremely rare, for women to work as blacksmiths, carpenters, cabinetmakers—or even as potters. In these trades women took on ancillary tasks: they decorated pottery, caned chair seats, painted tinware.

Occasionally, American printing offices saw women—usually printers' wives and daughters—setting type or reading proof. The best-known female mechanic in a traditionally male trade during the early nineteenth century was undoubtedly the remarkable Lydia Bailey, who ran a printing office in Philadelphia for thirty years after her husband's death. She trained numerous apprentices—but all of them were male.

The "needle trades"—seamstressing, embroidery, dressmaking—provided employment for some poorer urban women. Their earnings were meager, rarely enough to support themselves as independent wage earners. A few highly skilled milliners, dressmakers and cloak makers achieved the status of independent craftswomen, with their own establishments catering to fashionable women. Some took on apprentices, advertising for "industrious girls" in the newspapers.

A great many American artisans were, like Brooks, not only part-time farmers but versatile rather than highly specialized. In the rural communities of the North, woodworking artisans usually practiced an extensive range of skills that in American cities or in Europe were separate trades—the making of chairs and other furniture, cabinetmaking, house building, general carpentry and coopering. Many country artisans went further, practicing an array of less closely related crafts—surely not with a master's skill, but well enough to do for themselves and their neighbors. Over three generations from 1760 to 1855, the men of the Dominy family of Easthampton, Long Island, maintained a remarkable tradition of versatile artisanship. Their accounts and the hundreds of surviving tools from their shop disclose that they combined the skills of clock- and watchmakers, cabinet-makers, carpenters, blacksmiths and millwrights.

In city and countryside, master craftsmen, like Everard Peck, lived as well as worked with their apprentices and journeymen. Custom, as well as the legal wording of indentures, put both formal and informal apprentices under "family government." They were bound to live with and obey their masters as they would their own fathers; masters were obliged to feed and clothe them, provide for their schooling and teach them the trade. These were not always harmonious arrangements, and their terms were often enough broken by one party or the other. Masters sometimes treated their apprentices poorly, beating them, providing them with worse food and clothing than other family members, or even refusing to instruct them in the craft. Responding to ill-treatment, or out of homesickness, youthful boredom and restlessness, apprentices sometimes ran away. If they were indented, masters had the legal power to pursue them and bring them back to the shop. More fortunate ones became members of reasonably comfortable families and were well instructed.

Each larger mechanic's shop was a world with its own rules. Seniority governed the status of journeymen and apprentices. It was "required of the youngest apprentice," as the Worcester, Massachusetts, cabinetmaker Purley Torrey wrote to the father of a prospective apprentice in 1828, "that he shall open the shop in the morning build and keep fires during the day wait on Journeymen and do all chores and go of all errands which are necessary for this shop," before he could begin to learn crafts skills. New apprentices might also have to undergo a ritual hazing at the hands of older ones. Newly arrived journeymen often had to give "footings" or treat their fellows to drinks for the day.

As places to work and live in, shops and their households varied enormously. Purley Torrey kept close control. "It is my wish that my apprentices may worship on the Sabbath with me," his letter continued, ". . . further that they become a member of some one of the Bible classes. . . . Such evenings as it is not customary to work I do not allow them to go where they please—it is my wish that they stay at the shop." The large country printing office that the Merriam family of Brookfield, Massachusetts, ran for fifty years, between 1798 and 1848, was a quiet and orderly place, but less regimented. The six to eight apprentices who worked there year to year shared meals, living quarters and work with the Merriam sons, who sometimes complained that they were pushed harder than the others to demonstrate the masters' lack of favoritism. The Merriams worked everyone in the shop long hours, and occasionally docked a worker for "staying abed" or breaking equipment. But they joked with their workers, allowed them time to visit their families, and were later remembered with respect and affection by many of the men whom they had trained.

Not far away, in Hartford, Connecticut, was the bookbinding and printing shop of Andrus and Judd. An anonymous young bookbinder there kept a personal "History of the Shop" for the years 1831–38, which depicted something very different: a disorderly, divided and sometimes violent world. There was a deep split in the shop between "one flock of sheep and another of goats." A few pious and orderly young men each received "a premium for his good behavior, minding his own business, etc.," while others climbed out of their rooms after hours to haunt taverns and got into "scrapes" with rowdies on the streets. For them life was a continuing series of squabbles with each other and confrontations with masters.

Angry exchanges between apprentices and journeymen in the shop started with "jawing" and then went to shoving or even brawling. Work discipline, too, could become violent. The foreman sometimes used a knotted piece of rope to chase the apprentices back to their work, and the master bookbinder Silas Andrus once threatened a discontented journeyman with an iron bar. The boys retaliated with ridicule. "One day," recounted the nameless apprentice, after the foreman had gone to dinner, "the boys took an old pair of pantaloons and stuffed them with shavings, put an old coat and cap which he used to wear in the shop on it, and placed it on a stool before his desk with the keys of the shop hanging out of one pocket. This did not sit very well upon his stomach but as he could not find out who stuffed it all he could do was to roll his eyes and hope for better days."

"Profitable Occupation": The New Worlds of Work

In the years just after the Revolution, some Americans were already experiencing change in the routines and circumstances of their work. In the decades that followed, ever-increasing numbers would find that their daily tasks had been in some way transformed. New factories and expanded workshops were signs that, in a shift that would take generations to complete, the traditional identification of household and workplace was beginning to break apart. Although it directly involved only a minority of mill hands, the mechanization of work had begun, with enormous significance. New tools and implements began to alter ancient, laborious patterns. On the farms work and family remained integrated, still inseparable, but oriented increasingly toward commerce and "profitable occupations."

Ever more crowded on their land—by American standards—as population grew, hundreds of thousands of families in New England and the Middle States left to take up farms in the West or moved to cities and villages. Those who left the farm went to labor in artisans' shops, warehouses, docks, stores, garrets and city streets. But those who remained in the Eastern countryside, and Western farm families when they came within reach of expanding markets, also changed the patterns of their work.

At the end of the eighteenth century, a significant number of American farms, depending on their location and the quality of their land, were already heavily commercial in their orientation; they produced wheat for breadstuffs, cheese and butter, livestock for city slaughterhouses, hay for horse fodder. Farms closest to cities and villages were producing meat, whole milk and vegetables. The urban population grew nearly eightfold between 1790 and 1840, and rural commercial and manufacturing villages added to the number of Americans who no longer produced most of their own food. Northern farm families as far west as Ohio turned toward more specialized and market-driven agriculture. In southern New England, it was universally noted, industrial growth had created "home markets in every valley." Transportation to markets near and far improved on roads and canals. By 1840, cheaper, high-quality flour from wheat grown on the more fertile soil of western New York and Ohio had replaced traditional New England breadstuffs even for many farm families.

In some communities farm families took up new kinds of production in the household. Women braided straw and wove palm-leaf hats to supply consumers across the country, and farmers' sons and daughters took up the making of shoes. In the Connecticut Valley of Massachusetts, some farmers took up the growing of broomcorn and made brooms all winter.

Plows as well as hoes, shovels, axes, forks, rakes and scythes, the traditional implements of American husbandry, had been made and endlessly repaired by country blacksmiths and farmers themselves. Men who worked with them remembered them later as heavy and awkward. Change began to come with improved designs and the appearance of agricultural implement shops that produced tools not one by one but by the dozens and hundreds. A new notion was dawning, that tools could save and lighten labor.

Traditionally the blades of shovels and the moldboards of

plows were made of wood and then "shod," or covered and edged with iron. In the new tools these critical parts were made completely of cast iron. They turned over or cut through the soil more easily, and were much harder to break. Other implements were remade with stronger handles, and lighter and more efficient blades and working surfaces. There was "scarcely a tool," wrote the *Farmer's Almanack* in 1839, "that has not been altered for the better in some way or other" since the turn of the century. With better manure forks, claimed the *Boston Cultivator* the same year, "one third the former labor of forking or shovelling is saved." Hand-cranked fanning mills appeared for separating grain from chaff after threshing, replacing the work of men or women with winnowing baskets. On many Northern farms, dairywomen adopted improved equipment: "rocking" or crank-powered churns that promised to speed the labor of butter making and improved cheese presses.

Great farmers and their hired hands, along with a few adventurous smaller farmers, were working with a complete range of the new implements by the 1830s. A small number of the most prosperous and progressive were experimenting with rudimentary mechanization. In the wheat-growing regions of the Middle States and Ohio they were trying out horse-powered threshing machines, which replaced the work of men with wooden flails, or horses stamping out the grain on the barn floor. Some with large hayfields were adopting "horse rakes," which promised to reduce the time and labor involved in turning and "making" hay after it had been cut.

"Relief . . . came to working men" with lighter and easier tools, as Francis Underwood observed, but gradually. They made their way out to Western farms as market production advanced. Slaves found their instruments of tillage little changed, except for the plows that planters were beginning to use more frequently. "Common" farmers in the North took up the new tools one by one. They began to use fanning mills, but adopted other machinery not at all. Everywhere, farming remained heavy manual work. Its most important and laborious tasks, cultivating and harvesting, were as yet unchanged. The reaper, cultivator and mowing machine were still on the horizon.

Many Northern women were abandoning some of their ancient household tools and tasks. They first gave up the arduous process of producing cloth from flax as machine-produced cotton fabrics became available. In southern New England, wrote the *New England Farmer* in 1835, flax was rarely grown anymore. It had yielded to "the extensive and daily increasing use of cotton." The production of woolens declined more gradually, because the process took longer to mechanize efficiently. But by 1830, the loom and wool wheel had begun to disappear, and within a decade country families were consigning their textile equipment to the attic. Outside the longer-settled parts of the North, this "great change in domestic life" took longer to become complete. In most of the West and South, and recently settled parts of northern New England, the production of cloth remained a critical part of the household economy and of women's work for decades longer.

The gradual disappearance of spinning and weaving from many Northern households troubled some male, upper-class observers, who feared that farm wives and daughters would have empty time on their hands. In reality, the great majority of women stayed hard at work. Some shifted from textile production to "outwork," others to more intensive dairying. American women and girls actually sewed more as their spinning and weaving declined. Industrial production made far greater quantities of fabric available, and they could make shirts, dresses, curtains, bedspreads, sheets and towels in greater numbers than their grandmothers had done. For some women, time that had once been spent in textile production was available for maintaining higher standards of housekeeping, so that they worked harder at keeping their houses clean.

For many city and village women, food preparation and cooking became increasingly systematic domestic arts, as they wrote down recipes, planned meals and strove for order and exactness in the kitchen. They could find guidance in a rapidly growing number of cookbooks. Almost fifty appeared between 1796 and 1840, with two or three new ones appearing on the shelves each year after 1824.

These women also had access to significant changes in cooking technology. "Tin kitchens"—open half-cylinders of tin in which meat could be spitted and turned in front of the fire—began to come into use around 1800. They roasted meat far more evenly than the old method of dangling a joint precariously over the hearth, and improved the taste as well. Even more important was the cookstove, which made its appearance in the kitchens of prosperous urban homes two decades later. Made possible by major improvements in the technology of cast iron, it marked the most significant change in the technology of cooking since the widespread adoption of the fireplace and hearth. By the late 1830s cookstoves were coming into use among middling city families and in Northern commercial villages. In 1838, "the year we had a new cooking stove, the first one in town," recalled Susan Blunt, who grew up in a bustling rural commercial center, "the neighbors said we would all be sick—taken off in rimmers as they called them." The Blunt family embraced the new contraption and its "different sised kittles" at waist height. Susan noted that "in a year or two all the neighbors had one, after they saw that we came out all right in the spring."

With their stove-top heating surfaces at waist height, their somewhat lighter-weight "boilers" and kettles of various sizes, cookstoves, as the editor of the *New England Farmer* noted in 1837, saved "much female strength, which over a fireplace has to be exerted over heavy pots and kettles." Women had to learn new ways of gauging temperature and judging cooking times, but they usually found the cookstove's even heat "generally more comfortable to cook over than a blazing fire." Mrs. Blunt, her daughter recalled, "was quite pleased with it; it was easier to cook on than the fireplace." The cookstove became the first major domestic appliance in American history.

Probably, most families did not adopt stoves simply to ease women's labor or even to provide more comfortable heat. Far more fuel-efficient than open fireplaces, stoves saved firewood that was growing increasingly expensive in heavily settled and deforested parts of the North. They reduced what households paid for firewood, and lessened men's and boys' work in hauling wood and chopping kindling. It took longer for farm families to make the change that city folk and villagers like the Blunts had embraced. As stove prices continued to decline while firewood prices rose, and stoves became symbols of domestic improvement, they gained much more acceptance in the Northern countryside by 1850. Where wood remained abundant, and cash scarcer, farm women remained tied far longer to the back-straining routines of the fireplace.

A number of American women were also looking differently at how they raised their children. Bearing and rearing children had always been intertwined with the multitude of other tasks which American women performed: "boiling and baking, turning the spinning wheel and rocking the cradle," as the *Farmer's Almanack* put it. Caring for children simply took its place in the daily round, important but not complicated. But a new conception of motherhood as a special and uniquely important form of women's work emerged in the Revolutionary years and was finding substantial acceptance in early nineteenth-century America. Ministers' sermons and other public pronouncements stressed the theme that motherhood was not just something natural, inevitable and to be taken for granted. Not only did Evangelical preachers charge mothers with preparing their children for salvation, but others maintained that the safety of the Republic itself, or, at the very least, success in the rapidly changing social and economic order were at stake; they depended on the strength of character and self-control that virtuous mothers-citizens alone could instill in their offspring. These admonitions were echoed in the child-rearing advice books that appeared in increasing numbers for a public of well-off and moderately well-off Americans. It is no wonder that many came to believe that motherhood was the most important part of a woman's life, a source of great satisfaction but also a "fearful responsibility."

Prosperous and middling women in cities and villages, and some living on farms, took these precepts very seriously. They devoted increasing time and attention to rearing their children. Their letters and diaries began to be full of careful and loving observations of their children's growth and activities, and anxious concern for their physical and spiritual welfare.

With expanded production for market in the countryside came increased amounts of cash in circulation, embodied not just in coins but in the bank notes produced by a great expansion of commercial banking. It led to the gradual erosion of the world of rural exchange. Households with larger amounts of cash had a wider range of options for purchasing goods and services. They became less firmly tied to long-term reciprocal relationships with their neighbors. By 1840, some rural New Englanders were giving up their account books, with their long-term records of work and commodities exchanged for "cash books," which simply recorded sums paid in and paid out on a daily basis. Applying labor and capital more intensively and single-mindedly to their fields, many farmers were also abandoning rituals such as corn huskings, which combined work and sociability. The economic threads that helped tie the social webs of country neighborhoods together became weaker.

The American world of reasonably widespread literacy but comparatively little reading was also changing. Starting late in the eighteenth century, well before the emergence of highly self-conscious "school reform" in the 1830s, American families in the North began to send their children—in particular, increasing numbers of girls—to school for longer periods of time. Pupils younger than four or in their late teens gradually became less common sights in schoolhouses. Textbooks became cheaper and much more widely available. Books, periodicals and newspapers of all kinds were pouring off the presses of the 1830s in enormous numbers compared to thirty years earlier, and rural printing as well as elaborate networks of book exchange brought them to the countryside as well as the city. In 1798 when his ministry began in the small country town of North Brookfield, Massachusetts, remembered the Reverend Thomas Snell, there was only one "channel of general intelligence" in town, a few weekly copies of "the one newspaper published in the county." Fifty years later, the mail brought "each week 342 newspapers, weeklies and dailies, under fifty different titles— together with fifty-five other periodicals every month."

Many Americans, however, were untouched by this increase of print and days of schooling. School enrollment in American cities did not keep pace with that in the countryside. Poor urban children were not much more likely to be learning to read and write in 1840 than they had been in the late eighteenth century. Southerners continued to have fewer schools, lower rates of literacy and less access to newspapers and periodicals than the Northerners. And in the early 1830s, slaves found even their previously meager opportunities for learning foreclosed when embattled Southerners, fearful of slave revolts and abolitionist propaganda, tightened the slave codes in almost every state. To be found reading, or trying to learn, "was a major crime," as a South Carolina slave remembered. "You might as well had killed your master or missus."

"The wheel starts at sunrise," ran the rules of one of Zachariah Allen's textile mills; "it is expected that every person will be at their places ready to work at the starting of the wheel." Work ended at sunset between April and October; otherwise the factory "lit candles" and worked to "half past seven." The factory bells in Lowell tolled out even more regular hours, starting at five o'clock and stopping at seven, and were silent only Sundays and three holidays a year.

The most dramatically new workplaces in the United States were the textile factories, where what Lucy Larcom called "the buzzing and hissing and whizzing of pulleys, and rollers and spindles" displaced the quiet of farm households and the traditional music of spinning wheels and handlooms. In the years after 1790 Americans had adopted and modified the English technologies of mechanized textile production. By the 1830s there were hundreds of water-powered factories, large and small, that performed the tasks of picking and carding, spinning and weaving, on a vastly larger scale and far more swiftly.

The planners and owners of the Lowell factories and other mills organized on the same large scale recruited their work force primarily from young unmarried women—partly in a well-publicized attempt to avoid creating a permanent factory class, but also to obtain cheap and tractable labor. Young women came to the mills in Lowell and Waltham, Massachusetts, Manchester, New Hampshire, and a few other fast-growing textile towns from the hill country of New Hampshire and Vermont. They lived for the most part in supervised boarding-houses that resembled large-scale households linked to their factory workplaces. Thousands of them, from ordinary but not impoverished farm families, arrived to work for a year or two before they married—sometimes to help their families, but more often to earn money for their own use.

The managers of smaller mills—which taken together accounted for more output and employment than the few large ones—had to adopt a different policy. "In collecting our help," wrote the mill owner Smith Wilkinson of Connecticut, "we are obliged to employ poor families, and generally those having the greatest number of children, those who have lived in retired situations on small poor farms, or in hired houses" without any land at all. Young single women made up part of the work force, but families were usually recruited together, fathers often doing outdoor labor while their offspring toiled in the mill. Unlike the Lowell factories, which paid cash, the "Rhode Island system" mills paid their workers in the account-book exchange of the rural economy, through trade at company and other local stores and in the rental of tenements. Fathers received their sons' and daughters' wages on account. These hard-pressed mill-village families proved as mobile as farm laborers and household "helps." They rarely stayed much more than a year with a single employer, often only a few months. Frequently they moved restlessly from one factory village to another, looking for "better situations."

The ringing of the factory bells summoned women and children into a world of precisely structured hours, close confinement and the noise of machinery.

"You cannot think how odd everything seemed," wrote a mill girl in the *Lowell Offering,* about her introduction to factory work. Even experience in hand spinning and weaving did not help much with the new machinery, and new hands sometimes felt that "the sight of so many bands, and wheels, and springs in constant motion, was very frightful." A new operative often emerged with "the noise of the mill in my ears, as of crickets, frogs and jewsharps, all mingled together in strange discord." The new industry retained the traditional sexual division of labor. A minority of men performed skilled and supervisory jobs; women, girls and boys found themselves "tending" machines. The youngest worked as "doffers" or "bobbin boys," replacing empty spindles of yarn with full ones on the spinning frames. The young doffers had to move quickly—Harriet Hanson Robinson remembered "racing down the valley between the spinning frames, in front of me carrying a bobbin-box bigger than I was"—but they had long intervals of play between their stints of work.

Older workers had no time for relaxation. They had to oversee the operation of drawing frames, spinning throstles or power looms, work which required concentrated attention; women had to scan their machines constantly for broken threads or empty shuttle bobbins. It took a month or so for most mill workers to become reasonably comfortable with the machinery. Success depended on vigilance, quickness and deft manipulation. Some never acquired it and had to give up the work.

Dressing frames, which prepared spun cotton threads to make the warp for weaving, were the most difficult to manage. Working in Lowell, Lucy Larcom remembered that hers "had to be watched in a dozen different directions every minute, and even then it was always getting itself and me in trouble." Demanding close concentration through twelve-hour days, early nineteenth-century factory work was less physically exhausting than it was draining and numbing.

Responses to the experience of work in the mills varied considerably. Some of the Lowell mill hands remembered their friendships there fondly, and recalled their strictly controlled work without resentment, although they all found the "long hours of confinement" wearing. Other young women were far more rebellious. They led or participated in "turn outs" to protest reductions in wages or increases in the cost of board.

Many in the first generation of workers in the smaller mills only reluctantly accepted the factories' clock and bell time, and did not always acquire machine-tending skills to their supervisors' satisfaction. N. B. Gordon, a "mill agent" who ran a small cotton factory in Mansfield, Massachusetts, in 1829 and 1830, was clearly frustrated by how rarely he was able to report "all hands" at work in his diary. Most commonly, one or more mill hands were "absent" throughout the day, and others "come in after breakfast," or "after dinner." More than once Gordon reflected sourly that there were "but few good hands in the mill." In January of 1830, there were "a poor lot of weavers at this time & bid fair to be worse." On "Election Day" in May, a traditional holiday in the Massachusetts countryside, he was forced to have the "Factory stopped"; angrily he noted that "I could not peaceably work the mill as all hands seemed determined to have the whole day." Worst of all was his discovery that a boy in the mill, probably hoping to slow the pace of work, had been sabotaging the factory's most complex machinery, the spinning mules. Lewis Kingman, whose job as a piecer was to tie broken threads on the mules, was secretly slipping the leather belts that powered the devices off their pulleys, and finally he was caught cutting them. "For Boldness and Cunning the above tricks surpass all description," Gordon wrote. Hiram Munger, who had also worked as one of the "poor children" in a small Massachusetts factory, might have spoken for young Lewis. He recalled his experience as "American slavery in the *second* degree."

As national markets for chairs, brooms, shoes, farm implements, books and hats emerged and expanded in the United States, many more men were becoming full-time producers of objects. But fewer of them worked in small shops linked to masters' households, or had the expectations of traditional craftsmen.

Americans continued to learn their skills in the workplace, but in a number of trades, apprenticeship and the traditional ladder of craftsmanship were dying institutions by 1840. In some trades, work no longer required the full range of a mechanic's traditional skills. The world of the skilled ladies' shoemakers of Lynn, Massachusetts, for example, was devastatingly transformed as the markets expanded for what they made. A system of "putting out" production arose that divided tasks ever more minutely and took control of materials and product out of the hands of the craftsmen and into those of merchant-capitalists. They were losing their prized status as independent artisans and being converted into pieceworkers. Yet for many new American shoe workers there was no comparable experience of loss. As shoe manufacturing expanded in Massachusetts it moved deeper into the countryside, recruiting many thou-

sands of men and women from farm households who had no
community or family traditions of shoemaking artisanship.

Where shops were increasing in scale and growing into
"manufacturing establishments," only a few men could afford
the capital investment required to start a business. The number
of individual small-shop owners was diminishing. Indented apprentices became ever rarer. In an increasingly cyclical economy, masters began to see them as liabilities who could not be
discharged when business was poor. It became increasingly
difficult for employers to run their businesses as "family" units.

Apprentices and journeymen were turning into employees.
Some trades were more resistant. Carpenters and house builders, for example, because their markets necessarily remained
local and their work difficult to subdivide, were able to stay
organized in traditional ways.

In this turbulent economic transition, many shops, like that
of Andrus and Judd, became places of rapid turnover, turmoil
and uncertainty. Journeymen and apprentices came and went,
as shops went out of business or changed ownership at short
intervals.

In American cities the longstanding linkage of household and
shop went sharply into decline. The single young men who
moved cityward to work were more and more likely to be living
on their own, not subject to the "family" care and discipline of
their employers. It had become uncommon, observed a speaker
to a group of Massachusetts mechanics in 1845, for apprentices
to "live under the roof" of their employers, and "the paternal
character of this connexion has become obsolete." American
cities were full of lodgers, who paid for meals and a room or a
bed in a household but worked as mechanics or clerks elsewhere. They became important parts of the economic life of
many poor and middling city families, who increasingly relied
on income from lodgers to help pay the rent.

More traditional arrangements persisted in the countryside.
Rural artisans continued to feed and lodge their apprentices

and journeymen in their households, and country storekeepers boarded their clerks. But rural mechanics found their work patterns changing as well. Some country blacksmiths, for example, enlarged their shops to become specialized ax, plow or scythe makers, or machinists for rural mills. Those who did not specialize found their work ever more restricted to simple repairs, as farmers bought ready-made tools and hardware. Occasionally, like two of the Merriam brothers in 1831, they moved to an urban location and greatly enlarged their scale of production. More often, they persisted in doing what they had always done, and saw their markets dwindle against the competition of cheaper, mass-produced goods.

Most Americans' hours of work had not become shorter or easier. The seasonal swings of farm labor did not change, and new tools and rudimentary machinery were just starting to have an impact. A large number of rural Americans were working more calculatingly and less socially. Many American women found their burdens reapportioned, but not dramatically lightened.

For all of those working in the industrial and commercial sectors of the economy, the rhythms of work became less episodic and irregular. Merchants and storekeepers had more business to do, and had to do it more quickly. Factory work brought not simply long hours but dismayingly regular, clock-governed times of work. And many mechanics, as they struggled to succeed by producing goods for a perilously uncertain commercial economy, worked very hard indeed. The "hours of work were long" throughout the year for printers in Springfield, Massachusetts, who were producing law books and dictionaries for the national market in the 1830s, "in winter getting breakfast and going to work sometimes before daylight was sufficient to see by, working until 8 o'clock in the winter evenings and in summer till nearly dark." But the work had also become unrelentingly intense. The "ten-hour" movement that gathered

momentum among urban workers in the 1830s, with only limited success up to 1840, implicitly recognized that older, more
episodic work rhythms were disappearing. It was an attempt
to gain some relief from a transitional world of work that
combined the "sun to sun" hours of tradition and the new
regularity.

There had been "a great multiplying and diversifying of the
occupations of society" in the years of the early nineteenth
century, as Goodrich said. The expansion of manufacturing and
commerce was also creating greater material abundance, providing greater comfort, raising the standard of living. But there
were more propertyless workers in city and countryside, artisans without the traditional hope of independence. One cost of
the process was increasing inequality. The most successful
American families in commerce and manufacturing were able
to garner an increasingly large share of the wealth. The
rhythms and routines of labor of America's "industrious population" were in the midst of a great transition that would last
through the nineteenth century.

2

THE RHYTHMS
AND LIMITS OF LIFE

꙰ _____

O N JUNE 16, 1806, there was a total eclipse of the sun across
the northern United States. "The people stood in silent amaze-
ment," wrote the Reverend Timothy Dickinson of Holliston,
Massachusetts, in his diary. Nine months later Dickinson recalled that extraordinary event in his journal, linking it to the
much more commonplace ones of pregnancy. In Holliston,
there were "a number of our married women in the straw about
this time! Four in one neighborhood! Some refer to the eclipse!"

It's far from certain that the eclipse of 1806 created a wave
of American pregnancies; very few other Americans commented in writing on the intimate rhythms of their lives. But
recurring patterns of marriage and birth, sickness and death—
what the demographers call fertility, nuptiality, morbidity and
mortality—shaped the experience of early nineteenth-century
Americans more surely than any sequence of remarkable
events. Too often expressed only in abstractions and numbers,
they yet have a deep human meaning. They defined the
rhythms within which ordinary lives moved and the limits
against which they struggled.

Because most Americans remained tied to the countryside
and its agricultural cycles, their lives were structured by insistent seasonal rhythms of planting and harvest, work and leisure.
The chances and seasons of dying, giving birth and marrying

were for the most part an inheritance from the early American past. But in the patterns of childbearing and the size of families, and in the rituals surrounding marriage, childbirth and death, there were the beginnings of dramatic change.

"A Great Many Marriages"

Weddings marked the creation of new families and sanctioned the beginning of a new cycle of procreation. Anxious "to see everything relating to the manner and customs of the country," an English couple invited themselves to a wedding in the western Massachusetts countryside in 1827. They found a company of kin and neighbors crowded into a farmhouse parlor, some perched on benches, others sitting on chairs "as if they were pinned to the wall." The bride and groom, with their bridesmaid and groomsman, sat facing the minister, who pulled up "a chair before him, on the back of which he leant." He then motioned for the company to rise, joined the couple's hands together and led them through a brief exchange of vows. Most American couples were wed by a clergyman at the home of the bride, in such informal ceremonies of republican simplicity.

American women began to marry in their late teens; around different parts of the United States the average age of marriage varied from nineteen to twenty-three. This was later than in most of the world's societies, but earlier than in Western Europe. The American population grew so quickly relative to those of Europe partly because American brides were generally younger than their European cousins, and so had more childbearing years, and partly because few American women remained unmarried.

Throughout the American countryside the bride's family traditionally invited the entire neighborhood to the wedding as a matter of course. "Alternate feasting and dancing, often till broad daylight," followed the ceremony in many American weddings. At a wedding in Georgia plantation country in 1829,

Henry Worth remembered "a large concourse of people" so thronging the yard that the wedding party had to "press our way thro' the crowds to the house." After the service and bridal supper there were courting games for the young people, and all except near neighbors "stayed all night; and the bedrooms being crowded with old women and children, they had to sit up," talking and courting all night. In Kentucky, recalled Daniel Drake, "weddings were often scenes of carousal, and merriment of no very chastened kind." From Illinois to Massachusetts, wedding guests often went on to "shivaree" or serenade the newly joined couple that night or the next at their new home, making noise below the nuptial bedchamber until they were invited in for more "entertainment."

American brides rarely received presents and only occasionally wore white; women who could afford wedding outfits much more commonly chose brown or dove-colored silk and were sometimes married in their traveling clothes. Most American farm couples married and then settled into their new homes to begin the work that would structure the rest of their lives together. If they married in the winter they occasionally took a few days to make a short round of visits to kin and friends. Men employed in commerce and the professions could afford a longer transition between courtship and the serious obligations of marriage; they and their new wives spent a few weeks visiting relatives who might have missed the wedding or receiving company at their new homes. As long-distance travel became easier and more affordable these prosperous couples began in the 1820s to take "wedding tours" or "nuptial journeys," sometimes to New York City or even "the Falls of Niagra." Poor Americans everywhere, who had little choice, went almost immediately back to their occupations.

Although slave marriages were not recognized in law, it was "very common for slaves to be married," as the ex-slave William Wells Brown noted. Slaves usually took permanent partners, and marked their unions with some kind of ceremony—one which mirrored the relationships of power in the slaves' lives, for it involved not informing parents or gaining their assent but obtaining the permission of the master. Most elaborately, slave couples wed in a full religious ceremony with a white minister or black plantation preacher "on the porch of the Big House." Episcopal clergymen in eastern Virginia and South Carolina sometimes performed more black marriages than white ones. Many slaves became man and wife less formally, in abbreviated services performed by their masters "at the cabin door." In St. Mary's Parish, Louisiana, "the only ceremony required before entering into that 'holy estate,'" Solomon Northup recalled, was to "obtain the consent of the respective owners." Often there were other observances in the quarters in which masters did not participate. Part of the ritual that sealed many slave marriages was "jumping the broomstick," or having bride and groom leap backwards over a broom held out by their friends —a practice whose roots in African or plantation culture remain obscure.

"It is marrying time," Elizabeth Ward of Shrewsbury, Massachusetts, wrote in April of 1823, as she listed the weddings in her town for her daughter. For Americans in the countryside the timing of marriage still followed predictable seasonal rhythms. Marrying couples in the rural North followed patterns that their ancestors had established in the seventeenth century. Overwhelmingly they chose to marry in the early spring months of March and April, or the after-harvest months of November and December, avoiding both the dead of winter and the months of heavy farm work from May through October. Most marriages came either in anticipation or in fulfillment of the cycle of planting and harvest. "A great many marriages in the country," wrote a reflective New Englander, "take place at Thanksgiving"; and the week in early December around the New England festival, which was both a Puritan day of prayer and an ancient harvest celebration, was the most popular of all times for Yankees to wed.

In urban places, where work schedules and habits of mind had little to do with agriculture, the seasons of marriage were far less marked. Except for a flurry around Thanksgiving, marrying couples in Boston spread their weddings fairly evenly throughout the year. And the trend of marriages in Concord, Massachusetts, a rural community near Boston which was coming into the city's commercial and cultural orbit, pointed in the direction of change. As the town's ties to the metropolis tightened after 1800, Concord's citizens began to marry increasingly without reference to the seasons.

American husbands and wives participated in another, more intimate cycle, one of procreation and sexuality. From the seventeenth century through the early decades of the nineteenth, every year saw a regular, rhythmic variation in the frequency of childbirth in rural communities. Babies were born most frequently to white American families in months of late winter and early spring, and least often in late spring and early summer. In some Northern communities, a second, smaller upsurge of births came in the early fall. When Americans looked backward nine months, as Timothy Dickinson did, to the moment of conception, they surely noticed—although rarely in writing—that couples were most likely to conceive in the planting season, between April and June, and that their fecundity declined steeply during the summer to a minimum between August and October.

But Afro-American slaves conceived and bore children to a different rhythm entirely. Slave births peaked in midsummer and reached a minimum in late fall and early winter. Slave couples conceived least often in the late winter and early spring, but most often in the early fall months—the same time at which white couples were least fertile.

These cycles of birth and conception, which have greatly diminished in the twentieth-century United States and other urban-industrial societies, were shaped by a complex and only partially understood interaction of biology and behavior. Long hours of labor in the fields may have had a cumulative effect by midsummer, exhausting men and women so much that they had sexual intercourse less often. The heavier burden of summer work may also have made it harder for women to conceive and increased their chances of miscarriage. Slaves' conception cycles were linked more to nutrition than to work; food supplies were scantiest in the spring, and dietary deficiencies may have affected women's fertility.

These cycles marked recurrent rhythms, altering only slowly, which were the enduring signatures of preindustrial, agricultural life. Yet marriages and births, as they waxed and waned in the life of each community every year, were in some places weaving a pattern of profound change—the beginning of an unprecedented decline in family size.

In the traditional world of childbearing in which many Americans of the early Republic still lived, children began to arrive within a year after marriage, at first following an average spacing of two to three years; the interval lengthened as mothers grew older. Couples who lived together through the wife's childbearing years could expect seven to eight children on the average, but the actual sizes of their families varied considerably. There were couples who had no children, or only one or two; but this usually reflected sterility or incapacitating illness. For many, miscarriages and stillbirths were repeated, routine events. Extremely large families of ten or more children were not typical, but they were common enough that some could be found in almost any community, and that a sizable proportion of nineteenth-century Americans would remember growing up in them—thus accounting for the widespread impression that most families in the past were truly enormous.

Yet for women and men in some parts of the United States, the size of their families had already begun to change. At the time of his marriage in 1801, Pliny Freeman of Sturbridge, Massachusetts, had a house built for him by his father. It stands today not far from its original location, at the center of a museum re-creation of an early nineteenth-century farm. The Freemans were ordinary folk in a small community, but their lives over three generations gave pivotal testimony to a great change, a revolution in childbearing. Pliny's parents, Comfort and Lucy Freeman, had nine children born to them between 1772 and 1790—a large family but far from unusual in eighteenth-century Sturbridge. Like other Sturbridge couples of their generation, Pliny and his wife, Deliah, had a smaller although still sizable family—seven children born between 1802 and 1819. Six of their children survived to adulthood and married between the late 1820s and the early 1840s. This third generation of Freeman marriages produced only four children each on the average, and none had more than five. The Freemans exemplified a process of decline in family size that would continue over almost two centuries into our own time.

In communities across the North, married couples had begun having smaller families than in previous generations; their fertility fell in ways similar to that of the Freemans, although not always as dramatically. In some places women were marrying at increasingly later ages, shortening their childbearing years and thus limiting the number of children they were likely to have. By the 1830s, the *Universal Traveller* observed, New Englanders had come to "seldom marry at as early an age as is common" elsewhere. Women in rural Massachusetts were wedding at over twenty-five, two years later than their mothers had thirty years before, and five years later than their grandmothers.

But local registers that record births and marriages eloquently reveal that many of these couples were also doing something far more revolutionary: once married, they were consciously choosing within marriage to limit the number of their children. Mothers in eighteenth-century America usually bore the last of their children in their early forties, ceasing to have children only when it was no longer biologically possible. In Sturbridge and other New England towns after 1800 women were undergoing their final pregnancies increasingly earlier each decade. Among the Quakers of southeastern Pennsylvania, couples were limiting their families by increasing the spacing between births rather than shortening the length of the childbearing years. Taken together, the decisions and actions of hundreds of thousands of American couples began to reshape the dimensions of their society.

Because Americans in the longest-settled eastern parts of the United States were the first to limit their procreation, an observant traveler going east to west in the 1830s could have noticed a marked increase in the size of families he or she encountered. In 1830, the people of Massachusetts and Connecticut averaged not much over five children per family, and those of Illinois, Indiana, Alabama and Mississippi—just behind the advancing edge of settlement—probably had seven or so on the average. A trip westward was almost a demographic journey back in time; family sizes in communities farther west mirrored those in much longer-settled places a generation or two previously. The women of Sugar Creek, Illinois, for example, were marrying four to five years younger on the average than those in Sturbridge or Deerfield, Massachusetts.

Only the birth and marriage records speak for early nineteenth-century American wives and husbands, because they were not articulate about such intimate decisions. But American families surely made their decisions, or came to believe that there were decisions to be made, in the light of available resources and standards for rearing children. Both were changing.

The three generations of the Freeman family, like other American farm families, strove while their children were young to accumulate resources, particularly land, to provide for them as they came to maturity. They faced a decline in the availability of good farmland in their community. Land had been cheap and plentiful when Comfort Freeman's father, Samuel, arrived in the early eighteenth century from eastern Massachusetts, and Comfort received a generous portion when he came to marry. Comfort was able to settle his children reasonably well but less abundantly, and Pliny Freeman and his brothers faced significantly more difficult choices in dividing smaller resources among their children. Many of those children left an agriculturally crowded Sturbridge to farm elsewhere or find other work. Each generation had looked at more expensive and less easily available land—and had had smaller families.

As the United States expanded westward, families were starting to reenact a similar cycle of the generations. New settlers' family lives were like those of the communities they had left behind as adults. Their sons and daughters born and marrying in the new country had large families. Succeeding generations in the same places had steadily fewer children.

But land could have been only part of the puzzle of American motivation. Their ancestors had faced similar situations in Europe long before without responding as they had done. Successive generations of Freemans, for example, were not only facing more crowding on the land, they were better schooled and better read. Americans like them seem to have been looking at family life and family size with a new purposiveness. Providing properly and decently for their children was a more complex problem in the early nineteenth century than it had ever been before. A powerful ideology of motherhood took shape in the early years of the nineteenth century and became widely disseminated. Books of advice to mothers increased in number and in circulation. Three works popular in New England in the 1830s—Lydia Maria Child's *The Mother's Book,* the Reverend John Abbott's *The Mother at Home* and William Alcott's *The Young Mother's Guide*—gave widely differing advice on discipline or infant diet but agreed on one central point: motherhood was an enormously important task which rightfully demanded most of a woman's time and energy. The women who read these books or joined the new maternal associations devoted to Christian child rearing were very likely to have a different view from their mothers or grandmothers about the optimum number of children to raise.

Rising standards of domestic abundance and order—in household cleanliness, furnishings, clothing, even better textbooks for young scholars—seem also to have made for increased concern with family limitation even as they raised American couples' sights beyond the material life of their parents. "The advances made in wealth and refinement," thought Samuel Goodrich, had actually made it "more difficult than it formerly was, to provide properly for a family." Men and women married later, attempting to set themselves up more securely before starting a family—and were increasingly reluctant to have more children than they could expect to launch safely into life. Some were not marrying at all. In the northeastern states, the proportion of women remaining unmarried increased substantially as the westward migration of men unbalanced the sex ratio. "Many more," Goodrich went on to note, "are remaining in celibacy than formerly." Comfort and Lucy Freeman had simply accepted the children that God had been pleased to send them; their grandchildren were counting the cost.

These new attitudes toward procreation may have made themselves felt in changing ceremonies of marriage as well. Over the first few decades of the nineteenth century many Northern women and men were making their weddings less inclusive, substantially more private events. Ceremonies in rural New England had been "far more numerously attended" at the beginning of the century, Horace Greeley observed four decades later, "than are the average in our day." In the years after 1820 many more American weddings became quiet, sober occasions in which the guests "all resumed our seats and . . . silence prevailed," as Margaret Hall noted of a ceremony in Northampton, Massachusetts, while they passed around the wedding cake and sedately congratulated the young couple. Some wedding parties diminished to the extent of involving only closest kin and a few friends—frequently even omitting the groom's parents if they lived any distance away.

American slaves lived in a world which provided no incentives to limit their fertility. They remained in the traditional pattern of childbearing far longer. Slave families were as large as or larger than those of whites in 1800 and their size remained unchanged until after Emancipation.

The revolution in childbearing was a lengthy, undramatic process, whose full significance was inevitably hidden from its participants. Gradually, American families to the west and south followed in the path of the northeastern pioneers of family limitation. Over the decades even the most prolific American families, those of the sons and daughters of frontier settlers, became smaller, as they, too, started to count the costs and benefits of rearing children.

"No Force Can Death Resist"

Simeon Dwight, Jr., died unexpectedly in 1816 at the age of twenty-seven. His slate gravestone, engraved with the urn and willow symbols of mourning, stands in the oldest part of a hilly cemetery in Warren, Massachusetts. It bears an inscription which encapsulated Americans' experience of death in four lines:

> Fix'd is the term to all the race on earth
> And such the hard condition of our birth
> No force can death resist, no flight can save
> All fall alike, the fearful and the brave.

Sickness and death were far more resistant to change than were the conditions of family size. Americans' life expectancies did not change greatly in the early nineteenth century, and were not to improve significantly until the widespread adoption of public health measures and antiseptic precautions decades later. The unhealthiness of daily life may well be the most striking of the great divides between the past and the present. Set against conditions almost everywhere else at the time, much of the early nineteenth-century United States was favored and fortunate territory in terms of the chances of life. Americans on the average lived as long or longer than any other people in the world. For some, primarily in the rural North, life expectancy was close to the maximum level that the medical and hygienic knowledge of that time could sustain. Yet it was not a world to which any American today would willingly go back.

Americans' life chances looked good when set against those of most European countries. But both place and race remained significant determinants of life expectancy. Earlier in American history, regional differences in life expectancy had been enormous. Seventeenth- and early eighteenth-century New Englanders had lived far longer on the average than Virginians and Marylanders along the malarial Chesapeake. Southerners came gradually to live longer over the eighteenth century, but because their warmer climate sustained more virulent diseases, they continued to have somewhat shorter life expectancies than Northerners. South of the Potomac, mosquito-borne malaria and yellow fever brooded, food was more difficult to preserve from infection, and parasitic diseases like hookworm attacked the shoeless.

Poorer diet and housing and devastatingly inadequate opportunities for infant care reduced the life chances of black Americans. Slaves did not live as long as Southern whites, and free blacks in the North, everywhere pushed to the economic margin by virulent prejudice, fared no better—although their life expectancies were higher than those of the West Indian slaves who faced brutal work regimes and inadequate diets.

Greater wealth was only in partial measure a guarantee of longer life. The prosperous could provide better nutrition and improve their resistance, but they could not easily buy real protection from infectious disease. Prosperous American families may have had better sanitary habits than their domestic help or slaves—but they lived intimately with them. The most expensive medical care available—that offered by well-known physicians in large cities—was not usually more effective against illness than the treatment of illiterate folk healers. But it was not always true that "no flight can save"; the wealthy could move most easily and quickly, and could sometimes escape disease. Well-to-do New Yorkers were the first people to leave the city in the cholera epidemic of 1832, and South Carolina planters reduced their families' risks by taking yearly journeys from the swampy, mosquito-ridden lowlands to higher and drier ground in the malaria season, leaving overseers and slaves behind.

"Fix'd is the term" was carved on Simeon Dwight's gravestone, but the life expectancies of early nineteenth-century Americans who survived to adulthood were not shockingly low. In the rural Northeast—where the vital statistics were the best kept and allow for such calculations—a white man or woman of twenty-one could expect to live into his or her mid-sixties; their late twentieth-century counterparts can count on living some seven years longer if male and fifteen years longer if female. These differences in life chances from those of today are not enormous or astonishing, but they had major consequences for personal experience. Most people did not survive much past the beginning of today's retirement age, and proportionately there were simply many fewer Americans around in their seventies and eighties.

Moreover, "all fall alike" from Dwight's epitaph was more than a conventional phrase. Death cut a considerably more even swath through the age levels of the population than it does now; people in their twenties, thirties and forties, although with a good chance of surviving into their sixties, still had death as a far more serious possibility in their lives. Most adults could have named at least one brother, sister or close friend who had died in early maturity. Widows and orphans were still commonplace; marriages were broken not by divorce but by death, and children were far more likely to experience the death of one or both parents while they were still young and dependent. Because childbearing still extended far longer through parents' lifespans, they rarely confronted the "empty nest"; most were unlikely to live very long together after their last child had left the household.

No Americans could forget "the hard condition of our birth." From the moment of birth children's lives were precarious, and the first year of life was, as it still is, by far the riskiest. One white American infant in six or seven did not survive to age one—approximately ten times the risk for a child born in the United States today. The years of childhood and adolescence, now the safest of all, were also a time of high mortality. Between age one and adulthood at twenty-one, another eight to ten percent of American children died, meaning that one white child out of every four or five would not survive from birth to maturity. Since parents could expect to have at the very least five children, the death of at least one child in a family was a commonplace and expectable occurrence. What is now a rare and disastrous stroke of fate was the experience of most families.

"But how long we shal be allowed to keep him," wrote a New York farm couple announcing the birth of their son, "is inknown to us." Because infants' lives were so fragile, many American parents invested less emotionally in their babies until they were a few months old and past the worst risks. They sometimes delayed naming them for several months, or warned each other about a new birth: "don't set too much by it." Some early nineteenth-century mothers, responding to new conceptions of the centrality and importance of motherhood, began to form strong bonds with their infants earlier, despite the risks. They found it difficult, in the words of an Alabaman in 1836, to "call off our affections from those dear second selves."

The death of children past infancy was always a shattering blow for parents. Lucy Buffum Lovell's anguished remembrance of 1840 registered how parents felt: "Two days after Caroline was taken from us, Edward became ill. I cannot again bear to tell the story of the suffering which came to this last of our children. Our despair was utter when the physicians told us that he was afflicted with scarlet fever, the disease which they had decided had taken Caroline. . . . We felt horribly hopeless and desperate."

Edward died within three days, and the Lovell family was to lose three young children in less than two years. The grim logic of infection meant that some families would be devastated by multiple deaths from the same disease, like that of the New Hampshire doctor who told Susan Blunt's mother in the 1830s that in a whooping cough epidemic "he had buried seven little children, all that he ever had." A more fortunate minority of families escaped childhood deaths entirely.

Among the slaves, infant and childhood mortality were fearful. One of three Afro-American children died in infancy. Black infants suffered from low birthweights due to inadequate prenatal rest and nutrition, from their mothers' lack of opportunities for adequate breast-feeding, and sometimes from unskilled care at the hands of very young girls. Not many more than half survived to adulthood. "I've lost a many," a slave mother whose child had just died "repeated over and over" to Frances Kemble Butler, "they all goes so." Several other mothers had been to see her, fearing the same event, "asking for advice and help for their sick children."

Death was a seasonal visitor as well. The late winter and early spring marked the highest risk of death from respiratory diseases. In the South, August and September were peak times for malaria-related deaths. Everywhere in the Union, from the smallest rural communities to the great cities, they were the "sickly months," the time of peak infant mortality from intestinal infections that flourished at summer's end.

"No force can death resist" was written everywhere, implicitly, in early nineteenth-century graveyards. The threshold of mortality could not be lowered even for the most privileged, because medicine and sanitation were not and could not be based on an understanding of microbial infection. Early nineteenth-century physicians were not willfully blind to what now seems the abundant evidence for mechanisms of infection and transmission; they lacked the accumulated body of clinical research that eventually gave medicine the ability to understand and treat disease. Bacteria and viruses, with their animal or insect hosts, were the invisible, intangible, unknown carriers of sickness and fatality. Contagion was almost a folk belief, widely held by ordinary people but frequently dismissed as superstitious. In the eyes of the medical profession, the vast majority of diseases showed no medically compelling evidence of contagiousness; of all the major illnesses, only smallpox was well established as clearly transmitted in some fashion from one person to another. Struggling for understanding, American and European medical thought looked for environmental causes in "miasmas," alterations in the composition of the atmosphere.

Before the antibiotics and immunizations of the twentieth century, infectious disease was the great killer. Newborns died in substantial numbers from birth defects and the effects of traumatic deliveries, but they primarily fell victim to galloping infections of the lungs and intestinal tract that ravaged their immature systems. When children passed beyond infancy they became vulnerable to diphtheria, whooping cough and scarlet fever that could ravage whole families. The ordinary viral diseases of childhood—measles, mumps, chicken pox—posed hazards from secondary bacterial infections that attacked already weakened victims. For adults, too, infections posed the greatest threat to life. Typhus and typhoid fever, bacterial dysentery, and bacterial and viral pneumonia, often as complications of influenza, struck at men and women in the prime of life as well as the young and the old.

Accidents—particularly ones which resulted in open wounds —were always alarming. Tetanus was always a deadly threat and infections leading to "mortification"—gangrene—or "blood poisoning"—septicemia—could not be checked. Working with edge tools, heavy loads and large draft animals, men from their midteens on were the most susceptible. Lewis Miller described how "a young woman threw an apple" at his eighteen-year-old brother who was running a cider mill. David Miller "turned around to see who threw, and his hand caught" in the mill's apple crusher. With his hand "dreadful ground up," he died of infection eight days later.

"Common as it is for children to be born," wrote Ann Jean Lyman of Northampton, Massachusetts, "so it is very common for mothers to lose their lives in this perilous enterprise." Having herself borne six children, she reflected in 1838 on a friend who "died as she had expected to,—under the most aggravated circumstances that a woman can leave the world. She never gave birth to her child, but died in the effort. In this dreadful manner have six of my youthful contemporaries departed this life." Women ran serious risks to life in hazarding repeated childbirths, where infectious complications from injury to the outer reproductive organs were frequent and protracted deliveries were very dangerous. Death in childbirth was a pervasive fear, which shadowed mothers' joy about bringing new life into the world, and even darkened young women's prospective views of marriage. Women's life expectancies for their childbearing years between twenty and forty-five were slightly lower than men's. The perils of work and masculine risk-taking were a little overbalanced by the even more harrowing passages of motherhood. For ages past forty-five, women's life expectancies rose slightly to match men's but did not surpass them.

The two great endemic diseases of the early nineteenth-century United States were malaria, usually called "intermittent fever" or "the ague," and pulmonary tuberculosis, then known as "consumption." Malaria was rare north of Virginia, but it affected a large portion of the South and extended far up the

Mississippi and Ohio river valleys. Wherever there was low-lying, swampy ground and a climate that fostered the year-round breeding of its host, the anopheles mosquito, it could thrive. The malaria parasite depended on human-mosquito contact to allow it to live out its extraordinarily complex life cycle. While in its victims' bloodstream malaria produced recurrent spasms of fever, chills and weakness.

Malaria was a disease that Americans lived with, for it usually debilitated its victims rather than killing them outright. In 1809, just as the British traveler John Melish took up a friendly glass of whiskey with his tavern-keeper host and a local doctor in Willton, South Carolina, he found that both his new companions had begun to shake violently with "ague fits," the violent shivering of malarial paroxysms. They treated it as a matter of no concern and within half an hour "they got clear of their shake, and we sat down to dinner." For many sufferers, it was less a disease than a condition of life. "To have the ague is in some places so common," claimed an observer in 1832, "that the patient can hardly claim the privilege of sickness."

Yet along with making its "pale and slow-moving" victims' lives burdensome, malaria rendered them far more vulnerable to death from other infections. The "intermittent fever" of the South was one disease that favored slaves at the expense of their masters. A high proportion of Afro-Americans possessed the gene for the sickle-cell trait in their red blood cells; it proved dangerous to some, but provided many blacks with a substantial degree of resistance to the disease.

As many as "one fourth . . . of all the deaths . . . in the Northern and Middle States," according to one of the most perceptive medical observers of the time, were due to the "frightful mortality" of "consumption" or tuberculosis. Probably no single disease accounted for more deaths before the Civil War. Figuring prominently in nineteenth-century art and literature that romanticized death, it was both debilitator and killer. The illness attacked young and middle-aged adults more virulently than it did children and brought death slowly by destroying the lungs. Because consumption produced no disfiguring symptoms, often struck young women and gave them a languorous air and the flush of low fever, its dying victims were easy to sentimentalize. "A more beautiful object I have seldom seen," wrote Jane Grey Jennings in 1828 of a consumptive teenaged girl who had "a hectic flush still lingering on her cheek." For the disease's victims, the reality was far from romantic. Jennings's friend was already "so feeble as to be unable to walk."

Just as diphtheria or typhoid could quickly devastate a family, tuberculosis often caught whole households in its slow but deadly grip; homes became focal points of infection and family members fell victim to it one by one, as they unknowingly passed the disease on to each other. In 1831, Ralph Waldo Emerson married the beautiful Ellen Tucker, whose father and brother had both died of consumption a few years previously. She had just begun to cough and "raise blood." The disease took her in less than two years, leaving Emerson inconsolable. Within four more years she was followed to the grave by her consumptive mother and sister.

Tuberculosis could strike anywhere but, because it was spread only by the sneezing, coughing and spitting of infected people at close range, it was more likely to attack those who did sedentary work in close confinement or lived in crowded conditions. "It prevails least among farmers," according to contemporary medical opinion, hit shoemakers hard in their crowded shops, and attacked substantially more women than men. There is no certain statistical knowledge from the sketchy public health records of the period, but physicians thought that the "white plague" was considerably less common among whites in the South and the states west of Ohio, although it had a higher incidence among blacks. The most vulnerable of all to consumption were probably poor urban women who lived in cramped, poorly ventilated rooms.

The diseases which cause most of the deaths in the modern

industrial United States—heart disease, stroke and cancer— were far less dramatically in evidence in the early nineteenth century. In part, the forces that predispose twentieth-century Americans to these degenerative ailments were weaker in the past. The sheer physical exertion required by most work and travel surely promoted cardiovascular health even if the diet— heavy in salt and animal fats—did not, and environmental carcinogens were much rarer. Just as important is the fact that infectious diseases were simply quicker killers; they carried off many early nineteenth-century Americans who today would have lived long enough to develop heart attacks and tumors.

Cities in the United States, as elsewhere in the world, were more dangerous places to live than the countryside. Diseases spread more rapidly among close-packed city populations, and sheer numbers allowed illnesses to become endemic which would have burned themselves out in smaller communities. Because dwellings were crowded onto small sites, privies and wells for drinking water were usually sited dangerously close together. Under such conditions city dwellers were at high risk for intestinal diseases like typhoid and cholera which were transmitted through flies and fecal matter. Boston was probably the healthiest of large American cities—but Bostonians' life expectancies were still five or six years lower than those in rural Massachusetts. Very likely the most dangerous place in the United States was New Orleans, the southernmost of American cities. Its semitropical climate and seaport traffic made yellow fever a repetitive visitor, its low and swampy location made for endemic malaria, and its sanitation was casual even by then-contemporary standards. The swampy municipal burying ground on the city's outskirts was kept continually busy; surprised travelers noted that many fresh graves were opened there every morning, "as if the ground could scarcely be opened fast enough for those whom the fever lays low," in the Englishwoman Harriet Martineau's words. They were usually needed before nightfall.

One alone of the great fear-inspiring diseases of previous centuries had been conquered, if not entirely eliminated. Smallpox—highly contagious, often disfiguring, frequently deadly—had been a great scourge throughout colonial America. But smallpox had lost much of its power to terrify by the early nineteenth century, for it was the one disease for which there was a preventive therapy.

In 1721 Boston physicians first began to inoculate or "variolate" patients in the face of one of the city's periodic smallpox outbreaks. They aimed at giving them a relatively mild, immunizing case of smallpox by injecting them with small amounts of disease material. Once inoculation had been shown to be effective, a gradually increasing number of Americans adopted the practice. Samuel Goodrich recalled that his parents decided to have their whole family inoculated in 1798, and a number of neighbors joined them. They made arrangements with a physician, and turned their Ridgefield, Connecticut, dwelling into a "pesthouse" in which the inoculees were confined for a couple of weeks while their disease took its course: "The lane in which our house was situated was fenced up, north and south, so as to cut off all intercourse with the world around. A flag was raised, and upon it inscribed the ominous words, SMALLPOX. . . . When all was ready, like Noah and his family we were shut in. Provisions were deposited in a basket at a point agreed upon, down the lane. Thus we were cut off from the world. . . ." By the 1790s enough American families had acquired immunity in this way to reduce the frequency of devastating epidemics.

Inoculation was risky, however. Many patients acquired fairly severe cases of the disease, and some died. In 1796, after discovering that infection with cowpox, a much milder disease, gave immunity against smallpox as well, the English physician Edward Jenner developed the procedure of vaccination. Within less than a decade many American physicians adopted vaccination and it spread rapidly through the North, becoming a commonplace family health measure throughout the country by

1820. Vaccination did not become widespread enough to eliminate smallpox entirely, but as higher proportions of succeeding generations were vaccinated the disease became much rarer.

Yellow fever, on the contrary, came to new prominence in the years of the early Republic. It had visited the cities sporadically in the eighteenth century, but took on a new ferocity in American seaports in the years between 1790 and 1860. Endemic in the tropics, the yellow-fever virus was transmitted by the bite of the *Aedes aegypti* mosquito, which was carried on shipboard from West Indian and South American ports in buckets and other water containers. Sometimes called the "black vomit," the disease produced a telltale jaundice and killed by destroying the liver and kidneys. "Confined almost exclusively to the seaport towns and cities," as the Philadelphia physician William Currie observed, yellow fever also produced great fear because it was exceedingly deadly, killing up to one-half of its victims.

The single most devastating American epidemic of the early national years was the onslaught of yellow fever that killed one out of every ten Philadelphians in 1793. During the summer and fall of that year Philadelphia, then both the capital and the largest metropolis of the United States, was a ghastly place, paralyzed with fear and with the gravediggers' cry "bring out your dead" ringing in its streets. "Acquaintances and friends," recalled the publisher Matthew Carey, "avoided each other in the streets. . . . A person with crape or any appearance of mourning was shunned like a leper."

The visitation left some Americans with a sense of imminent doom and others with the fear that urban epidemics might make city living impossible. Through the 1820s yellow fever returned several times to Philadelphia, made assaults on Baltimore and New York, and brushed New Haven and Boston—although never with the devastating force of the 1793 epidemic. It then, somewhat mysteriously, retreated from Northern ports. In New Orleans, however, the black vomit became an annual visitor from 1796 until after the Civil War. North of the Gulf Coast it never penetrated into the countryside.

For almost four decades after 1793, no outbreak of disease had a comparable impact on public consciousness. It was not until 1832 that a national-scale epidemic appeared, bringing with it some of the terror of the once-recurrent waves of small-pox or the Philadelphia catastrophe. It was a new disease, Asiatic cholera, which had originated in the Indian subconti-nent and was making its way west. The speed of cholera's spread, ironically, was greatly increased by one of the early nineteenth century's most vaunted achievements, the increas-ingly rapid pace of ocean and overland transport in the United States and Western Europe. Cholera arrived first in Quebec and Montreal in early June of 1832 and reached New York City by the end of the month, Philadelphia and Cincinnati by mid-July, Boston and Baltimore by mid-August, and New Orleans by early October. Few urban communities south of Boston es-caped entirely.

A virulent bacterial disease of the intestinal tract, cholera caused intense diarrhea and dehydration, and sometimes took its victims in a matter of hours. Cholera was not quite the wholesale killer that smallpox had been, or yellow fever in its earlier assaults, but it was deadly and frightening enough. When the disease struck New York, over twenty-five hundred citizens died in the course of two months, and the city's com-mercial economy and social life were brought to a standstill. "Deaths exceed a hundred a day," wrote the young editor Henry Dana Ward to his parents, safely deep in the New En-gland countryside. "People are sad, some out of employ that know not how to live without day labor, others have sick friends to nurse with trembling for their own lives, and others are taken like lightning from the midst of their families and daily work."

Ward went on to describe how a visiting friend "took the cholera bad" in the course of his stay and in a few days "sank into the arms of death, in spite of every effort we could make to save him." New England cities escaped lightly, but Philadelphia, Baltimore and other towns in New York and New Jersey were similarly hard hit. New Orleans suffered most severely; its losses to the cholera relative to population were three times as high as New York City's. Following the main transportation routes, and thriving in dense populations, cholera spared most of rural America. Yet it terrified the nation as a whole, adding emotional distress to its physical dangers. Information traveled quickly enough in 1832 that increasingly anxious Americans were able to follow the progress of this new "scourge of the world" in the newspapers for months as it moved relentlessly through Europe to the New World and then was discovered in place after place.

"Occasionally Taking a Dose of Medicine"

Homer Merriam, a young printer, began to feel ill with "dyspepsia, jaundice" in the fall of 1833, and embarked on his own therapeutic odyssey. He began "by occasionally taking a dose of medicine somewhat at random," and then settled on a journey west "hoping the change of climate might give me good health." Returning to Massachusetts unimproved, he tried self-medication again, and next put himself "in the hands of Doctor Woodward," a traditionally trained "orthodox" physician, and "was largely dosed by him, to no good effect." Increasingly concerned, he sought out a botanical physician and began to hope that this doctor's regimen would "complete my restoration to health." Yet his symptoms began to return, and "in a sort of desperation" Merriam "decided to try the skills of an Indian doctress." He spent four months living in her tiny, cramped house, taking the "preparations of roots and herbs" that she prescribed for him. Finally discharged by the old lady, he left, and remained "in comfortable health."

Merriam's illness remains obscure, but his nearly three-year search for health illuminates the diversity of America's practitioners of healing, who set their efforts against the threats of disease and death. The medical horizon of the early nineteenth century was enormously different from our own. From Edinburgh- or Harvard-trained physicians to neighborhood women, the practitioners shared some basic assumptions, many forms of treatment—and a common inability to cure decisively.

When American men and women fell sick, they often turned first to their own resources, or to lay healers in the household or neighborhood. In his part of Kentucky in the 1820s, an ex-slave recalled, "there were no doctors back there" for white or black. "If you got sick, you would go dig a hole and dig up roots and fix your own medicine." European as well as Native American and African traditions of folk medicine were very much alive in Indian "doctresses," slave "root doctors," frontier Illinois "granny women" and New England farmers with a knack for doctoring. In many communities there were midwife-healers, experienced and skillful women who were sent for in serious sickness as well as childbirth. Rural America was "full of people who practiced with herbs," treating illness with preparations from their household gardens. Many Americans used their almanacs not only to plant their crops but to dose by astrological correspondence. "The twelve signs of the zodiac presided over the twelve signs of the living body," in Daniel Drake's recollection; each limb and organ had its sign, which determined the herbal remedy for its ills.

Many American families remained wholly within the world of folk medicine. Some lived on isolated farmsteads or in tiny, dispersed communities simply out of reach of physicians, while others distrusted doctors' skills or wanted to avoid their fees. Slaves frequently resisted the attempts of masters to bring white physicians out to treat them, preferring their own black healers and root medicine. Other families, particularly prosperous ones, called on physicians routinely, while still others only brought them in if an illness looked extremely serious. But across the country as a whole, the professional practice of medicine was gaining at the expense of self-dosing and neighborhood healing. Between 1790 and 1840 the number of men who called themselves physicians and attempted to make full-time careers of treating illness was increasing four times as fast as the American population. By the 1820s their training varied enormously—there were men with formal medical education, many who had learned through apprenticeship to another physician, and practitioners who were self-instructed and self-certified.

Yet in terms of the certainty of cure, there was little to choose between popular and learned forms of medicine. The remedies and procedures of family and neighborhood healers were actually not so radically different from those of physicians.

Still part of the way most Americans understood sickness was a long-lived inheritance from the ancient world, the Galenic theory. It held that the body was a dynamic system of four circulating fluids, or "humors," and that illness occurred when they were out of balance. European medicine had evolved a wide variety of drugs and treatments over the centuries which attempted to cure disease by restoring the balance, increasing or decreasing the quantity of one or more of the humors— blood, phlegm, bile and black bile—in the body. Even as the specific concepts of the humoral theory were gradually abandoned, and less and less literally believed, the therapeutics based on them—almost always involving removing humoral fluids from the patient's body—remained.

In the early nineteenth century, most trained American physicians held to a different theory of illness, but one whose origins in old humoral ideas were still evident. They saw sickness as resulting from a "morbidly overstimulated state of bodily excitement," as contemporary medical writing phrased it, that underlay and caused the sufferer's specific symptoms. They strove to counter it by depleting the patient's excess fluids— using exactly the same drugs and procedures that traditional theory called for. Many of the most widely used folk remedies acted in the same way. They compelled the sick body to produce dramatic and visible signs of the treatment's efficacy, signs that onlookers, healers and patients themselves could see and find reassuring.

"Bleeding and blistering, purging and puking" were the remedies that American physicians, and many other healers, offered their patients. The most dramatic was bleeding or venesection. The practitioner opened one of his patient's veins with a sharply pointed lancet and let the blood flow into a basin until he judged that a therapeutic amount had been withdrawn. For localized injuries and infections patients were "blistered"; a caustic substance was applied to the skin to raise a blister and produce a serous discharge. Some physicians reached even deeper into tradition and bled by applying leeches—bloodsucking invertebrates—to the skin. The most common remedy of all was "purging"—administering massive doses of cathartics, or powerful laxatives. Almost as frequent was "puking," or dosing heavily with emetics to induce copious vomiting. Other drugs produced different forms of fluid emission like salivation, sweating or frequent urination. Blood, pus, vomit, feces, sweat or urine were the tangible evidence that the dose had "operated." In describing illnesses and their treatment, ordinary Americans sometimes went into graphic detail about the copiousness and consistency of the patient's discharges.

"The most active remedies are to be used," wrote Dr. Isaac Rand, in managing cases of hydrocephalus, or the buildup of fluid around the brain. He bled "at the arm or jugular vein," and proceeded to "apply leeches to the temples, and behind the ears; scarify and cup the temples; excite a hemorrhage at the nose; scarify and cup the nape of the neck, give gentle cathartics . . . assist their action with stimulating blisters. . . ." Continuing his struggle with the patient's condition, he felt compelled to "shave the head and bathe it with ether . . . blister the whole head, and keep up the discharge with the vesicating ointment;

blister the nape of the neck, the temples, and behind the ears. . . ." Rand's hydrocephalic patients died, because their condition was intractable without cranial surgery. The course of treatment they were subjected to was extreme, but not unique. Although many doctors bled and dosed more moderately, and a few avoided bleeding altogether, Rand was one of a substantial number of American physicians who practiced "heroic medicine," intervening as vigorously as possible to deplete their patients' overstimulated systems. They bled heavily, often removing a pint of blood at a time and repeating it daily for a week. Under heroic treatment many patients suffered presumably well-intentioned but sometimes astonishingly severe and protracted assaults on their bodies.

In the 1820s and 1830s American physicians practicing "orthodox" medicine were challenged by "sectarian" practitioners who attacked the regimens of bleeding and purging. Many of them—"Thomsonian," "physiobotanic" and "eclectic" physicians—offered strictly botanical remedies, claiming that they were far safer than bloodletting and "mineral" drugs. "Homeopathic" doctors prescribed the traditional drugs, but in very diluted doses. Growing skepticism among overdosed patients, along with increasing competition between healers in many communities, was pushing some traditionally trained physicians away from heroic practice by the 1830s.

But the sectarian therapies, although they gave many Americans a wide and sometimes bewildering array of medical choices, did not involve any really new approaches to treating disease. Homeopathic doctors, for instance, merely offered less of the same. Botanical medicine simply took what herbal practitioners had always done and made it systematic. Some of the most important of the botanic remedies, like lobelia, were emetics, which operated on patients just as traditional doses did.

In all its diversity, early nineteenth-century medical practice was only sporadically effective in curing disease and easing pain. Many of its treatments were not only uncomfortable but potentially dangerous to patients. Although minor reductions in blood pressure actually promoted muscular relaxation, high-volume bloodletting, like violent purging, often seriously weakened patients who needed their strength to fight off infections. Some herbal remedies were effective in assisting the body's own healing processes, and almost all had considerably less potential for doing harm. In the light of today's pharmacology, the early nineteenth-century arsenal of drugs was feeble. Cinchona bark—quinine—was available against the symptoms of malaria, but it was not universally used and was often prescribed for other "fevers" which it could not help. Very few other drugs had much therapeutic value as determined by later clinical research, and some were positively dangerous. The most widely prescribed of all drugs was calomel, a powerful cathartic. Calomel was actually mercurous chloride, which was highly toxic in large doses. More than a few calomel-taking Americans added mercury poisoning—evidenced by the destruction of their gums and the loss of their teeth—to their existing ailments.

For all the real intelligence and energy devoted to it, early nineteenth-century medicine seems today uncomfortably similar to astrology or magic—an elaborate but largely ineffective set of techniques. Confidence in an individual healer or the specific treatment he or she offered undoubtedly helped many individuals get better. But in terms of actually arresting disease processes, medical treatments—except for quinine for malaria, tooth extraction and bone-setting, and some successful surgical procedures—were irrelevant to the outcome of illness.

Most practitioners were not charlatans and most patients were not fools. Within their horizons of understanding, they could believe, usually on rational grounds and often on the best evidence available, in the efficacy of treatments which now appear useless or even dangerous.

The number of those Americans was growing who, like

Homer Merriam, occupied themselves with an insistent and sometimes desperate search for health. If seventeenth- and eighteenth-century Americans often simply took their doses and waited for God's will to be disclosed, men and women of the early nineteenth century were likely to try a wide variety of "cures" in succession. In the mounting numbers and variety of physicians, the expansion of medical education and medical publishing, and the enthusiastic marketing of patent medicines for self-dosing were the clear signs of change for age-old patterns of resignation and passivity in the face of illness. Both patients and healers seemed increasingly eager to take action of some kind—any kind—hoping to cure rather than endure.

"As Well as Common"

"We are all as well as common," began many of the letters sent between 1802 and 1821 by the Searle family between Massachusetts and northern New York State; they then usually proceeded to list their various painful ailments. Americans bore with many nonfatal but painful and debilitating chronic afflictions. Many men and women did their daily work on limbs that were twisted and painful from dislocations and poorly set fractures. Chronic infections and inflammations of the skin, the stomach, the ears and the genitourinary system could not be treated. Early nineteenth-century people surely had a higher threshold of pain than their descendants, born of long, matter-of-fact endurance of discomfort. The Maine country merchant Zadoc Long, born in 1800, suffered all of his adult life from a chronic infection which produced recurring abscesses on his legs and chest; he underwent periodic bouts of excruciating pain, and had several times felt that his "life was in some peril." Yet Long could say, summing up his life, that he had enjoyed "generally good health." When suffering became acute, there were only a few options besides endurance. One of alcohol's attractions for Americans was as a painkiller. Strong drink and opium derivatives, both addictive and dangerous to health in heavy use, were the only effective pain relievers available.

Because most remedies and procedures were designed to produce dramatic and visible bodily results, the treatment of illness frequently made the sufferer even more uncomfortable. When Zadoc Long's wife Julia suffered a sudden and intense bout of the "bilious cholic" while traveling, he took her to the nearest tavern and "physicked" her with thoroughwort, a botanical emetic. The dose, he noted with relief, operated to "puke her." Her treatment, administered with great concern by a devoted husband, consisted of being forced to vomit violently while she was in the throes of what was probably an acute gallbladder attack.

Without antiseptics or anesthetics surgery was a desperate expedient, usually undertaken only in life-threatening situations. Operating with breathtaking speed, a skilled surgeon could amputate a gangrenous limb or remove kidney stones to relieve intolerable pain, but the risk of death from shock or uncontrollable postoperative infection was very great. Even at the hands of the most highly skilled "operator" a surgical procedure was extraordinarily dangerous and painful, and speed was the only recourse.

Henderson's Almanack for Raleigh, North Carolina, assured its readers in 1801 that common "nervous headaches, are frequently cured by extracting some decayed stumps that have not been painful in a dozen years." Hundreds of thousands of Americans had at least some of their teeth badly rotted, a source of chronic pain and foul breath to many, with extraction its only cure; the hollow-jawed visages in many folk portraits may well reflect the condition's prevalence. Some Americans brushed their teeth regularly; there were toothbrushes for sale in many country stores by 1820, and the Scotsman Patrick Shirreff, while visiting the town of Detroit, "remarked dozens of storekeepers . . . washing their teeth in the mornings at the door." Many did not. *Henderson's Almanack*'s urgent and detailed instructions to its audience about brushing clearly assumed that they were unfamiliar with the practice. Decades later, books of advice on health and etiquette were still not taking it for granted. In 1835, Frederick Marryat maintained that the dental hygiene of the ordinary Americans he met while traveling was still very poor; he was often mistaken for a dentist, he claimed, because he carried a toothbrush in his dressing case.

Dentistry, which most rural American physicians practiced, was by far the most effective form of surgery; extraction was a decisive and relatively safe procedure (although infection always posed some risk). Americans with painfully decayed teeth, then, were at least one group likely to be considerably better off from the ministrations of a physician.

To all Americans, illness, whether in oneself or others, was a matter of virtually certain occurrence but uncertain outcome. Beyond the questions of doses and symptoms were the routines and social rituals of watching and waiting, which enveloped major and minor illness, childbirth and death itself.

Most seriously ill individuals were enmeshed in a web of concern, with family and neighbors constantly watching by the bedside—a form of care modern Americans have delegated to hospital staffs. In one of the commonest of American social rituals, neighbors took turns staying through the night at the sickbed to allow exhausted family members to sleep. Watchers could administer medicine when needed, but, far more important, they provided a continuous comforting presence—as well as witnesses who could quickly gather the family around if death seemed imminent. Friends and kinsmen, particularly those who did not have full responsibility for another household, arrived to do their part. For several weeks, as Joseph Ward lay dying of consumption in Shrewsbury, Massachusetts, a different pair of neighbors—one man and one woman—arrived each evening to watch the night with him. While in her late teens, Pamela Brown of Vermont recorded "watching the night" with sick neighbors and relatives an average of eight times a year from 1835 to 1838. Archibald Knode, a Maryland storekeeper in his twenties, watched in three "last sicknesses" in the course of only four months in 1834—those of a friend, a friend's child and a cousin. These arrangements could even spring into place for a stranger; when a Boston merchant became seriously ill while passing through Worcester, Massachusetts, the young lawyer Christopher Columbus Baldwin took over his care on one day's acquaintance, spending more than a week "sitting up with the sick stranger" until he recovered sufficiently to travel home.

"Called Her Women Together"

As the Maine midwife Martha Moore Ballard repeatedly phrased it in her diary, an American mother-to-be "called her women together" when her time was approaching, summoning the midwife who would preside over the delivery along with kin and neighbors. She expected to give birth at home, in the company of other women. In most American households around 1800 children were born in a warm and crowded room, usually the parents' bedchamber. A circle of women surrounded the expectant mother, talking to her in low tones or encouraging her as she groaned in labor. An American woman about to give birth did not lie down but remained partially upright. She squatted on a low midwife's stool, sat on two chairs put together to provide support for the legs, or even stood while supported by two helpers.

In the South, birth often crossed barriers of color and servitude; the children of many plantation mistresses were delivered by slave midwives in a female circle that mixed black and white. This world of birth was by custom a female one. Husbands normally spent little time in the birth chamber during the hours of labor and usually avoided the hours of delivery. But on the trail westward, or on truly isolated frontier farmsteads, they were sometimes the only birth attendants available, and women might even give birth sitting on their husband's laps for support.

Midwives in America rarely had any formal training, but had learned their art from older practitioners and in the course of attending births from early womanhood. Like that of male physicians and other healers, their skillfulness varied. Ballard, for example, was a confident and resourceful practitioner whose diary records hundreds of successful deliveries. In most births there was relatively little to be done except to give the expectant mother support and encouragement, receive and wrap the baby, tie off the umbilical cord and deal with the placenta.

But if childbirth pointed to the certainty of new life it also carried with it the possibility of death for mother or child. When deliveries became difficult the midwife called her skill and judgment into play. Sometimes simply waiting proved the wisest course. If a fetus would not pass through the birth canal, she would turn it and deliver the child feet first. But if that failed, her only recourse was to remove the fetus piecemeal—or allow both mother and child to die. Although most childbirths ended successfully for both mother and child, many were exhausting and traumatic experiences which weakened mothers for months; an infected perineal tear or a prolapsed uterus could destroy a woman's health permanently.

After birth, the ideal was a month's "confinement," a period of bed rest and almost ritual separation from the life of the household. But it was not always possible for a mother to get a full month's rest; most women—indeed, all but the well-to-do —found it difficult to leave their crucial household tasks for very long, and many returned to their routines sooner.

It was worst for black American mothers. Most white women could at least remain close to their infants while working in the home, but "constant childbearing and hard labor in the fields at the same time," as Frances Kemble Butler observed, was the lot of most slave women. Particularly on large plantations, slave mothers worked in the fields until near the time of delivery, and then returned to labor within a few weeks after birth. "Nancy" —a young slave woman on the Butlers' Georgia plantation— "has had three children," Frances noted while recording slave petitions. "Two of them are dead. She came to implore that the rule of sending them into the fields three weeks after their confinement might be altered."

The great majority of American women breast-fed their infants, beginning soon after birth—although if a mother died or lost her milk supply it was possible to "bring up a child by hand" with cow's milk, broth and "pap" or gruel. Wet-nursing was common only on larger plantation households, where a black woman was often chosen to suckle her mistress's babies as well as her own. Medical writers recommended one year as the age for weaning, and most American women took their children from the breast around this time, or a few months later. Frances Kemble Butler believed that many mothers, fearful of high infant mortality in the "sickly season," nursed their babies "until after the second summer." Advice books also suggested that the process be a gradual one, but mothers often acted much more abruptly. Julia Long of Maine weaned her son John just after his first birthday by suddenly separating herself from him for four days.

Some American women had already left the traditional all-female world of birth and accepted physician-assisted childbirth. Beginning in the 1760s, a few male physicians in Philadelphia, Boston and New York began to deliver babies as part of their practices. These American "man-midwives" were English-trained; they brought back with them the obstetrical forceps which, in the hands of a skillful operator, made it possible to assist babies out of the birth canal in difficult deliveries without seriously injuring them. Over the next four decades most upper-class women in American cities turned to physicians during childbirth. "Man-midwifery" then spread more widely after 1800 as an increasing number of doctors outside large cities added obstetrics to their practices. In many American communities physicians were successful in challenging the old ways of birth—probably because many women were seeking greater safety in childbirth and became convinced that doctors, with their formal medical training and the forceps, would deal better with difficult births.

Midwives lost ground to physicians from the 1790s; physician-assisted childbirth by 1840 was almost universal among comfortably-off families and widely accepted in the Northern countryside. But midwifery never came close to disappearing in the nineteenth century. Most rural folk in the West and South, almost all the slaves, and the urban poor continued to "call the women together."

Midwives and obstetric physicians both varied widely in competence, so that it is hard to know, in terms of health and safety, what women lost and gained. In problematic deliveries, skillful male physicians using the forceps may have been more effective, their interventions saving a significant number of mothers and babies. Letting nature take its course, midwives were far less likely to intervene in the birth process. They probably managed normal deliveries with fewer injuries, and less chance of infection, than doctors did who were sometimes overeager to use their techniques.

The spread of obstetric medical practice, however, greatly changed the social context of childbirth. What the circle of women had always regarded as a natural although sometimes difficult and dangerous process became, with the doctor's presence, something more akin to an illness. Embarrassment and constraint became part of the birth process; physicians were greatly hindered, as midwives had never been, by firmly established canons of female modesty. Men could not look directly at their patients' genitals, but had to examine them only by touch while they remained fully clothed. Often deeply uncomfortable with a bedchamber full of women looking on—sometimes critically—doctors tried to persuade expectant mothers to clear them out of the birthing room. The new way of child-birth gradually became less a communal female ritual than a private matter between a woman and her doctor.

"The Last Wants of Our Poor Mortality"

Death was still an early nineteenth-century commonplace, not a hushed, almost secret event in a hospital or nursing home. All families, from the most affluent to the poorest, experienced death at home, dealt there with the corpse and participated together in rituals of mourning.

American rituals of death were spare ones, for the most part. Families completed the final watch with their dying members at home. Infants died in their mothers' arms. Men and boys fatally injured in accidents were often carried home to their families "on a plank." The prospect of dying and being buried by strangers was a truly frightening one.

Along the social networks of town or neighborhood, the news of death began to make its way. In rural New England the town sexton tolled the meetinghouse bell in well-understood codes. He rang out the sex—in many communities there were nine strokes for a man, six for a woman and three for a child—and the age of the deceased. "It was seldom that we could not tell who was the deceased person," Lyndon Freeman remembered of his Massachusetts town. Friends and people living nearby would gather at the house; "neighbors fell into one another's hands," wrote Harriet Beecher Stowe, "for the last wants of our poor mortality."

They came to "render the final offices from which the more nervous and fastidious shrink," but in which others "took an almost professional pride." They "laid out" the body, washing it as an act of purification and removing any unpleasant evidences of the final throes, trimming the hair and shaving men. The neighbors then dressed the corpse in its shroud—a long white linen or cotton garment with open back and long sleeves.

Both shroud and coffin had to be swiftly measured to the deceased and quickly made; corpses were not embalmed, and funerals could not wait long. Surviving shrouds in fact show signs of great haste in their sewing. The poor were simply wrapped in a "winding sheet"—a single long piece of sheeting fabric.

If a carpenter or cabinetmaker was nearby, he was immediately commissioned to make a coffin—which, though rarely used among ordinary Americans in the seventeenth century, was nearly universal by the 1790s. Twice during Edward Jenner Carpenter's first year as a cabinetmaker's apprentice in Greenfield, Massachusetts, he noted that he had "stayed up all night" to make one. Where an artisan was not available a neighbor, or even the grieving father or husband himself, would set to work. Through the first half of the nineteenth century coffins retained their characteristic and unmistakable shape—flat-sided, with a tapering hexagonal profile that fit the body. While wealthy Americans were sometimes buried in carefully finished coffins of mahogany, for most "few coffins better than plain pine painted black were used." Pine was the predominant wood for coffins because its easy workability made for rapid assembly.

Preparing bodies for burial had traditionally been a strictly sex-divided task, as men and women separately laid out corpses of their own gender. In some larger communities women had begun to perform this work for both sexes alike, and men withdrew from it. Sometimes the same women who healed the sick might be called on to lay out the dead. In the increasing anonymity and complexity of city life, providers of these services were emerging as paid specialists: the Philadelphia city directory of 1810, for example, listed fifteen women as "layers out of the dead."

In most American communities, deaths were rents in the social fabric which concerned far more than the immediate family. "Funerals were attended by nearly everyone who seasonably heard of them," Horace Greeley observed of rural New

Hampshire and Vermont around 1810. A wide variety of communal, sometimes rough-edged ways still surrounded funerals, which had not yet been split off from other forms of social interaction by the introduction of professional managers of mourning and interment. Americans of Scotch-Irish descent conducted whiskey-passing wakes where houses, as Greeley recalled, were "often filled through the night with sympathizing friends who proceeded to drown their sorrows in the strong drink supplied in abundance—whereby strange transformations were wrought from plaintive grief to exuberant and even boisterous hilarity." New Englanders and Pennsylvania Germans offered lavish funeral feasts with abundant drink. Virginians and Dutch New Yorkers escorted the coffins to their burial places with musket volleys.

The coffin usually lay "open in the best front room" before the funeral—often surrounded on the table with tansy and rosemary leaves to ward off danger from the corpse. The principal mourners sat with the coffin and received the condolences of the community. In the mourning households of New England images were shrouded like bodies; looking glasses and pictures were customarily covered with white cloth. Services were rarely held in churches; before forming a procession to the gravesite, mourners assembled at the house, often full to overflowing, to hear a prayer and sometimes a sermon. At funerals in Narragansett County, Rhode Island, "women and children filled the rooms; the men were chiefly grouped in the entries, looking in the windows or standing by the door."

American mourners had originally traveled even to distant gravesites wholly on foot; the bearers literally carried the coffin on their shoulders, pausing briefly to rest. But as wheeled vehicles became available, it grew customary to carry the coffin on a hearse; more prosperous mourners rode behind it in carriages, while those at poorer folks' funerals simply walked. At the gravesite itself the bearers lowered the coffin into the newly dug grave, and "there followed the usual sounds, so terrible to

the ears of mourners," Stowe recollected, "the setting down of
the coffin, the bustle of preparation, the harsh grating of ropes
as the precious burden was lowered to its last resting-place."
Sometimes, as Nathaniel Hawthorne noted, straw was strewn
on top of the coffin, because "the clods on the coffin-lid have an
ugly sound."

In newer settlements, funerals were by necessity sparer affairs; it was difficult to bring many mourners together and not
always possible to have a minister present. Unsupported by kin
or community, many American families conducted their funerals alone. They read from the Bible, uttered a prayer or silently
interred the body; sometimes, "without text, prayer or hymn,
the dust was forever given to its fellow dust."

The slaves, in their plantation communities, practiced a different way of death. When the slave Shadrach died on Pierce
Butler's Georgia plantation, Frances Kemble Butler was asked
for "a sufficient quantity of cotton cloth to make a winding sheet
for him." A day later, "just as the twilight was thickening into
darkness," she attended the funeral. Shadrach's coffin "was laid
on trestles in front of the cooper's cottage, and a large assemblage of the people had gathered round, many of the men
carrying pine-wood torches." The whole assembly of mourners
then lifted their voices "in the high, wailing notes of a hymn,"
and followed the bearers on the trek to the swampy "people's
burial ground." The slaves' custom of burying their dead at
night, with funeral processions by torchlight, was in part dic-
tated by their lack of control over their daylight hours, yet it
also suggests how different their sense of the fitness of things
really was; European-Americans, given the depth of their traditions about night and the spirits of the dead, often found torchlight funerals troubling, even frightening. Black mourners did
not keep silence; they sang together on the way to the burying
yard and at the burial, and often would pick up a more cheerful
tune on the way home. Even more reflective of the funeral
practices of West Africa was the custom of some slaves, who

waited a month or more after the burial to commemorate the death with singing and dancing.

Black was traditionally the color of death for white Americans, and it marked coffins, the cloths that sometimes covered them and the clothes that some mourners wore. At most American funerals it was still rare to see all the mourners in black; in some, "the outward tokens of woe . . . were few or none." At a child's funeral in North Adams, Massachusetts, Hawthorne saw "most of the men in their ordinary clothes, and one or two of them in their shirt sleeves." Black, formal clothes and "a cloud of crepe veils" were for those who could afford it and "were the nearest relations of the deceased." Poorer families often dispensed with them altogether.

Mourning was particularly a woman's affair, and even more particularly focused on widows. After losing their husbands, many American women were expected to wear black for from six months to two years—although some adopted mourning attire for life. Less fettered than women, American men frequently wore no more than a simple crepe armband as a sign of mourning.

More permanent than mourning clothes as reminders of those who had died were the graves themselves and their markers, set in the daily landscape. "Wherever there is a solitary dwelling" in the western United States, observed Harriet Martineau, "there is a domestic burying place." Community graveyards—for a neighborhood, town or religious congregation—were commonest in the North. Large plantations customarily had their own burying grounds for both whites and blacks.

Family graveyards were sometimes "delicately kept" at first, but they often fell into neglect or obliteration within a few decades as farms passed to new owners. Most larger graveyards in the United States before 1830 were rank and weedy places, if not worse. Burial places, as many observers saw them, were covered with "monuments half buried in the earth, or broken, or overgrown with grass," and some town burial grounds in New England, as late as 1840, were simply unfenced sections of the central common, over which pedestrians tramped and cows grazed. City graveyards were enormously crowded, and their physical integrity was constantly threatened by urban growth. Philadelphia's burying yards were often simply unused plots of ground on the city's expanding edge; as the land became more valuable for other uses they were simply razed and turned into building lots. The upkeep of burying places was rarely a concern of anyone's, because Americans traditionally shunned their graveyards and visited them only when they had to. "It is uncommon to see any person" in the graveyards of New England, Goodrich noted in 1832, "except at burials."

But some Americans began to see both neglected graveyards and the communal, widely inclusive, sometimes almost festive funeral practices of tradition as inappropriate responses to death. "In the cities" of the North, "a great change has occurred in the manner of observing funerals," a Bostonian remarked in 1833; they were "now conducted with little publicity." Genteel urban families and those who followed their lead—"in the country," he continued, "the change is going on"—confined attendance at funerals more tightly within the circles of the family and close friends. "The custom to have ardent spirits" they made "obsolete," and some had begun to give up the funeral supper entirely. They moved toward a mourning ritual of somber restraint, and traveled to the gravesite increasingly in wheeled funeral processions, which sealed the mourners off from passersby. Diminishing funerals as occasions of community, they made them increasingly elaborate as services of worship. Ministers lengthened their sermons and prayers and added more elaborate graveside benedictions to the grim simplicity of traditional interments. Mourning became caught up in patterns of fashionable display. Under the guidance of fashionable magazines for affluent households such as *Godey's*

Lady's Book, some families were having elaborate and expensive mourning wardrobes made for them that extended even to small children.

In the 1830s, beginning with Mount Auburn in Cambridge, Massachusetts, and Laurel Hill in Philadelphia, these same prosperous urban families subscribed to build not graveyards but "rural cemeteries" on the cities' edges; they were painstakingly landscaped and carefully maintained. Built to walk around and linger in, these new burying grounds were the theaters not just for increasingly private funerals but for new rituals of memorial visiting that went along with increasingly elaborate mourning.

The rhythms and limits of American life changed gradually and unevenly. All Americans continued to confront the intractable limits of life set by death and disease, although many had begun to struggle vigorously against them. For most, the seasonal clock still shaped patterns of fertility and the timing of marriage. In the midst of rapid population growth some Americans began to take decisive action to limit the size of their families. Some chose to reshape their traditional ways of dealing with the occasions of marriage, birth or death. They shifted from communal habits to ways of "little publicity," moving momentous but intimate occasions into an increasingly private world.

3

"COMFORTABLE HABITATIONS":
HOUSES AND THE DOMESTIC
ENVIRONMENT

꙳꙳

Iɴ 1828 George Olds of Brookfield, Massachusetts, contracted with the carpenter Joel·Upham to build a house for his family. Like many dwellings built in the New England countryside for generations, it was a one-story dwelling with a chimney at its center, "to be 32 feet from north to south and 22 feet from East to West," with "a cellar under the South end." The "South room" of the house was the kitchen, with "a fire place, oven, and ash hole"; the "North room," with a fireplace and decorative molding, was to be for sitting, taking many meals, entertaining guests, perhaps some kinds of work. Behind these rooms were two smaller ones—a "bedroom," probably for Olds and his wife, and a "back room" with unfinished walls and ceiling and a sink, for storage and work. Other Olds family members would sleep in the unfinished garret spaces above.

Written building contracts like this one, usually with a simple sketched plan, have survived in some numbers for early nineteenth-century America, even for houses as ordinary as the one Upham was building. In similar agreements, written and unwritten, householders and housebuilders—more by tradition and common practice than by conscious innovation—together shaped the spaces in which American families would live.

The house, as it still does today, enfolded the most basic routines and experiences of everyday life. Just before 1800 a nationwide tax assessment revealed close to six hundred thousand dwellings in the United States; by the time of the next national count in 1850, there were well over three million houses—scattered in country neighborhoods, perched on the edges of forest clearings, clustered in villages, packed tightly in cities. In a great variety of forms and sizes, they were the setting of common experience—eating and work, sexuality and socializing, prayer and children's play.

"To Be Done in a Workmanlike Manner"

"All to be done in a workmanlike manner," Upham agreed. The creators of American houses spanned a wide range in both skills and self-consciousness. A few professional architects were working in the cities by 1800: men who saw themselves as artist-designers, and would draw up elaborate plans for their clients and carefully supervise their builders. Only a tiny minority of house-building Americans could afford their services, although as time went on the example of their work would affect the design of much more ordinary housing. Most American builders used nothing more than a quickly sketched plan that showed the placement of major features; almost none used detailed scale drawings. Today, the form of a house is generated by an elaborate set of architect's drawings or standardized construction plans; most early nineteenth-century houses still took shape out of local tradition, based on shared, unwritten, perhaps even unspoken assumptions about how houses should be built and organized—what archaeologists have called "mental templates" for building.

Most Americans timber-framed their houses in ways descended from traditional English techniques. They built them as frameworks of heavy wooden posts and beams, held together with interlocking, often intricate joints in which a protruding tenon was carefully cut out of one timber to fit precisely into a corresponding mortise in the next. Builders covered the massive frame with boards known as sheathing, then sided it with clapboards—overlapping narrow lengths of thinly split wood—and covered the roof joists with wooden shingles. In most parts of rural America, brick and stone houses were rare, usually erected only by a few of the most affluent families. Americans made fullest use of those Old World skills of building which made a good fit with the New World's abundance of timber. Only in eastern Pennsylvania and adjacent parts of Maryland and New Jersey did builders, primarily following German traditions, work extensively in brick and stone. As a result, Pennsylvania could boast a comparatively enormous population of stonemasons and bricklayers; the 1850 census of occupations counted nearly three times as many in proportion to population as in any other American state. Outside Philadelphia, Baltimore and New York, even the houses in American cities were still largely built of wood.

Many Western and some Southern Americans built log houses, using a much simpler and less laborious technology than timber framing. They usually squared the logs off into timbers but avoided the complicated carpentry of planning and joining the frame, and the materials and labor involved in sawing and nailing up the sheathing. Instead, they laid logs atop one another horizontally, and joined them by notches cut at the corners. Log construction was not an English building tradition, and did not make its appearance in the first settlements in New England and the Chesapeake. Although the Swedes built log houses in their isolated settlements in what later became Delaware, it was the Pennsylvania Germans who were responsible for their wide adoption by American settlers. German log-building techniques were taken up in the eighteenth century by the many thousands of settlers of English- and Scots-Irish descent who passed through eastern Pennsylvania on their way west and south. Later, some of the Yankee settlers of upper New York and northern New England borrowed log construction methods from the West.

Wherever new land was being taken up, many thousands of Americans, like Jonathan Drake in Kentucky and Ezekiel Greeley in western Pennsylvania, learned the techniques of log construction. Both men had been small farmers, not builders. But as their sons remembered, they built their own one-room cabins, armed with the farmer's basic woodworking skills and the urgency of need. In most places settlers chose the log house as an expedient, the quickest and least laborious way of putting up shelter; they expected to progress from log to timber-framed houses as they built roads, established full-scale agriculture and found markets—even if it often took longer than they hoped. Everywhere but in the hills and hollows of the upland South a landscape of log cabins meant a community expecting a rapid transition. There—in that agriculturally marginal region extending from western Virginia and North Carolina through Kentucky and Tennessee, and even into parts of southern Illinois, Indiana and Ohio—families built log houses and lived in them for two generations or more.

But most of America's houses were created neither by scholarly professionals nor ordinary householders, but by a large body of skilled craftsmen. When Americans' occupations were first counted in 1850, there were almost two hundred thousand carpenters and joiners, not even considering the additional thousands of slave artisans. Building in the cities was largely the province of builder-contractors who employed numerous journeyman craftsmen. The bulk of American builders were country carpenters, ranging from men like Joel Upham, who worked most of the time at their trade and built a house or two a year, to men who combined it with farming, cabinetmaking or even coopering and built only a few structures over their lifetimes. Illiterate yet skillful black craftsmen shaped many of the houses of the slave South, building everything from sizable plantation homes to their own cramped cabins.

All learned as Upham had, to build "in a workmanlike manner," acquiring their skills through some sort of apprenticeship —varying from formal long-term indentures to shorter and more casual arrangements for observing, imitating and working along with more experienced craftsmen. They learned the traditional techniques and construction materials of their own regions and localities. Some carpenters worked almost entirely by eye and ear; others drew on the carpenters' guides and architectural pattern books that were flowing off the increasingly productive presses of the early nineteenth century, looking for designs and details that would please their customers.

Americans' technologies of building in the first decades of the nineteenth century had evolved gradually from those of their seventeenth- and eighteenth-century ancestors and for the most part would have been recognizable to earlier generations of housewrights. But a radically new way of putting buildings together appeared in the early 1830s, probably first developed by carpenters struggling to keep pace with the rapid growth of the settlement of Chicago on the tree-poor Illinois prairie. "Balloon framing" replaced the massive timber frame with a structural skin of numerous light, weight-bearing members, later standardized as two-by-fours, which were simply nailed together, not intricately joined. Carpenters could put up a balloon frame more quickly and could use much smaller-dimensioned lumber. Balloon framing was adopted first by builders in fast-growing Western cities and commercial towns, for whom speed and economizing on materials were highly important. It was slower to arrive in older, Eastern cities and took even longer to arrive in the countryside, where it did not really begin to replace the old ways until after 1860. Eventually rapid construction with lighter lumber triumphed almost everywhere; traditional timber framing and log construction had almost disappeared by the end of the nineteenth century.

"The Habitations of Those Days"

The examples of domestic architecture that have survived, preserved and restored, into the present, do not provide an accurate picture of the conditions under which most Americans have lived in the past. Old houses have usually survived in proportion to their size and expensiveness, and the fame of their owners; those built by or for the least prosperous folk have only rarely escaped abandonment or destruction. Despite the best efforts of museums and historic sites, the character of surviving buildings almost inevitably suggests that most early nineteenth-century Americans lived in dwellings that their descendants in the late twentieth century would find comfortable, even highly desirable. But this was far from the truth.

In 1798, as the still-new United States became embroiled in escalating disputes with France, its former Revolutionary ally, Congress levied a "Direct Tax" on all American households to meet the pressing financial demands of national defense. This first federal property tax proved widely unpopular; but it left behind an extraordinarily valuable historical record, since the tax assessors were instructed to describe and assess not only land and slaves, but every free family's dwelling house. The 1798 Direct Tax provided a description of American housing conditions that has never since been equaled; its schedules noted not only the value of each house but its size, number of windows, number of stories and type of construction. Study of the tax schedules reveals a landscape of American housing striking in its small scale, its plainness and its inequality.

Houses that would be sizable, comfortable and well-maintained by the standards of the later twentieth century represented the dwellings of a minority. Most American families lived in houses that were much smaller and barer than it is easy to imagine today. Many homes were genuinely squalid, starkly reflective of the world of scarcity in which their owners lived.

Just before 1800, housing was less equally distributed among the families of the United States than it is today; the differences between rich and poor were profoundly and visibly expressed in the landscape. Even leaving out the cabins of the slaves, which were not described at all, the wealthiest ten percent of American households lived in dwellings which, taken together, were worth just over half the total value of all the nation's houses. In 1970, in contrast, the most prosperous one-tenth of American families would own no more than thirty percent of the total value of the country's housing.

As the assessors saw it in 1798, the two best houses in the United States were the three-story, fifteen-room mansion of Elias Hasket Derby, the Salem, Massachusetts, merchant who had made a great fortune in overseas trade, and the equally imposing house of Peter Stuyvesant, the wealthy Dutch-American who lived along the Hudson River outside New York City. Each house was valued at over thirty thousand dollars; all by itself either one was worth more than the total value of all the structures in many small farming communities. On the other side of an enormous social and economic gulf were the more than a quarter of a million houses, over forty percent of the total, that were valued at one hundred dollars or less.

Many of these were the homes of the frontier—log dwellings with only one or two rooms, often with no more than two windows. Daniel Drake recalled that the Kentucky cabin his family was living in was half-built in 1798, "without a window . . . with a half-finished wooden chimney—with a roof on one side only." But the contrast was not confined to the humble houses of the West and the opulent homes of seaboard cities. Disparity in housing was evident everywhere in the United States. In newly settled Mifflin County in western Pennsylvania, houses ran the gamut from an eight-room brick house worth fourteen hundred dollars to dozens of tiny one-room log shacks valued at less than ten dollars each.

Even in long-settled areas the majority of houses were surprisingly small, and meanly built and dilapidated structures were often numerous. In older rural places, like the communities of Worcester County, Massachusetts—settled for three generations—housing standards varied greatly. The houses of the first parish of Mendon, Massachusetts, situated on relatively rich farmland, were on the average twice as valuable as those of nearby Douglas, where farmers contended with thin soil and steep slopes.

While houses in the rural North were larger than Western cabins, many artisans and small farmers lived in roughly finished dwellings of two or three rooms. Visiting one such meager habitation in central Massachusetts a few years after the 1798 assessment had been taken, Asa Sheldon noted that "it had two rooms on the base, and was one story in height." There were "two small glass windows in front and a board one in the rear that could be taken down at pleasure." The hearth was "rough stone," Sheldon continued, and in the center of one room there was a pine post used to support the garret floor; over the years it had been whittled down "almost to a splinter" for fireplace kindling.

The two-story houses that figure so prominently in surviving American architecture were actually relatively uncommon. In the fifty country towns of Worcester County, two out of every three homes had only one story; the two-story house was a striking symbol of prosperity in the landscape. One Worcester County house in four was valued at under one hundred dollars; many of these, with three to six windows, and dimensions of 20 by 24 feet or 20 by 18 feet were dwellings like the one Sheldon saw: structures described by the assessors as "an old poor house" or even "one building 20' by 18' called a house." A rare sketch of one of these tiny dwellings, *A Scene in Preston, Connecticut,* testifies to their size and appearance. (See illustration no. 18.)

Throughout the South, great plantation mansions were rare although impressive sights, for Southerners lived in generally smaller houses than New Englanders. In 1798, close to half of the dwellings in St. Mary's County, Maryland, were no larger than twenty-four by sixteen feet. These figures exaggerated the small scale of Southern housing, for Americans south of Pennsylvania, responding to their warmer climate, customarily built kitchens as separate structures. Still, most slaveholders owned homes that were more modest in scale than those of prosperous Northern farmers. Enormous numbers of these small dwellings remained three decades later; the house of a Maryland family who owned three slaves, Frances Trollope reported in 1832, "looked as if the the three slaves might have overturned it, had they pushed hard against the gable end. It contained one room, about twelve feet square, and another adjoining it, hardly larger than a closet."

In 1798, only one white American family in ten lived in a house valued at seven hundred dollars or more, which was roughly equivalent to a substantial but plain, two-story, central-chimney New England farmhouse of six or seven rooms. Only one in a hundred owned a dwelling of over three thousand dollars in value, corresponding to a large and elegantly finished new house in the Federal style, with paired chimneys, a spacious central hallway entrance, and ten to a dozen rooms. Throughout most of the country such houses were actually rarer; although some of them could be seen in smaller commercial towns or in the midst of the best Northern farmlands, they were heavily clustered on the best streets of cities and in the wealthiest plantation districts.

Cities not only had the young Republic's most distinguished examples of domestic architecture, but also narrow back alleys filled with tiny, flimsy structures, in which the poorest city dwellers lived. Impoverished households headed by day laborers or widows without resources were often jammed into small, fetid, one- or two-room tenements. "Snowtown" was a neighborhood in Providence, Rhode Island, where the city's most marginal people had come to live starting in 1797; it was a good example of housing conditions at the bottom of the urban world. Although Snowtown's early houses did not survive much past 1840, archaeological investigation has revealed them as tiny and impermanent structures, built without foundations or cellars on posts set into the sand of the city's North Cove. They were as small and impermanent in form as the first houses of

America's seventeenth-century settlers. Buildings no larger than fourteen by seventeen feet housed one or two families. Slightly larger but equally wretched dwellings were crowded with multiple households, lodgers or the carousing patrons of taverns and bawdyhouses. Only a short walk away, excavators have identified the foundations of much larger houses with full cellars; these were the homes of a respectable city neighborhood of merchants and craftsmen.

The houses of the slaves everywhere ranked with the smallest of white people's dwellings. Throughout the plantation South, where whites almost universally built framed and clapboarded dwellings, the majority of blacks lived in log huts, equivalent to the housing of impoverished urban whites or poor families on the frontier. Most slave families lived in one-room unpartitioned cabins, with crude hearths, and two families often shared a single structure. The slave huts on a Georgia plantation in 1838 ranged from twelve by fifteen feet to "ten feet square"; the larger dwellings had one main room and two tiny closets for sleeping, divided by thin wooden partitions. Many were completely windowless, "having no light but what they admitted by the open door or an occasional separation between logs." Small planters' slaves, like house servants on larger plantations, often slept in the separate kitchen building.

The nationwide housing assessment of 1798 was never repeated, so that it is impossible to be as precise about the housing of the American people in later years. Over the next five decades, Americans built nearly one and a half million new houses, and surviving architecture gives strong evidence that they rebuilt and added on to many existing dwellings. With the quickening of the pace of commerce and the maturing of settlement, American houses surely grew larger, on the average. As Western communities moved past the first decades of settlement, they replaced small log houses with larger ones and then with more substantial framed dwellings. Two-story houses became more common across many parts of the countryside; a

rare dwelling-house map for Shirley, Massachusetts, reveals
that their proportion in that community increased from just
over a third in 1798 to well over half by 1832.

Another sign of improvement was the decline of dwelling-
house sharing in the Northeastern countryside. In 1798, one
rural house in five was occupied by two families, who shared the
same roof but kept their living quarters separate; this suggests
that even some of the larger-seeming houses were cramped. By
1850, the census for those same districts showed that the proportion of houses shared by two households had dropped to one
out of ten. By 1832, the *Universal Geography* could maintain
that "the universal manner of building" in the countryside was
"that one house shall accommodate but one family; and more
than one family seldom live together, even among those nearly
connected by affinity."

In cities and manufacturing villages, however, families were
increasingly living two or three to a house. By the 1840s, the
majority of New Yorkers, residents of the densest and most
dynamic of American cities, lived in multiple-family housing; at
least one family in four in Boston, Baltimore, Philadelphia and
New Orleans shared space with others.

But as the housing of many Americans improved, inequality
remained very great. Numerous "small and mean" houses remained visible across the American countryside of the 1830s.
Families on the frontier in the 1830s, now hundreds of miles
west of what had been the edge of settlement in 1798, still
lived in small log cabins. In the cities, as great American fortunes grew, the gulf between the most opulent and the poorest housing grew ever wider. Slave housing may have shown
some improvement, with a few families living in two-room,
single-family houses with windows and wooden floors by the
1830s; but these were the showpieces of plantation life and
very rare, while truly wretched dwellings—"very crazy,
wretched cabins," as Charles Dickens saw them—remained in
great numbers.

"The Common Form . . . of All the Houses"

"Houses in the southern states," observed the Scotsman James Stuart while passing through Georgia in 1831, "are very different in their mode of construction from those of the North." While traveling in New England, Stuart had surely seen houses built around massive central chimneys, some "story and a loft" with a double-pitched gambrel roof, or lean-to houses, "with two stories in front, and a long roof, sloping down to one behind." In eastern Pennsylvania he would have passed square brick dwellings, often with two front doors. But in Georgia, "the common form . . . of all the houses that you meet with on the roadsides" was something else entirely. Each house had "two square pens," or rooms, "with a large open space between them, connected by a roof above and a floor below." These dwellings of the deep South were often called "saddlebag houses" because of their form; in their large, open entryways, Stuart said, Georgia families chose to "take their meals during the fine weather."

Across the United States, in communities in New Hampshire, Pennsylvania or Georgia, neighbors could "read" each others' houses without difficulty. Without having to enter them, they knew how the rooms were laid out, what their uses were and how to find their way around inside them. But as such folk ventured farther from their own locales, they would have found many of the houses they saw increasingly difficult to understand at first glance. In outward shape and interior plan most of the houses early nineteenth-century Americans built still varied strikingly from one part of the country to another. Their "common forms" had been shaped by the traditions of various regions of Britain and Germany, by widely varying climates and by the slow development of shared local practices. The dimensions and placement of their rooms, the position of doors and windows, staircases and chimneys, and innumerable details of construction were part of the taken-for-granted marks of local distinctiveness.

Except where they have been self-consciously preserved, the wide variety of unwritten designs that created most American dwellings before 1840 have disappeared. With rapid-assembly construction technology, standardized plans and mass-produced and catalog-ordered fixtures and fittings, American housing has lost most of its localism.

Despite their diversity, most of the houses of the early nineteenth century shared elements of design that set them apart from those of early colonial America. Before the middle of the eighteenth century, American housewrights built without much thought for symmetry and the appearance of orderliness in the placement of doors and windows, or privacy in the arrangement of rooms. They changed or added on to dwellings in ways that appear haphazard to later symmetry-seeking eyes. Most dwellings had no entryways, and even more were without internal passageways. Family members passed through one room to enter another, and visitors usually walked directly into the household's living space. Dwellings in the countryside were commonly built with their backs or sides to the main road; older houses in Rhode Island, Esther Bernon Carpenter thought, "stood half-cornerwise, with no particular reference to the road or anything else." What she may not have noticed was that they were often oriented to the points of the compass; some New England dwellings faced south, for warmth and light for their primary living spaces, and turned their kitchens to the north.

Toward the middle of the eighteenth century the leaders of colonial American society introduced a new house form into their communities from England. They began to build in the balanced and orderly way, inspired by classical Greek and Roman architecture, that much later came to be called the Georgian style in honor of the then-reigning English monarchs; its continuation after the Revolution has been designated *Federal*. Over several decades it profoundly influenced the shape of most subsequent American dwellings. The Georgian style imposed a three-part symmetry on houses, putting doorways at the center and flanking them with identically placed windows. A fully developed Georgian house was two rooms wide, two rooms deep and two stories high; its symmetrical facade balanced identical numbers of windows around a prominent central doorway. Within, a wide central entryway and staircase provided access to first- and second-floor rooms.

When contrasted with older forms, the Georgian way of building clearly suggested a new concern not only with balance and order, but with privacy. The impressive, symmetrical facade was meant for display to passersby and faced the road. The entrance separated the living spaces of the house from the outer world of the road; visitors now entered through a transition area while family members could prepare to receive them. The entryway also changed the way in which people moved within the house, by enabling them to reach any room without passing through another.

Only the well-to-do could build a house on the complete Georgian or Federal plan. But during the later eighteenth century American householders and builders, in increasing numbers, gradually accepted its assumptions of symmetry and separation—and adapted them to each region's mode of construction. Balanced and symmetrical house forms became badges of gentility that builders and their customers agreed upon.

American housewrights learned the new rules first by looking, and later, in part, by reading carpenter's guides such as Asher Benjamin's *American Builder's Companion*, first published in 1806 and in its sixth edition by 1827. Builders began to make the facades of their houses more orderly and symmetrical, and more often provided them with separate entry halls—transition spaces between the living quarters and the outside. They increasingly built houses to face the road. While houses built in the new way gave families greater separation and privacy from visitors, their new orientation turned entrances and facades toward the highway and its flow of commerce and travel.

Some Americans adopted these changes more slowly and partially than did others. Into the first decades of the nineteenth century, some country housewrights were building small houses that were balanced or "genteel" only from the road. Visitors entering would still find no entryway, and with the rooms still oriented, regardless of the road, to the points of the compass, they might find themselves walking directly into the kitchen.

These conventions of house building were widely accepted by the 1790s, but they did not really erode local distinctiveness. Between 1790 and 1830, American country builders everywhere built vigorously within their regional traditions.

But after 1830 many families in the rural North were abandoning the "common forms" they had been building and living in for generations. Joel Upham's building contracts show that like other Massachusetts country housewrights he was beginning to build a different house form, which he and his customers called an "end house." These dwellings were designed in the Greek Revival style which in earlier decades had triumphed in the design of urban public buildings and the residences of the wealthy; in shape and orientation end houses broke sharply with how American dwellings had previously looked.

Almost all American houses, for two centuries, had been oriented longways; the main door, and the facade the house presented to visitors, was set in the long side of the structure, parallel to the roofline. Greek Revival design, imitating the form of Athenian temples, reoriented the house a full ninety degrees. Unlike any dwelling previously built in the countryside, the end house presented its gable end, and the peak of its roof, to the road. Visitors usually entered through a door asymmetrically placed on one side of the gable end and passed through a long side hall to enter rooms that were located behind each other, no longer paired on either side of the doorway. The new design provided perhaps even greater separation and privacy, and also sharply symbolized a a clear-cut break with the past.

Gable-end orientation was becoming the new look of the Northern landscape. In New England, meetinghouses or churches had been the first country structures to be "turned," or built in the new fashion, as early as the 1790s; they were followed by stores and even schoolhouses, shops and barns, and last, by dwellings. Builders like Upham not only learned this new style quickly, but they worked in it with far less of the regional variation that marked earlier American building. In this they contrasted sharply with previous generations of carpenters who gradually incorporated the Georgian ideas into long-established and locally diverse ways of putting houses together. From imposing pillared mansions to one-story shoemakers' cottages, end, "side hall" or "temple front" houses, as Americans in other areas called them, became the most commonly built rural dwelling north of Pennsylvania and as far west as Illinois. They gave architectural form to the advance of commerce in the countryside. Across this wide region, more traditional Northerners continued to build in the older styles of their localities, but in steadily diminishing numbers. By the 1840s there were very few. Southerners remained attached far longer to their traditional house forms; only a relatively small number of wealthy planters and townspeople built in the Greek Revival style.

Other new forms of American housing appeared where the pace of economic change was quickest. In Baltimore and Philadelphia connected brick row houses came to fill street after street; from the great townhouses of wealthy merchants to the three- or four-room dwellings of artisans, their citizens lived in dwellings organized vertically on narrow urban lots. In the textile-mill villages of the Northern countryside, employers were building two- to four-family houses for their workers.

They were dwarfed by the long lines of the great brick boardinghouses of new industrial cities like Lowell, built to house
young women workers from rural New Hampshire and Vermont. Sometimes housing a hundred women, the boarding-
houses organized living space on a scale almost as large as that
of the factories themselves.

"Beds in Every Room of the House"

Around "the cabin hearth . . . of my mother" in Kentucky,
remembered Daniel Drake, the entire domestic scene would
have been apparent to any visitor: he would be "setting the
table" for breakfast while she "sat nursing the baby in the corner" and his sister Lizy was getting the younger children out of
bed and helping them dress. The single-room house—in which
almost all medieval Europeans had lived, and contemporary
African villagers still did—remained a reality for many early
nineteenth-century Americans. The households of most slaves,
some poorer whites and many new settlers lived "corporately,"
carrying out all the activities of life in sight and hearing of one
another. Slaves lived most densely of all, sometimes putting two
families in one room; on a plantation in coastal Georgia, Frances
Kemble Butler noticed one dwelling, "not ten feet square,"
where "three grown-up human beings and eight children stow
themselves by day and by night, which may be called close
packing, I think."

Such houses did not have physical partitions, but spaces set
aside for sleeping, eating, working and socializing, with un-
marked but perceptible boundaries. A North Carolina white
family living in a single-room house in the 1830s cooked and ate
around the fireplace at the end of the house farthest away from
the door. Their beds were in another corner, and opposite them
was the space for sitting and entertaining, furnished with a
clock and chairs.

Given the sizes of their households as well as their houses, most Americans still lived in close quarters. Their living spaces expanded and contracted in both seasonal and daily rhythms. At night, the meagerness of light available from candles or oil lamps drew people close together or sent them to bed. In the Northern winter, even relatively large houses contracted to one or sometimes two crowded spaces as family members clustered around the hearth. They learned from early childhood how to move in small spaces, how to adjust for the presence of several people close to the same source of light and heat, and how to carry on multiple activities in close proximity.

While passing through Maryland in 1832, Frances Trollope "went into the houses of several of the small proprietors." She found them not to her taste, but interesting enough to describe, and recounted taking tea with a small planter's wife in a room she estimated as "twelve feet square." Adjoining it was a smaller chamber used as "the lodging-room of the white part of the family," and a "loft without windows," where, her hostess explained, visitors or "staying company" slept. "Near this mansion" was a separate kitchen where the blacks lived.

Most American families living in houses of more than one room separated their living spaces in this way—into public and private, outer and inner, and sometimes ordinary and ceremonious. One room—in colonial America often called the "hall," although early nineteenth-century Americans gave their rooms a great diversity of names—was the space for eating, indoor work, sitting, sometimes sleeping and cooking if there was no separate kitchen. The second room—sometimes called "parlor" or "chamber"—was first of all a space for sleeping: sometimes for the entire family as in the houses Trollope visited, sometimes simply for the parents, while other family members slept in the "hall" or the loft. Southerners usually kept this inner room a bedchamber, but for New Englanders it often served two functions that today might seem profoundly incompatible. It was not only the parents' bedchamber, but also a formal and ceremonial space, which contained the family's most valuable possessions, and might be used for entertaining on important occasions. Among ordinary families in rural New Hampshire before 1820, a local historian recalled, "a parlor wasn't considered well furnished unless it had a bed in it." Displaying their "best bed" in the "best room," couples could put a premiere household possession on public view, and give visual expression to the authority and centrality of their role in the household.

Americans who built larger houses could afford the more specialized use of space to separate the activities of their families. They set off food preparation and heavy domestic work into a separate kitchen, and then added "back rooms," for food and equipment storage and dairying. Still larger dwellings expanded sleeping space by providing rooms designated as bedrooms or bedchambers; second-floor rooms in two-story houses were almost universally used for sleeping.

Sleeping and sleeping space only slowly became individualized and private. Families in one- or two-room houses necessarily slept within sight and hearing of each other, even for parents' sexual intercourse. In most larger dwellings, parents were still the only family members to gain private sleeping quarters. In 1800, only a few wealthy households provided individual rooms for anyone other than the heads of the household, or occasionally a widowed grandparent. In the great majority of American families, the concept of one's own room, and often even one's own bed, would have been a strange one. Children and other adults living in the household slept together in hall, garret or bedchambers, although they usually separated the sexes if there was enough room. Where bedchambers were separate rooms they were rarely heated or furnished for anything but sleeping and storage.

Given the size of early nineteenth-century households and the practice of long-extended visits, it was possible to find people sleeping almost anywhere in most houses, including the kitchen. Even the wealthy were not exempt, particularly in

rural areas. The western Massachusetts lawyer Charles Sedgwick had such an abundance of family, household help, laborers
and visitors in his large house in 1823, noted a guest, that "there
are beds in every room in the house, except one parlor."

Some American infants slept in cradles, but it was common,
noted the physician and reformer William Alcott in 1830, for an
American mother "to sleep with her infant on her arm," and
children often shared the parental bed until they were weaned.
Older children were less likely to sleep with their parents, except under the pressure of pioneering conditions or dire poverty. But children and dependent household members rarely
slept alone; sisters and female domestic help routinely shared
beds, as did brothers, apprentices and laborers. Phineas T. Barnum, of Bethel, Connecticut, whose father was a middling
farmer and tavern keeper, remembered that in the 1820s he
and his brother customarily slept three in a bed with the Irishman who labored on his family's farm. Susan Lyman Lesley of
Northampton, Massachusetts, recalled the pain of parting with
an older sister, "for I had slept with her from the time of my
infancy." Accustomed to the presence and warmth of another
person's body since early childhood, many an American became uneasy at the prospect of sleeping alone. Edward Jenner
Carpenter noted in his diary that he was trying to "find someone to sleep with tonight" when another apprentice who
shared his room in lodgings was away.

In the decades after 1800, some Americans were dealing
differently with bedchambers and beds. More American families in the upper echelons of society began to provide separate
bedchambers for adolescent or grown but unmarried sons and
daughters—giving them spaces to which they had a personal
claim and might withdraw. These prosperous Americans were
the beneficiaries of the economic achievement and family limitation that made larger houses and smaller households possible.
Only these well-to-do families, the architectural writer Andrew
Jackson Downing noted in 1848, could use their "second-floor

apartments for the purpose of passing the time," as individuals' rooms; farm families still went "into them merely for the purpose of sleeping."

Casual bed sharing among adult houseguests and travelers in taverns also declined, as some men and women of higher status adopted the mores of the English travelers whose "one person, one bed" requests so surprised country tavern keepers. One sign of change was the transformation of the habits of the New England lawyers who followed the courts on their circuits from one county seat to the next. At the beginning of the nineteenth century they customarily slept two to a bed in the taverns where they lodged; by the 1820s they were insisting on sleeping alone.

Since 1811, when they set up housekeeping in their recently built small one-story farmhouse, Stephen and Olive Walkley of Southington, Connecticut, had slept, as well as entertained formal company, in the "best room." Their children slept upstairs in unfinished spaces separated only by blankets hung from the rafters. In 1831, Mrs. Walkley carried out a minor domestic revolution: she had the upstairs plastered and partitioned into bedchambers, moved the parental bed out of its place of honor in the "best room," and replaced it with a new parlor carpet. In this way the Walkleys made their own transition from the old style of domestic space to the new. They came to see the bed, with its reminders of sleep, undress and sexuality, as inappropriate for display.

By moving the bed out of the parlor and adding bedchambers, the Walkley family adopted a pattern of room use that was becoming typical for middling and prosperous Northern families: a pair of rooms furnished for sitting, eating and socializing, usually called "sitting room and parlor," one for everyday use, the other for display and entertaining on special occasions. Southern families created a similar pattern by adding a dining room to pair with the "hall."

Northern families were resolute in setting their parlors, "best rooms" or "great rooms" aside from everyday activities. Most households came to use them ever more exclusively for displaying the best and the newest of their possessions, for receiving formal visits like ministers' calls, and for the observance of such ritual occasions as, the *New England Farmer* observed, "the solemnization of a marriage or the obsequies of the dead." Many autobiographers remembered entering their families' shut-up parlors once a week, on Sundays, to sit in uncomfortable silence on rarely used furniture. Wealthy families, whose extensive social lives involved a good deal of formal visiting, naturally used their parlors much more frequently. In contrast, most Southerners were more expansive than Northerners in their use of domestic space. They were much less likely to draw formal boundaries between the use of hall and dining room.

Few houses in the early nineteenth century had single specialized rooms set aside solely for eating; as they had in the eighteenth century, most Americans continued to take their meals in spaces throughout the house. The household inventories of larger American dwellings frequently show two or three rooms furnished with enough chairs, tables and crockery for taking a meal. In some ordinary farmers' houses, "the whole family assembled at meals" in the kitchen, recalled a Connecticut man, "save only when the presence of company made it proper to serve tea in the parlor." Into the 1820s, Edward Everett Hale recalled, even well-to-do families in Boston "dined in their back parlors," or sitting rooms—where many rural Northern families ate through most of the nineteenth century. Even the dining rooms of larger Southern houses had a variety of other uses and family members sometimes took meals in their chambers.

Most elaborate in their specialized use of space were the great city houses. Elias Hasket Derby's house, the most valuable on the 1798 tax list, had fifteen rooms. The great Boston merchant Thomas Handasyd Perkins built seven houses in succession as his fortunes increased, each one larger and more expensive than the last. His final residence, completed in 1832, was of four stories with twenty-three rooms. In addition to parlors for the family, workrooms, kitchen and bedchambers, there were formal drawing rooms for the reception of company, a formal dining room, a library, a third-story room solely for the appreciation of art with "its wall covered with elegant prints," and a billiard room on the fourth floor. While most American families crowded the activities of their lives into a few small spaces, members of the Perkins household, and a few others like them, found themselves having to choose which room to sit in next.

"When Lilacs Last in the Dooryard Bloom'd"

At the beginning of the nineteenth century, American houses were only rarely the neat and meticulously arranged habitations that the preserved and restored fragments of the past now often suggest. "When Lilacs Last in the Dooryard Bloom'd," Walt Whitman entitled his great dirge for the death of Abraham Lincoln, and the poet pictured himself "in the dooryard fronting an old farm-house near the white-wash'd palings," where stood "the lilac-bush tall-growing with heart-shaped leaves of rich green." Whitman framed his poem with an image of the domestic landscape that would have been familiar, even seemingly traditional—the farmhouse was "old"—to his Northern readers in 1865. But it would not have been so at the beginning of the nineteenth century. The dooryard itself, the "white-wash'd palings" of the picket fence, the lilac bush—the familiar rural landscape of later years—were then artifacts of a new domestic order that was just emerging.

Around American farmhouses, the English agricultural reformer William Cobbett observed in 1818, there was "a sort of out-of-door slovenliness. . . . You see bits of wood, timber, boards, chips, lying about, here and there, and pigs tramping about in a sort of confusion." Not only were many dwellings "indifferent," "poor and old" or "small and mean," but the surrounding landscape was often barren, rough and disordered. Few houses boasted grassy lawns or enclosed front yards. The unfenced spaces in front of dwellings were most often trampled and bare, or sprouted straggling uncut weeds. Many farmhouses long remained "devoid of shade," a consequence of long generations spent clearing the forest; "for as the early settlers found the forest an enemy," the *Universal Geography* noted, "their descendants seem to inherit the hostility, and will not let a tree remain." Even the greatest houses and their grounds fell far short of the manicured perfection of some suburban residences of today.

Far more often than they noticed architectural gems, travelers reported dwellings that were "gray or dingy with neglect, and rifted or 'chinky' with dilapidation," doors that would not shut, and broken windows often casually repaired with hats, bags or old rags.

The houses of ordinary Americans contrasted sharply with the homes of the better off not only in size but in paint and finish. Log houses were "rude dwellings, in which the cracks are filled up with mud," and sometimes still showed peeling strips of bark. Smaller framed houses in the countryside were, as Francis Underwood noted, "rarely painted, and dusky with weatherstain." Most American families allowed their dwellings' clapboards to weather to the uncertain color they usually called "brown." In a landscape of brown dwellings the painted houses of the well-to-do in white, yellow, "stone-colour" or occasionally dark red stood out.

Open fireplaces, dirt roads and the proximity of the barnyard meant that the houses of the early nineteenth century were inevitably dusty and dirty; without window screens, every room was full of flies and flyspecks in summer.

Dogs and cats had the run of most American farmhouses, just as they did of churches, taverns and courthouses; occasionally they were listed in farmers' inventories as productive assets. Other domestic animals were rarely seen in the dwellings of British-Americans or German-Americans, who carefully separated their living quarters and their livestock. But Afro-Americans and the Irish immigrants starting to arrive in the 1830s had more relaxed attitudes about proximity to farm animals. In crowded Ireland, poor families living in sod huts and without the means to build tight pigsties sometimes gave their animals houseroom; it was held against them when they occasionally repeated the practice in sod huts or urban shanties in the new country. Slaves rarely kept pigs, but sometimes lived with domestic fowl; "the back door of the huts" in the slave quarters on a South Carolina plantation were "left wide open for the fowls and the ducks, which they are allowed to raise, to travel in and out."

Inundated with the daily tasks of farm households, rural women sometimes struggled with dirt, and more often ignored it. Travelers found dirt and litter on the floors, and household belongings in disorderly piles. In the countryside, the archaeological record shows, housewives still tossed broken vessels and trash out the most convenient door or window, and threw bones and food scraps into the yard to be picked over by their pigs and chickens. Patterns of convenient use clearly governed, not concern for the look of the domestic landscape. In the first two decades of the nineteenth century the great majority of American families had not yet come to see the environment immediately around the house as anything but a workspace.

But change was coming. Samuel Goodrich and other observers felt that "better taste" was "dawning both in houses and grounds." "I was glad to hear," wrote Mary Pease of Boston to Pliny Freeman of Sturbridge in 1840, "that you had your house painted and a dooryard." Freeman's house had been built at the time of his marriage in 1801, and for almost four decades had gone without paint or fence. Yet eventually Freeman had yielded to a thoroughgoing reformation of the domestic landscape, a deep but largely unspoken shift in the way many American families in the North saw and treated the spaces immediately around them. Over the years between 1800 and 1840, Francis Underwood recounted, households in his boyhood community of Enfield, Massachusetts, took on "a more general air of neatness in houses, dooryards, and gardens," planted "more ornamental trees," cleaned up their "old straggling heaps of wood" and had them "cut and piled undercover"; an increasing number of farmers were seeing to it that their houses "were painted and in good repair."

Many farm families came to make these extraordinary efforts to impose order on their surroundings. First those of the "better sort," then middling, then even humbler families took on the genteel trappings of house paint and ornamental plantings. They repaired windows, trimmed the grass and called in carpenters to build protective dooryard fences with their "whitewash'd palings." Within these ornamental enclosures they put climbing roses on trellises or planted "the lilac-bush tall-growing." Rural households gradually took up the city and village custom of dumping their refuse in well-defined pits instead of scattering it broadcast. By the 1830s there were street improvement and rural improvement societies in many country villages, organized to plant shade trees along the roads.

The houses of the American countryside took on color. They were not gaudy, variegated hues—New England meetinghouses in the eighteenth century had sometimes been painted in contrasting shades of pumpkin orange, pea green or chocolate brown—but strikingly uniform, light, neutral colors. As white lead paint became less expensive, Americans used it to create the landscape of white-painted commercial villages on many Northern main roads, "clean, airy and neat" in Patrick Shirreff's words. Most foreign observers joined Charles Dickens in regarding them as "the most favourable specimens of rural America."

More American families also began to take up the battle

against household dirt. Widely distributed domestic advice books appeared which vigorously invoked cleanliness and order. Lydia Maria Child's *The American Frugal Housewife*, dedicated not to the affluent but "to those who are not ashamed of economy," was published in 1832 and was already in its twelfth edition by 1833. Readers were admonished to value "neatness, tastefulness" as well as "good sense" and to see "the true economy of housekeeping" as the "art of gathering up all the fragments." Child filled her book with recipes for cleaning and scouring as well as for preparing economical meals.

The rapid growth of an American market for mass-produced brooms testified to an increasing number of households who were putting such urgings into practice, and wanted efficient tools for cleaning up domestic dust and litter. Beginning with a few hundred broomcorn brooms commercially produced in the Connecticut Valley of Massachusetts in 1798, the annual output of brooms sold in the American market had grown to around two million by 1840. The new attitudes toward landscape and domestic interior, emulating the ways of the well-to-do, were adopted most easily by those who had resources to spare; the poor clearly had no time for them. Women freed from most of the tasks of textile production in their households may have had more time to spend on cleanliness and order. But, more importantly, the change involved a different way of seeing house, grounds and the tasks of daily life; neatness and order, as well as food and clothing, became goals of domestic work.

But if multitudes of American families participated in these changes, perhaps more did not. Americans outside the North were clearly slower to take up the new and more exacting standards. There was general agreement among travelers in the 1830s that, while there were some elegantly kept and maintained homes, clutter and disorder in the landscape as well as household dirt increased as they went south of Philadelphia or west into the "new states." The disheveled cabins of the West were a signature of pioneering conditions. As for the South, "it does seem amazing to think," said Frances Kemble Butler, comparing the homes of Georgia planters with the houses of substantial New England farmers by the late 1830s, "that physical and moral conditions so widely opposite should be found among people occupying a similar place in the social scale of the same country." She found an "air of neglect, and dreary, careless untidiness" in and around the planters' houses; some of their domestic settings she regarded as "but a few degrees less ruinous and disgusting" than the slave cabins themselves.

But the mistresses of these plantations did not really deserve her moralistic condemnation as women made slack and lazy by slavery; in fact, they lived in a domestic world more like that of women on the frontier. They were far more directly involved in supervising the household production of food and clothing for family members and slaves alike, and carrying out some of its tasks themselves, than Northern housewives of comparable wealth. Less reliant on commercial exchange, Southern and Western women were more firmly bound to traditional routines of work and also to a traditional acceptance of dirt and disorder. They had not yet begun to see imposing order and cleanliness as crucial household tasks.

"For the Great Comfort of Your Family"

While paying a circuit-riding visit to a community near Sangamon, Illinois, a decade or so after its settlement in the early 1820s, the Methodist preacher Peter Cartwright was invited into a dwelling whose interior deeply disturbed him. "There was but one chair in the house," which he was given; the rest of the household sat on rough benches. Their table was a hewed section of log, and the hearth was merely earth, with a deep hole worn just in front of the fire. For eating utensils there were "wooden trenchers for plates, sharp-pointed pieces of cane for forks, and tin cups for cups and saucers . . . but one knife besides

a butcher's knife, and that had the handle off." The beds were
mere pallets on rough boards. Cartwright had seen many such
scanty, makeshift domestic scenes before among his many
Western congregations, but he knew that the head of this
household had "money hoarded up" and had the means to do
better. He preached an impromptu sermon on domestic decency that was also a shopping list. "Now, brother, do fill up this
hole in the earth, and go to town and get you a set of chairs,
knives and forks, cups and saucers, and get you a couple of plain
bedsteads and bed-cords. . . . Give your wife and daughters a
chance," argued Cartwright; he urged his parishioner to furnish
his house "for your own comfort, and the great comfort of your
family."

When Cartwright returned to the area a few months later,
"everything was done about right"; the new furnishings had
been purchased, and the interior of the house had been transformed. Cartwright was a rough-hewn revivalist who disdained
college education for clergymen, too much attention to refinement in dress or deportment, and anything else he considered overgenteel. But here he found himself evangelizing on
behalf of a powerful ideal of domestic comfort and decency. His
list summed up the minimal requirements for domestic respectability in the early nineteenth-century United States, even on
the Illinois frontier: chairs for all members of the family to sit
on, substantial wooden bedsteads, knives and forks for all to eat
with, a set of English ceramic plates, drinking glasses, and the
teapot and cups used in the social ritual of taking tea.

Earlier in American history, what angered Cartwright would
not have much surprised any visitor to an ordinary farmer's
home. Goods that were once the trappings of luxury in early
colonial America—reasonably well-assorted sets of sitting and
eating furniture, and comfortable beds—had gradually become
widespread in their ownership. By 1800, it would have been
reasonable to expect them in most white American households
in settled communities. In a long, slow process of change that

had begun in early Renaissance Europe, American families since the time of first settlement had on the average, over the generations, improved the material conditions of their domestic life. The gradual growth of commercial networks in early America, the slowly decreasing cost and greater availability of household goods, made possible an awakening interest in domestic consumption and comfort.

As household goods became less costly and more widely available, they moved outward from fashionable city life to the houses of the hinterlands, and Americans continually redrew the boundaries between the genteel and the common, the special and the ordinary. Each household's furnishings constituted a material world that defined the limits of comfort, heating and lighting, and filled functional needs for sitting, sleeping and eating; but they also spoke of Americans' economic status and aspirations.

Early nineteenth-century Americans did not invent this ongoing, long-term rise in material standards. But they accelerated it, and, like Cartwright, often gave it moral urgency. Achieving domestic comfort and abundance became a major American preoccupation.

A few months after the head of a household died in most parts of early nineteenth-century America, three duly sworn men, usually neighbors, arrived to take inventory of the possessions of the deceased in order to ensure a fair and lawful settlement of the estate. They looked over the house and outbuildings, the land, slaves, and livestock, the shop, store or office, and tools or stock in trade. They then turned to the household furniture, walking carefully through the house, sometimes accompanied by a family member, counting chairs and dishes, opening chests, valuing beds and kitchen utensils. Later they made a fair copy of their listing, signed and dated it, and presented it to the local court of probate.

Inventory takers created not only a legal record but a minute anatomy of the household's material surroundings. County courthouses across the United States still contain lists of the possessions of hundreds of thousands of families: beds and chairs, candlesticks and crockery, looking glasses and pictures, curtains, carpets and clocks. These inventories have so far only been studied in small samples for the early nineteenth century, but coupled with rare paintings, drawings and descriptions, they allow a tentative, approximate reconstruction of what American families had in their homes.

These sources reveal that the material world of most white Americans during the first decade of the nineteenth century met Cartwright's standards for "comfort" and decency, with more possessions than their colonial ancestors had had; but by those of later generations the interiors of their houses were still bare, sparsely furnished, often dark and sometimes cold.

"The people of this age," wrote Sophia Tyler in 1850, "know little of the horrors of winter." She was looking back on a time when "appliances for heat," as Ann Jean Lyman wrote of her girlhood in the 1790s, "were not what they are now." Even in the rigorous climate of inland Massachusetts, inventory takers rarely found more than two sets of fireplace andirons in a house, and very often there was only one. A single fire warmed many households through the winter, and most rooms were never heated at all. Northern families faced the winter with "large open chimneys and wood fires" that Mrs. Lyman recalled were "cheerful to the eye" but in severe weather "not warming to the body" even though they burned enormous quantities of wood. Even though the cavernous fireplaces of the seventeenth century had gradually given way to somewhat smaller and more efficient ones, the roaring hearths of the early nineteenth century could not keep drafty, completely uninsulated houses warm. On bitterly cold days, the hearth fire would warm only a very limited space around it. "Standing with her back so near the blaze as to be uncomfortably warm," as Harriet Beecher Stowe described her, a New England housewife "yet found her dish-towel freezing in her hand."

Only the Germans of Pennsylvania had a more efficient solution; they used stoves made of cast-iron plates to heat their homes, devices common in the Rhineland and Palatine regions of their ancestry. Their "large close stoves," Benjamin Rush observed in 1789, rendered German houses "so comfortable, at all times, that twice the business is done in every branch of the family" than in other Americans' dwellings "where every member crowds near a common fireplace, or shivers at a distance from it."

During the day, Americans depended on direct sunlight entering through windows or open doors. They read, sewed, and did other close work near windows, and moved their tables and chairs to follow the sun around the house.

At night, most Americans walked in darkness between the flickering fire and the "feeble circle of light" that Harriet Beecher Stowe remembered, made by "the dim gleam of a solitary tallow candle." Inventory takers usually numbered candlesticks on their lists, for they supplied illumination for the great majority of American families. Dim and flickering as they now seem, candles were in fact relatively expensive in terms of the beef tallow and household labor that went into making them; on his parents' farm, said Daniel Drake, tallow was often "too scarce to afford sufficient candles." Poor backwoods families and slave households saw by firelight alone, or used burning pineknots and rush lights; the urban poor often sat in darkness after their scanty supplies had been exhausted. Almost all Americans used candles sparingly; in a group of central Massachusetts inventories taken between 1790 and 1810, for example, over half of the households owned only one or two candlesticks, and those having more than four candles were very rare. Wealthy families could awe others with a prodigal lighting display of nine or a dozen candles.

For elderly people, and others with poor sight, the visual world created by these small islands of illumination was shadowy at best. Readers straining to make out the words sometimes set their books or newspapers on fire by holding their candles too close. The Germans' English-speaking neighbors in Pennsylvania may have resisted replacing their open fires with stoves because they provided no additional light.

The floors and windows that inventory listers saw or the painters of domestic interiors portrayed were bare and unadorned, for the most part. In 1800, "carpets were then only known in a few families," Samuel Goodrich recalled, the most affluent in each community. Many American housewives kept their kitchen floors "strewn with sand"; the most meticulous even brushed it into decorative patterns before retiring for the night. Window covering were equally rare. Rural Massachusetts inventories for the great majority of households show no floor coverings and not even a single pair of curtains.

"Most walls were bare," as well; American houses were strikingly poor in images. Appraisers found fewer than one household in ten with a painting, print or engraving. Only looking glasses, or framed mirrors, broke the empty expanse of walls, and most houses had no more than one or two. Their rarity made them important objects, prominently placed in the parlor or sitting room. Not only was a looking glass crucial for respectable grooming—a family without one surely faced some difficulty in looking presentable—but it also helped eke out scanty illumination by throwing back reflected candlelight.

Most households at the turn of the century had enough chairs for family members to sit down to meals or to offer seats to visitors; inventories of Massachusetts and Pennsylvania farm households usually showed at least half a dozen, and the majority of families had nine or more. Prosperous households treated them not just as seating furniture but as items of repetitive display; they lined them up along the walls of parlors and sitting rooms, and put them in entryways and even in bedchambers. When inventoried in 1801, Elias Hasket Derby's opulent Salem house had over one hundred chairs marshaled in its rooms and corridors. Poor families, with only two or three, often had to sit on beds or chests, or to socialize while leaning against walls or mantelpieces.

"Best bed—$11. Second bed—$8. Third bed—$7," wrote the listers of John Rogers's estate in Palmer, Massachusetts, in 1809. This careful hierarchical grading testified to the beds' importance; not only did the feathers with which they were stuffed make them valuable, but they were rare sources of bodily comfort in houses without cushioned seating. Men making their wills often divided their feather-filled beds, along with their frames or bedsteads, specifically and painstakingly among their heirs.

The greatest social gulf in sleeping furniture was between sleeping on feathers, a sign of at least modest comfort, and bedding down year-round on a straw tick, a scratchy and uncomfortable reminder of poverty. Most Americans did not sleep in the elaborate beds whose high-post bedsteads and curtains turned them into small separate sleeping chambers. They were expensive, because bed hangings used a great deal of cloth and represented countless hours of often complicated sewing. Many households had none at all, and in most only the parents' best bed would be "fully hung," providing the parental pair with not only warmth but privacy for conversation and sex. Children, apprentices and household help slept in "low beds."

Curtains in the best room, a tall case clock, long rows of chairs, a carpet and an engraving on the wall, a half-dozen candlesticks, and two or three fires were the marks of real affluence around 1800, a standard that only a few could even expect to achieve.

"All This Is Changed"

"But all this is changed," wrote Newton Hubbard of Massachusetts, reminiscing about the transformation of the domestic world from the vantage point of the mid-nineteenth century. Curtains "protect the windows and ornament the house, carpets cover the floors, and stoves are through the house." New technologies of mass production, as well as of heating and lighting, created a quiet domestic revolution for those families who prospered in the expanding American marketplace. As textiles, carpeting, wallpaper, chairs and looking glasses became less expensive in proportion to their resources, these women and men filled the rooms of their houses and embellished bare walls, windows and floors. As consumers, they created a new world of domestic abundance and comfort. Yet Americans shared very unevenly in these changes, depending on their wealth, their race and their engagement in the commercial economy. Some had little part in it or none at all.

Lambert Hitchcock of Connecticut was marketing factory-made "fancy chairs" in the thousands by the mid-1820s and underselling the local cabinetmakers of the countryside who made chairs for ordinary folk. But he was only the most famous of dozens of artisan-entrepreneurs, inventive New England mechanics who adapted water-powered lathes and saws to the production of standardized chair parts. They created both gain and loss. With mass-produced chairs selling for thirty to seventy-five cents each, Northern families bought them in increasing numbers; the average number of chairs per household, central Massachusetts probate inventories show, almost doubled between the 1800s and the 1830s. Old habits of domestic display thus became democratized; many families of fairly modest wealth could fill parlor and sitting room with matched sets, as only more prosperous ones could have done earlier. This increase also extended the social capacity of the household. Families could entertain larger groups and offer them uniform and genteel seating. Households with eighteen or twenty-four chairs rather than six or ten could entertain not only the minister but the Masonic Lodge, not only the neighbors but a full meeting of the Ladies' Charitable Society.

In their shape, construction and detailing, chairs, like other furniture in American households, had previously borne the stylistic stamp of local crafts traditions. The local distinctiveness of household furnishings began to erode with mass production and long-distance distribution. The "hearts and crowns" motif, for example, characterized almost all the chairs made and used in the communities of coastal Connecticut throughout the eighteenth century; but by 1820, after more than a hundred years, their unmistakable shapes were no longer being produced.

Wherever she went in the United States, Margaret Hall discovered, her American hostesses would beg her "to take a seat on the 'sofa.'" She found the sofas in prosperous American parlors of the late 1820s uncomfortable compared with those of London, but her hostesses were proud of them. Very rare before the 1820s, upholstered furniture such as sofas and easy chairs were now appearing in well-appointed parlors; by the 1830s, they could be seen in the houses of merchants and lawyers in the countryside. They provided a new standard—or at least a new expectation—of comfortable seating.

By the 1830s, sleeping habits were changing as hung beds began to become unfashionable among prosperous Americans, marking the start of their gradual disappearance from American bedchambers. Popular works of medical advice, like William Alcott's guides for young men and young women, were voicing concern about the unhealthiness of the closely confined and unventilated sleeping spaces traditional "best beds" created. Those married couples who gave up their high-post beds for "French low post" ones were those who lost the least in the exchange; they were prosperous folk, most likely to have warmer houses and greater privacy in their bedchambers.

Around 1820, improvements in stove design and an awakening desire for better heating came together with the continuing rise in the cost of firewood in Northern cities, the result of a century and a half of land clearing and deforestation. Stoves burned far less wood than open hearths—Rush thought "but a fourth or a fifth part of what is commonly burnt in ordinary open fireplaces," and the true figure was at least one-third.

Northern Americans living in cities and villages began to install cookstoves to replace their kitchen fireplaces, and accepted the most significant change in the technology, and the experience, of domestic heat since the fireplace itself had come into common use in the late Middle Ages. By the late 1830s, even modest artisans' households in cities and country villages were adopting stoves to economize on expensive wood. Farm families, who cut wood from their own lots, were much slower to abandon their hearths and brick up their fireplaces. Inventory takers recorded few stoves in farmers' houses in Massachusetts until after 1840, and they were rare in the South and West for decades longer.

Together, cookstoves and the ornamental parlor stoves that were taken up a few years later displaced the traditional functions of the hearth and changed the way an increasing number of families used their houses. Stoves stood near the center of the kitchen, parlor or sitting room, radiating heat evenly and invisibly, enlarging the room's usable space during the winter.

As the price for gains in comfort and efficiency, the cookstove imposed an emotional, perceptual loss. For hundreds of years, the hearth had been the warm, bright center of the household, the provider of cooked food, heat and light and a symbol of the family's shared life. Many of those whose families abandoned the fireplace when they were children remembered it with regret. "What magic it seemed to me," recalled Lucy Larcom, "when I was first allowed to strike that wonderful spark, and light the kitchen fire." And when Susan Blunt's mother, a village blacksmith's wife, got a stove in 1828, "we children missed the bright fire in the evenings with the big back log and fore stick and pine knots between; it made our great kitchen look very bright and cheerful." The more practical weighed gains and losses differently. Sophia Tyler was, she said, "disposed to vote for a monument to the memory of the first inventor of family stoves."

Houses built in the early nineteenth century were a little brighter during the day because their windows were larger;

panes of window glass continued to increase in size and decrease in cost from the "dark days" of the seventeenth century. Nighttime seeing became easier, as more American households were able to move beyond Stowe's "feeble circle of light." Farm families, who continued to make their own candles, saw better because they were using more of them; they owned an extra candlestick or two on the average by the 1830s. Inventories show oil lamps appearing in city and village homes after 1810, fueled by the rapidly expanding American whaling industry. By the 1830s, many nonfarming families had a pair or two of lamps and were buying lamp oil at stores. Lamps burned brighter and more evenly than candles and threw back the darkness considerably better.

A far more dramatic improvement in illumination came with the development of the Argand lamp in 1798 and its successor, the "astral lamp." Expensive to buy and burning highly refined and costly sperm oil—the precious commodity for which the whale ship *Pequod*'s crew hunted in *Moby Dick*—each was equivalent to about ten candlepower, far more than the total lighting most households could produce. They were rare and splendid objects to ordinary folk; Blunt remembered the astral lamp her mother had received from a wealthy relative as the most precious thing in the house. As they bought one or two for their parlors, prosperous American families of the 1820s and 1830s moved farther out of nighttime darkness than had any previous generation.

A very few wealthy households could go beyond astral lamps to lighting so dazzlingly bright that it was beyond the imagination of their ordinary fellow citizens, let alone previous generations. First in Baltimore in 1821, and by the 1830s in Philadelphia, New York and Boston, some affluent city dwellers had their houses fitted with gas lighting supplied by central coal-distillation plants. Philadelphia's gaslight system had almost seven hundred customers by 1836, whose installation fees and gas bills cost more than many poorer families paid for yearly rent. Gaslit houses with ten lighting fixtures of several candlepower each, like those in Philadelphia, were each brighter than an entire neighborhood in the countryside. Probably nothing could express the inequality of Americans' living conditions more starkly: the poor struggled to see by firelight, while the wealthy could now keep their entire houses ablaze throughout the evening.

The application of the power loom to the weaving of carpets made them far more common in American parlors—within reach, the inventories suggest, of one household out of four or five by 1830. The parlor carpet, adding a soft texture to a previously hard, bare floor, became, along with the sofa, a crucial symbol of genteel comfort, and aspiring families often looked for substitutes. Olive Walkley completed the transformation of her farmhouse parlor in 1831 by weaving a "rag carpet" as a stand-in for the expensive real thing, and other country families bought painted canvas floor cloths, or even painted their parlor floors with carpet stripes.

The pianoforte, the direct ancestor of today's piano, became the most decisive piece of American parlor furniture. That small minority of families—less than one in a hundred—who were able "to beautify the room by so superb an ornament," as a cynical music teacher suggested in the Boston *Musical Intelligencer,* had acquired the ultimate "badge of gentility . . . the only thing that distinguishes 'decent people' from the lower and less distinguished" whether it was ever played or not.

Cheaper machine-made textiles put window curtains within reach of an expanding number of families. Window curtains became widely used in cities and villages, where they gave families some visual privacy from passersby on increasingly busy roads; they were also part of the house's facade, speaking to those same passersby about the household's standard of living. In the countryside, all but the most prosperous homes adopted curtains more slowly than in closer-set communities.

An improving technology of machine production and printing had also brought the price of wallpaper down to levels many more households could afford. Traces of paper on the walls of many surviving houses, as well as evidence in the ledgers of country stores, attest to its growing availability in the rural North.

American houses were less barren of pictures. Wealthy families could hang more art on their walls than in 1800, because there were many more painters in the United States in the 1830s, from highly successful European-trained artists to itinerant painters who traveled the countryside. "Most works," Edward Everett Hale recalled, "were portraits"; American artists were primarily engaged in supplying prosperous householders with likenesses of themselves or other family members, while booksellers ran an increasing trade in engravings of heroes and statesmen like George Washington, Andrew Jackson and Napoleon Bonaparte. Landscapes and scenes of work and social life, although fascinating as historical evidence, were much rarer, and religious art was almost wholly unknown.

Before the advent of cheap lithographs in the 1840s, professionally produced art was still for a relatively small minority; no more than one Massachusetts house in five had even one painting or engraving on its walls as late as the 1830s. But looking glasses ceased being singular objects on American walls; households had two, three or more. And more families were decorating their walls with other images: most commonly printed or hand-drawn records of marriages, births and deaths, or schoolgirl-produced "mourning pictures" that memorialized departed family members.

The likeliest place to look for pictorial expression in American households after 1820 was on the dining table or in the cupboard. Another new technology, the "transfer printing" of images on relatively inexpensive mass-produced English pottery, brought depictions of English, European and oriental scenery into many thousands of homes which had seen nothing before except small woodcuts and engravings in books. Emerson Bixby of Barre, Massachusetts, was a farmer and blacksmith living in a three-room house in the countryside; yet by the 1830s, archaeology has revealed, he and his wife and daughters were eating off plates marked with "select views" of the manor of "Eashing Park" and the "Wilderness of Kent" in England, of "Batalha, Portugal," and of the city of Verona in Italy.

The presence of clocks in American households became less a symbol of affluence than of time consciousness. Tall case clocks and others with finely finished brass movements remained expensive and relatively rare, but the development of mass-produced clocks with inexpensive wooden works, beginning with Eli Terry's Connecticut "shelf clock" in 1806, brought them within reach of a wide range of families. Rural Massachusetts estate appraisers found clocks in the homes of storekeepers and professional men and two-thirds of craftsmen by the 1830s; farmers were slow in accepting stoves and oil lamps, but many more of them, about half, had clocks in their houses by 1830.

By the 1830s, prosperous commercial and professional families, along with those of some successful farmers and artisans, lived with this abundance of chairs, mirrors, wallpaper, sofas, engravings; they had, as the traveler Francis Grund observed, "large airy parlors, nice carpets, and mahogany furniture."

The households of most farmers and craftsmen, however respectable, lived in smaller rooms, with bare floors, and chairs and tables of less expensive wood; but on the whole they had more than their parents and grandparents—a set of "fancy chairs," a shelf clock, more light at night, bright images on their crockery. But there was a great and widening gap between the wealthiest and the poorest, who had a very small share in all of this or none at all.

Frances Trollope was normally blunt in her evaluation of American domestic deficiencies. But "the houses of the higher classes" in New York City, she remarked in 1831, were "extremely handsome, and very richly furnished." There were chairs covered in "silk or satin," and the mirrors were "as handsome as in London" and the "marble tables as elegant." The homes of the urban wealthy were becoming lavish, even spectacular by earlier standards. Henry Sargent's *A Tea Party,* painted in the 1820s, illustrates how those at the apex of American urban society were able to live. (See illustration no. 27.) The scene is a late afternoon party in an upper-class Boston home, probably Sargent's own. The large drawing room is abundantly lit and full of well-dressed men and women, and the chairs are gilded pieces in the latest fashion. The carpet is sumptuous, and the walls are lavishly hung with paintings.

Comfort and abundance came to wealthy plantation households as well. The main house of the Skirving family plantation on the Combahee River in South Carolina, which Margaret Hall visited in 1828, had "everything that is luxurious," with "snow-white quilts and draperies" and a "delightful arm chair and sofa" even in the bedrooms.

But five hundred yards away from the Skirving main house, with its armchairs and sofas, were the twenty-nine earth-floored "negro huts" of the slave quarters, without windows or candles. The domestic world of American slaves remained, as it had been, dark at night, crowded with people and sparsely furnished, in an intricate intertwining of their material deprivation and their African inheritance. Many masters did not provide slaves with "furniture of any nature or description," in Solomon Northup's words. "Chairs, tables, plates . . . they had none," a traveller observed of Georgia field hands. Primarily left to furnish their cabins on their own, slaves occasionally had a cast-off chair or table, but far more often sat on rough benches and stools, or could be seen "squatting on their hams" around their hearths and outdoor fires. In squatting, Afro-Americans used a posture that white Americans found uncomfortable and alien, but was a common practice among African farming and herding peoples. They built three-legged stools that could be made easily out of scanty materials, but were also a form of seating furniture known in West Africa.

Some slave cabins had wooden floors but most were "not boarded, but merely the damp hard earth itself." Slave households sometimes had one or two rude bedsteads, pallets of wooden boards, to raise their straw or cornhusk mattress ticks off the floor. More often they simply spread them on the ground. The most poorly supplied had even less. "My pillow," Northup remembered of his life on a Louisiana plantation, "was a stick of wood. The bedding was a coarse blanket and not a rag or shred beside." Most slave households completed their furnishings with some hollowed-out gourds for storage, a single cooking pot, and a few scavenged utensils and broken pieces of pottery or clamshells.

The urban poor often lived little better. They slept on straw mattresses in "habitations," as a minister described the quarters of the poor in Massachusetts cities, "not ventilated at all," with entire families "in a single room, and sometimes in one bed." During the day they sat on their beds, or eked out a couple of old chairs with a broken barrel or two. Like the slaves, they usually saw at night only by firelight.

In the log cabins of the Kentucky hills, Charles Dickens noticed in 1841 families still living as sparsely as Peter Cartwright's errant parishioner had, with "homemade dressers standing in the open air without the door, whereon was ranged the household store, not hard to count, of earthen jars and pots."

But away from the massive disparities of the slave South and the cities there were great contrasts even in small rural communities. In the country town of Shrewsbury, Massachusetts, two men, near neighbors, died in their late thirties within a few years of each other. Both Gerry Dudley and Calvin Stone were farmers' sons but they had found new occupations in their region's expanding commercial economy. Dudley was a shoemaker, one of thousands who produced cheap, heavy shoes for the national market. Stone was a country merchant with a store near the town common, who just before his death had been planning to move his mercantile business west to St. Louis. The

Stone family owned a two-story, eight-room house in the full Federal style, with a central hallway and double chimneys; it was worth five times as much as the Dudleys' one-story dwelling with its three small rooms. Stone's household of six had forty-three chairs, an elegant brass timepiece, carpets in parlor, hall and best bedchamber, five looking glasses, mahogany tables and bureaus, a cookstove and an abundance of bedding, silver, china and glassware. Dudley's family was just as large, but it lived with three chairs, two small, battered tables, no clock, bare floors, a single looking glass, an old chest for storage, meager dishes and eating utensils worth less than one-twentieth of their neighbors'. One of their three beds was a skimpy straw tick; another, although of feathers, was "old and worn" and almost valueless.

The Stones's domestic world was not as opulent as the one Sargent painted, but its comfort stood for solid, reasonable success in the 1830s; they lived as well as all but two or three in their community. The Dudleys' home, like those of agricultural laborers and many artisans, was painfully sparse; the family could not have sat around the dinner table together.

Across the immense territory of the United States the American people lived in domestic scenes of enormous variety. Many —slaves, some farmers and artisans, laborers—still lived in small, crowded, scantily furnished dwellings. Other Americans had participated far more fully in what some of them called "an advance in civilization." Most of them lived between abundance and bitter austerity, in a world that was more comfortable, but also more unequal, than that of their ancestors.

4

"THE MASKS WHICH
CUSTOM HAD PRESCRIBED":
INTIMATE LIFE

WHEN two farmers met" in New England, remembered
Francis Underwood, "their greeting might seem to a stranger
gruff or surly, since the facial muscles were so inexpressive,
while, in fact, they were on excellent terms." Even in courtship
and marriage, he recalled, rural men and women were equally
constrained, with couples "wearing all unconsciously the masks
which custom had prescribed; and the onlookers who did not
know the secret would think them cold and indifferent."

Of all the "infinite details" of American life the most taken-
for-granted and often most elusive were the bodily ones: not
only the daily facts of food and clothing, but those parts of life
—appearance and posture, cleanliness and hygiene, and sexuality—rarely talked of at all, or hidden behind custom's masks.
But Americans, and observers of their society, left behind fascinating fragmentary traces of their intimate lives.

Underwood noted a pervasive physical as well as emotional
constraint among the people in his boyhood town of Enfield; it
was rooted, he thought, not only in the self-denying ethic of
their Calvinist tradition but in the nature of their work. Like
other rural Americans, New Englanders moved heavily. The
great physical demands of unmechanized agriculture gave men
a distinctively ponderous gait and posture. Despite their

strength and endurance, farmers were "heavy, awkward and slouching in movement," and walked with a "slow inclination from side to side."

These Yankee visages were captured by itinerant New England portraitists during the early nineteenth century, as successful farmers, storekeepers, physicians and master craftsmen became the first more or less ordinary Americans to have their portraits taken. New England had seen little in-migration since the seventeenth century, so that its people had shared not only the cultural inheritance but the genetic pool of the Puritan settlers for several generations. The portraits caught their caution and immobility of expression as well as recording their angular, long-jawed features, creating reasonably good collective likenesses of whole communities.

Almost everywhere in the American countryside east of the Alleghenies, the "masks which custom had prescribed" concealed much. Ordinary white people in the South were no easier to read than "heavy, awkward" Yankees. "In these Southern states," Margaret Hall complained, "the manners of the secondary classes are more disagreeable, gruff and boorish than anything I ever saw elsewhere." A group of North Carolinian men and women who came to see their first railway car in 1838 were "fierce, poor and wildlooking" to the train's passengers, and their facial expressions seemed to them to betray "a stupid kind of dismayed wonder" at what they were seeing. Such observers took the country people's ungiving expressions, slowness of speech and unyielding posture as evidence of ignorance and hostility.

Even by their own impassive standards, Yankees found New York Dutchmen and Pennsylvania German farmers "clumsy and chill," or "dull and stolid." But "the wild Irish" stood out in America for precisely the opposite reasons. They were not "chill" or "stolid" enough, but loud, boisterous and gesticulating. Their expressiveness made Anglo-Americans uncomfortable.

Of the slaves celebrating at a plantation ball, it was "impossible to describe the things these people did with their bodies," Frances Kemble Butler observed, "and above all with their faces." She sympathized deeply with the slaves she saw in Georgia, but the limits of her understanding were clear. Black Americans moved, spoke and gestured in ways which ethnocentric whites could not interpret accurately or fairly. Blacks' expressions and gestures, their preference for rhythmic rather than rigid bodily motion, their alternations of energy and rest, made no cultural sense to observers who saw only "antics and frolics," laziness, or "savagery." Sometimes perceived as obsequious, childlike and dependent, or alternatively as sullen and inexpressive, slaves also wore masks—not "all unconsciously" as Northern farm folk did, but as part of their self-protective strategies for controlling what masters, mistresses and other whites could know about their feelings and motivations.

A physical expressiveness alien to most other Americans as well as the stigma of poverty and low status made both blacks and Irish vulnerable to caricature. Illustrated comic almanacs and broadsides of the 1830s often portrayed them both as brutal and apelike.

American city dwellers, whose daily routines were driven by the quicker pace of commerce, were easy to distinguish from "heavy and slouching" farmers attuned to slow seasonal rhythms. New Yorkers, in particular, had already acquired their own characteristic body language. The clerks and commercial men who crowded Broadway, intent on their business, had a universal "contraction of the brow, knitting of the eyebrows, and compression of the lips . . . and a hurried walk," Frederick Marryat reported. It was a popular American saying in the 1830s, he went on, that "a New York merchant always walks as if he had a good dinner before him, and a bailiff behind him."

Northern and Southern farmers and city merchants alike, to say nothing of Irishmen and blacks, fell well short of the ideal of genteel "bodily carriage" enshrined in both English and American etiquette books and the instructions of dancing mas-

ters: "flexibility in the arms . . . erectness in the spinal column
. . . easy carriage of the head." It was the ideal of the British
aristocracy, and Southern planters came closest to it, expressing
the power of their class in the way they stood and moved.
Slaveowners accustomed to command, imbued with an ethic of
honor and pride, at ease in the saddle, they carried themselves
more gracefully than men hardened by toil or preoccupied with
commerce. Visiting Washington in 1835, the Englishwoman
Harriet Martineau contrasted not the politics but the posture of
Northern and Southern congressmen. She marked the confident bearing, the "ease and frank courtesy . . . with an occasional touch of arrogance" of the slaveholders alongside the
"cautious . . . and too deferential air of the members from the
North." She could recognize a New Englander "in the open
air," she claimed, "by his deprecatory walk."

Americans' countenances also became more open, travelers
agreed, as they went West. Nathaniel Hawthorne found a dramatic contrast in public appearances only a few days' travel
west of Boston. "The people out here" in New York State just
west of the Berkshires, he confided to his notebook in 1839,
"show out their character much more strongly than they do
with us," in his native eastern Massachusetts. He compared "the
quiet, silent, dull decency . . . in our public assemblages" with
their wider gamut of expressiveness, "mirth, anger, eccentricity, all showing themselves freely." Westerners in general,
Henry Ward Beecher observed, had "far more freedom of manners, and more frankness and spontaneous geniality," than the
city or country people of the eastern seaboard, as did the "odd
mortals that wander in from the western border" whom Martineau observed in Washington's political population.

Americans had their own ways of talking as well. The Gaelic
and Dutch that were noticeable in the eighteenth century were
rapidly disappearing. Pennsylvania Deitch, Louisiana Cajun
and the Gullah speech of Sea Island slaves did not die out, but
proportionately fewer Americans spoke them in 1840 than had

in 1800. In their own way, the great majority of Americans spoke English, as British travelers often somewhat reluctantly acknowledged. Most visitors, bearing in mind "the various dialects that are used by the lower classes in different parts" of Britain, agreed with James Stuart that the speech of ordinary Americans was far more intelligible and relatively uniform "all over the country." But American men and women anxious to testify to their country's "refinement" went further maintaining that there were no real differences between "educated speech" in the United States and in the mother country. Most of their visitors disagreed vehemently. All Americans, not simply Southerners, "drawled," they insisted, giving their vowels a long and painful drawing-out. Even the cultivated Sedgwick family of Massachusetts—lawyers, statesmen, and novelists—observed Margaret Hall, accustomed to the speech of London, had "an extraordinary portion of drawl." To the ears of upper-class Britons, Americans in the Northern and Western states added an unpleasant "nasal twang." Hall described an evening at the house of New York's Governor De Witt Clinton in Albany, with many of the state's most eminent men "asking me through their noses whether I should at all have detected them as Americans."

Britons found the American pronunciation of many words peculiar as well. Even among some in "the educated and respectable class" in American commercial cities, observed Thomas Hamilton, "the word *does* is split into two syllables, and pronounced *do-es. Where,* for some incomprehensible reason, is converted into *whare, there* into *thare.* And I remember, on mentioning to an acquaintance that I had called on a gentleman of taste in the arts, he asked, 'whether he *shew* (showed) me his pictures.' Such words as oratory and dilatory, are pronounced with the penult syllable, long and accented; missionary becomes *missionairy.*"

Many travelers delighted in collecting examples of how American pronunciation, usage and vocabulary differed from their own, although things rarely if ever reached the point of mutual unintelligibility. These comments stung Americans eager for foreign approval, but in reality simply showed that their speech, like their society, had developed along its own path.

Americans did speak more alike across their vast territory than villagers in England, but they heard their own speech in more subtle gradations than their transatlantic cousins could. All Americans sounded drawling and provincial in London drawing rooms, but there were great differences between the speech of ordinary farm households and that of the educated classes. The varieties of "chimney corner English" spoken in the regions of rural America were, as Underwood observed, the "result of the fusion of many illiterate British dialects" over a couple of centuries. The settlers of central Kentucky—immigrants from New Jersey, Maryland and Virginia—spoke what Daniel Drake described as "a dialect of old English, in queer pronunciation and abominable grammar." Rural New England's Yankee dialect, with its sharp nasality, its "local and obsolete terms, half-articulated contractions, and clipping of words," was the prevalent speech of ordinary country folk. Its "peculiar twisting of accent," Underwood claimed, became more evident the farther into the hills, or the lower on the social scale, a listener went. New England ministers spoke with far less "rustic intonation" than most members of their congregations.

When commerce, an increasing flow of books and newspapers, and city fashions in clothing made their way into the countryside, the city's standards of educated speech arrived as well. In his subsequent career as a distinguished physician and educator in Cincinnati, Drake had unlearned his parents' speech, and taken on more "correct" pronunciation and grammar. As young people who had learned the "speech of the educated world" returned to their rural communities, even for visits, families and schoolteachers began to emulate them, and gradually to "uproot bucolic speech."

The great majority of slaves spoke America's most distinct dialect of English. Slave speech put *hab* for *have, dat* for *that.* Slaves often dropped the initial syllables of words, changed many uses of the verb "to be," and simplified possessives, plurals and references to gender. Ethnocentric whites regarded these changes and simplifications as ignorant corruptions of the language, some calling it "nigger gibberish." Striving to show whites that a black man could write and speak as well as they, the ex-slave and abolitionist Frederick Douglass found the ordinary speech of his fellow Southern blacks an embarrassing sign of ignorance and tried to excuse it. But blacks were not speaking ignorantly, just differently, by modifying English pronunciation and grammar in the direction of African syntax and speech rhythms—rhythms that were helping to shape some of the familiar cadences of white speech in the deep South as well.

The traditional signs of deference before social superiors— the deep bow, the "courtesy," doffed cap, lowered head and averted eyes—were a part of social relationships in colonial America. Although less deeply ingrained and widespread than in England, they were still often found when people of humble station were confronted by "the rich, the high-born and the able." "Forty years earlier," wrote Lydia Huntley Sigourney in 1824, there were still "individuals . . . in every grade of society" who had grown up "when a bow was not an offense to fashion nor . . . a relic of monarchy." But in the early nineteenth-century United States such signals of subordination were rapidly falling away. It was a natural consequence of the Revolution, she maintained, "which in giving us liberty, obliterated almost every vestige of politeness of the 'old school.' "

Shaking hands became the accustomed American greeting between men, a gesture whose symmetry and mutuality signified equality. The Englishman Frederick Marryat found in 1835 that it was "invariably the custom to shake hands" when he was introduced to Americans, and that he could not carefully grade the acknowledgment he would give to new acquaintances according to their signs of wealth and breeding. He found instead that he had to "go on shaking hands here, there and everywhere, and with everybody." Americans were not blind to inequalities of economic and social power, but they less and less gave them overt physical expression. Bred in a society where such distinctions were far more clearly spelled out, Marryat was somewhat disoriented in the United States; "it is impossible to know who is who," he claimed, "in this land of equality."

Other well-born British travelers encountered not just confusion but conflict, when they failed to receive the signs of respect they expected. Margaret Hall's letters home during her Southern travels outlined a true comedy of manners. At every stage stop in the Carolinas, Georgia and Alabama, she pressed country tavern keepers and their households for deferential service and well-prepared meals; she received instead rancid bacon and "such an absence of all kindness of feeling, such unbending frigid heartlessness." But she and her family were more responsible than they realized for creating the reception that they encountered. Squeezed between the pride and poise of the great planters and the social debasement of the slaves, small Southern farmers often displayed a prickly insolence, a considered lack of response, to those who too obviously considered themselves their betters. To the proprietors of a roadside tavern in Georgia, plain fare and short words may well have seemed no more than a haughty aristocrat deserved. Greatly to her discomfort and incomprehension, Mrs. Hall was experiencing what a Briton more sympathetic to American ways, Patrick Shirreff, called "the democratic rudeness which assumed or presumptuous superiority seldom fails to experience."

Deferential manners survived much longer among American children, who could still be pressed to make obeisance to adults. The children he passed along the road in New England and western New York, observed the British army officer Edward Coke in 1833, were "remarkable for their decorum of manners, bowing and making courtesies to the passengers as the coach passed." Lyndon Freeman recalled that pupils "made their manners" to the schoolmaster or -mistress every morning, and that "if a boy did not doff his cap on meeting a person on the road and 'make a bow' or the girl a courtesy they were sure to answer for it." Growing up in Kentucky, Daniel Drake remembered, he "had often run to the roadside to make my bow. . . . If a man overtook us or met us, we all stepped aside, stopped in a row, [and] took off our hats." But gradually, children too abandoned this fossilized version of the deference that their elders had once given the powerful. Edward Everett Hale recalled seeing young people "make their manners" for the last time in New England in 1842. A few years later, Drake thought the practice, although surviving "in remote places," was "never seen in cities." It had been "ominously neglected" by the rising generation.

"Dirty and Slovenly to a Degree"

Early nineteenth-century Americans lived in a world of dirt, insects and pungent smells. Farmyards were strewn with animal wastes, and farmers wore manure-spattered boots and trousers everywhere. Men's and women's working clothes alike were often stiff with dirt and dried sweat, and men's shirts were often stained with yellow rivulets of tobacco juice. The location of privies was all too obvious on warm or windy days, and unemptied chamber pots advertised their presence. Wet baby "napkins," today's diapers, were not immediately washed but simply put by the fire to dry. Vats of "chamber lye"—highly concentrated urine used for cleaning type or degreasing wool—perfumed all printing offices and many households. "The breath of that fiery bar-room," as Underwood described a country tavern, "was overpowering. The odors of the hostlers' boots, redolent of fish-oil and tallow, and of buffalo-robes and horse-blankets, the latter reminiscent of equine ammonia, almost got the better of the all-pervading fumes of spirits and tobacco."

Densely populated, but poorly cleaned and drained, America's cities were often far more noisome than its farmyards. City streets were thickly covered with horse manure and few neighborhoods were free from the spreading stench of tanneries and slaughterhouses. New York City's accumulation of refuse was so great that it was generally believed that the actual surfaces of many streets had not been seen for decades. During her stay in Cincinnati, Frances Trollope thought she was following the practice of American city housewives when she threw her household "slops"—refuse food and dirty dishwater—out into the street. An irate neighbor soon informed her that municipal ordinances forbade "throwing such things at the sides of the streets" as she had done; "they must just all be cast right into the middle and the pigs soon takes them off." In most cities hundreds or even thousands of free-roaming pigs scavenged the garbage; one exception was Charleston, whose streets were patrolled by buzzards. By converting garbage into pork, pigs kept city streets clearer than they would otherwise have been, but the pigs themselves befouled the streets and those who ate their meat—primarily poor families—ran greater than usual risks of infection.

Boston probably had the best sanitary regulations of any large American city; its scavengers' carts and manure-collecting farmers kept its streets, as the English visitor John Lambert noted in 1808, "for the most part clean and in good order" by contemporary standards. Yet the city still made powerful assaults on the nostrils of its citizens. Dead animals were sometimes thrown in the Frog Pond on the Common, and the area around the wharves and Faneuil Hall market were putrid with the decayed residues of vegetables, meat and fish. Although Boston's hogs were not allowed to roam at large—comparing it to New York, the printer David Clapp called it the "swineless city" in his 1832 diary—one of the city's scavenging contractors often carted away the offal to feed his own large herd, kept in an unsavory and prominently situated pen.

Humbler folk lived in close, matter-of-fact proximity to odors that disturbed the more fastidious minority. Stopping to eat at a house on the Pee Dee River in South Carolina in 1810, the traveler John Melish had just begun to eat when "I heard a violent retching in the adjoining room, the door of which immediately open'd, and out came such a smell as filled the room with a perfume somewhat different from that of Arabia Felix." Melish "could not bear it," and tried to leave the scene, but the two stage drivers traveling with him "seemed to be accustomed to these sort of scenes," and finished their meal "with all the composure imaginable."

The most visible symbols of early American sanitation were those most anonymous of buildings, privies or "necessary houses." But Americans did not always build them or use them. Many rural households simply took the closest available patch of woods or brush, just as families in some traditional farming communities of Ireland do today. Extremely careful archaeological investigations of small farmsteads, for example, have often found no privy sites, and they were not usually built in slave quarters. Men and women working in the fields or traveling simply answered the body's call when and where they could. Lewis Miller's sketches provide graphic evidence that the male inhabitants of York, Pennsylvania, at times relieved themselves in the street or against the walls of houses.

But in more densely settled communities, and regions with colder winters, privies were in widespread use. They were not usually put in out-of-the-way locations. "The fashion of some" Northern farm families, according to the *Farmer's Almanack* in 1826, had long been to have their "necessary planted in a garden or other conspicuous place." Other country folk went even further in turning human wastes to agricultural account, and built their outhouses "within the territory of a hog yard, that the swine may root and ruminate and devour the nastiness there-

of." The *Almanack* was a longstanding critic of primitive manners in the countryside and roundly condemned these traditional sanitary arrangements as demonstrating a "want of taste,
decency, and propriety."

Families following Thomas's advice and trying to exemplify
"decency" were becoming concerned about shielding privies
from sight, or at least ensuring that they did not take too prominent a place among their farm buildings. Some larger and
newer Northern farmhouses were built with necessaries made
architecturally invisible by attachment to the house; they were
separated from the living quarters by a succession of work and
storage rooms. Catharine Beecher's *Treatise on Domestic Economy* of 1841, a bible of refined domesticity, actually included
a plan for such an indoor privy. Rural sanitation, however, had
its advantages. With their abundance of room, farm households
could avoid putting living quarters, well and kitchen too close
to the "back-house." Rural privies could be moved when the pit
filled up and had to be covered over; on some farms a succession
of fruit trees around the home lot marked previous locations.

Living in much closer quarters, urban families were often
painfully conscious of their privies, which usually sat in their
small backyards. The better-arranged necessaries of the prosperous emptied into vaults which could be opened and cleaned
out. The dripping horse-drawn carts of the "nocturnal gold-
finders," as a Boston newspaper called them, who emptied the
vaults and took their loads out for disposal or occasionally to
sell to farmers—most Americans would not use "night soil" as
manure, but some did—were a familiar part of nighttime traffic
on city streets. Those privies more poorly constructed sometimes opened directly on a stream or pond, or simply over-
flowed their pits, making the yard "a sink of filth."

The humblest pieces of American household furniture were
the chamber pots that allowed people to avoid a dark and often
cold nighttime journey outdoors. Kept under the bed or in a
corner of the room, "chambers" were used primarily upon

retiring and arising, or by invalids unable to walk to the privy. Collecting, emptying and cleaning them out were an unspoken but daily part of every housewife's routine.

Nineteenth-century inventory takers became considerably more reticent about naming chamber pots than their predecessors, usually lumping them together with other miscellaneous "crockery," but most households probably had a couple of chamber pots; genteel families reached the optimum of one for each bedchamber. English-made ceramic pots had become cheap enough by 1820 that few American families within the reach of commerce needed to go without one. "Without a pot to piss in" is still a vulgar tag of long standing for extreme poverty; those poorest households without one, perhaps more common in the warm South, used the outdoors at all times and seasons.

The most decorous way for householders to deal with chamber-pot wastes accumulated during the night was to throw them down the privy hole. But more casual and unsavory methods of disposal were still in wide use. Farm families often dumped their chamber pots out the most convenient door or window—sometimes, the archaeological record discloses, letting the pot slip as well and leaving its broken pieces on the ground. In a more densely settled community like York, Pennsylvania, the results could be more serious. In 1801, Miller drew and then described an event "in North George Street," when "Mr. Day an English man" (as the German-American Miller was quick to point out) "had a bad practice by pouring out of the upper window his filthiness. . . . One day came the discharge . . . on a man and wife going to a wedding, her silk dress was fouled."

Sleeping accommodations in American country taverns were often dirty and insect-ridden, from Isaac Weld's "filthy beds swarming with bugs" in 1794 to Charles Dickens's "a sort of game not on the bill of fare" in 1840; complaints increased in intensity as travelers went south or west. Tavern beds were uniquely vulnerable to infestation by whatever insect guests travelers brought with them, and the bedding of most American households was surely less foul. Yet it was dirty enough. New England farmers were still too often "tormented all night by bed bugs," complained the *Farmer's Almanack* in 1837, and books of domestic advice contained extensive instructions on removing them from feather beds and straw ticks.

Journeying between Washington and New Orleans in 1828, Margaret Hall became far more familiar with intimate insect life than she had ever been in the genteel houses of London or Edinburgh. Her letters home, never intended for publication, gave a graphic and unsparing account of American sanitary conditions. After sleeping in a succession of beds with the "usual complement of fleas and bugs" she and her party had themselves become infested: "We bring them along with us in our clothes and when I undress I find them crawling on my skin, nasty wretches." New and distasteful to her, such discoveries were commonplace among the ordinary folk with whom she lodged. The American children she saw on her Southern journey were "kept in such a state of filth," with clothes "dirty and slovenly to a degree," but this was "nothing in comparison with their heads" which were "absolutely crawling!" In New Orleans she observed women picking through children's heads for lice, "catching them according to the method depicted in an engraving of a similar proceeding in the streets of Naples."

After Andrew Jackson's election in 1828 the White House, at the center of American government, became far more than ever before a place of democratically mixed public assembly. President Jackson's "levees" or public receptions, open to all citizens, broke down olfactory boundaries as well as social ones. These "singular and miscellaneous assemblages," Harriet Martineau observed, juxtaposed diplomats, public officials and prominent local citizens, whose hands were washed and whose clothing was clean, with soldiers "redolent of gin and tobacco" and "men begrimed with all the sweat and filth accumulated in their day's—perhaps their week's labour," who gave the hot and crowded drawing rooms "odours . . . more pungent than agreeable."

But many even of the best-turned-out visitors at Jackson's levees would have not have passed unnoticed at a social gathering today. Americans were not "clean and decent" by today's standards, and it was virtually impossible that they should be. The furnishings and use of rooms in most American houses made more than the most elementary washing quite difficult. In a New England farmer's household, wrote Underwood, each household member would "go down to the 'sink' in the lean-to, next to the kitchen, fortunate if he had not to break ice in order to wash his face and hands, or more fortunate if a little warm water was poured into his basin from the kettle swung over the kitchen fire." Even in the comfortable household of the prominent minister Lyman Beecher in Litchfield, Connecticut, around 1815, all family members washed in the kitchen, using a stone sink and "a couple of basins."

Southerners washed in their detached kitchens or, like Westerners in warm weather, washed outside, "at the doors . . . or at the wells" of their houses. Using basins and sinks outdoors or in full view of others, most Americans found anything more than "washing the face and hands once a-day," usually in cold water, difficult, even unthinkable. Most men and women also washed without soap, reserving it for laundering clothes; instead they used a brisk rubbing with a coarse towel to scrub the dirt off their skins. The minority of Americans who used soap joined the English travelers who so frequently surprised everyone by asking for it at taverns.

Most Americans were dirty by modern standards, but black Americans came in for the harshest scrutiny and description. Judging by the standards of upper-class London or Philadelphia, some native and foreign observers who found field hands and house slaves "perfectly filthy in their persons and clothes" and "intolerably offensive." Of all Americans, slaves had the most meager utensils for washing and laundering and the most limited opportunities to keep clean. Southern blacks and whites alike shared a climate that fostered insect life and heavy sweating. White masters may have washed more frequently, but these same "offensive" slaves were a routinely accepted part of the plantation's domestic environment, and came into the closest physical proximity with white family members as waiters at table, cooks, wet nurses and sometimes even bed partners. Surely, ethnocentric commentators found it considerably easier to describe how black folks looked and smelled than how white back-country farmers or urban laborers did.

In matters of cleanliness, the practice of the most advanced American households differed sharply from that of the majority. Catherine Webb was the daughter of a wealthy New York City merchant who boarded with the Beechers for a time; she found these arrangements "a great trial" because it was impossible to take anything like the complete bath to which she was accustomed—and the Beechers clearly were not. Pioneers in cleanliness sometimes suffered derision. When Frances Kemble Butler bathed her two young children during a Philadelphia-Savannah boat trip in 1838, a fellow passenger thought it "excessively ridiculous"; Butler noted that her critic had completely "abstained" from washing even her hands during the two-day journey.

But gradually Catherine Webb's practice of complete bathing was spreading beyond the topmost levels of American society and into smaller towns and villages. Increasingly this became possible as families moved washing equipment out of kitchens and into bedchambers, from shared space to space that could be made private. As more prosperous households furnished one or two of their chambers with washing equipment —a washstand, a basin and a ewer or large-mouthed pitcher— family members could shut the chamber door, undress and wash themselves completely. The daughters of the Larcom family, living in Lowell, Massachusetts, in the late 1830s, began to bathe in a bedchamber in this way; Lucy Larcom described how her oldest sister began to take "a full cold bath every morning before she went to her work . . . in a room without a fire," and that the other young Larcoms "did the same whenever we could be resolute enough." By the 1830s better city hotels and even some country taverns were providing individual basins and pitchers in their rooms.

At a far remove from "primitive manners" and "bad practices" was the genteel ideal of domestic sanitation embodied in the "chamber sets"—matching basin and ewer for private bathing, a cup for brushing the teeth and a chamber pot with cover to minimize odor and spillage—that American stores were beginning to stock. By 1840, a significant minority of American households could show chamber sets, and washstands to hold them, in their bedchambers. For a handful, there was the very faint dawning of an entirely new age of sanitary arrangements. In 1829, the new Tremont House hotel in Boston offered its patrons indoor plumbing: eight bathtubs, and eight "water-closets." In New York City and Philadelphia, which had developed rudimentary public water systems, a few wealthy households had water taps and, more rarely, water closets by the 1830s. For all other families flush toilets and bathtubs remained far in the future.

The American people as a whole moved only slowly toward cleanliness. In "the backcountry at the present day," commented the fastidious author of the *Young Lady's Friend* in 1836, custom still "required that everyone should wash at the pump in the yard, or at the sink in the kitchen." Writing in 1846, William Alcott rejoiced that to "wash the surface of the whole body in water daily" had now been accepted as a genteel standard of personal hygiene. But, he added, there were "multitudes who pass for models of neatness and cleanliness, who do not perform this work for themselves half a dozen times—nay once—a year." As the better-off became cleaner than ever before, the poor stayed dirty. In cleanliness, as in much else, Americans' material lives were becoming increasingly unequal.

"The Odious Practice"

"Everyone smokes and some chew in America," wrote Isaac Weld in 1795. Americans turned tobacco, a new and controversial stimulant at the time of colonial settlement, into a crucially important staple crop and made its heavy use a commonplace —and a never-ending source of surprise and indignation to visitors. Tobacco use was widespread in the United States because it was comparatively cheap, a homegrown product free from the heavy duties levied on imports by European governments. A number of slave rations described in plantation documents included allotments such as "one hand of tobacco per month." Through the eighteenth century, most American smokers used clay pipes, which are abundant in colonial archaeological sites, although some men and women "dipped" snuff, or inhaled powdered tobacco.

Where the smokers of early colonial America "drank" or gulped smoke through the short thick stems of their seventeenth-century pipes, those of 1800 inhaled it more slowly and gradually; from the early seventeenth to the late eighteenth century, pipe stems became steadily longer and narrower, increasingly distancing smokers from their burning tobacco.

In the 1790s, cigars or "segars," tightly wrapped cylinders of tobacco leaf, were introduced from the Caribbean. Prosperous men widely took them up; they were the most expensive way to consume tobacco, and it was a sign of financial security, or extravagance, to puff away on "long-nines" or "principe cigars at three cents each" while the less well-off used clay pipes and much cheaper cut plug tobacco. Unlike the pipe, the segar put the smoker's mouth in direct contact with the "noxious weed"; but it was positively genteel compared with tobacco chewing.

In the streets, barrooms, stores and public conveyances of the United States after 1800, chewing was widespread, almost inescapable; it was often not easy to avoid in private dwellings. Even as pipe smokers distanced themselves from their tobacco, a growing number of chewers directly ingested it. Chewing extended tobacco use, particularly into workplaces; men who smoked a pipe at home or in the tavern barroom could chew while working in barns or workshops where smoking carried the danger of fire.

Americans took tobacco and liquor in close association. Alternate pulls on the pipe or segar and the glass, or intervals of drinking and chewing, were part of the daily ritual for countless men. Every tavern had its rack of pipes and a floor liberally stained with tobacco juice. It is no surprise that Americans began chewing tobacco most copiously just when they were drinking more heavily than ever before or since. But even after temperance reform had reined in American drinking habits, chewing declined much more slowly.

"In all the public places of America," winced Charles Dickens, multitudes of men engaged in "the odious practise of chewing and expectorating." Chewing stimulated salivation, and gave rise to a public environment of frequent and copious spitting, where men every few minutes were "squirting a mouthful of saliva through the room." The scenes, indoors and out, created by large groups of men with chaws in their cheeks are still difficult to reconstruct without distaste. Spittoons were provided in the more meticulous establishments, but men often ignored them, and more frequently they were missing entirely. The floors of American public buildings were not pleasant objects to contemplate. Thomas Hamilton found a courtroom in New York City in 1833 decorated by a "mass of abomination" produced by "judges, counsel, jury, witnesses, officers, and audience." The floor of the Virginia House of Burgesses, said Margaret Hall in 1827, was "actually flooded with their horrible spitting," and even the aisles of some churches were black with the "ejection after ejection, incessant from twenty mouths," of the men singing in the choir. In order to drink, an American man might remove his quid, put it in a pocket or hold it in his hand, take his glassful, and then restore it to his mouth. Women's dresses might even be in danger at fashionable balls; "one night as I was walking upstairs to valse," reported Mrs. Hall of a dance in Washington, "my partner began clearing his throat. This I thought ominous. However, I said to myself, 'surely he will turn his head to the other side.' The gentleman, however, had no such thought but deliberately shot across me. I had not courage enough to examine whether the result landed in the flounce of my dress."

"Incessant, remorseless spitting" could be found throughout most ranks of American society, from the frequenters of back-woods taverns to members of the New York bar. Some men preferred pipes or segars exclusively, and a number avoided tobacco altogether; others refrained at home or in the company of women. Mrs. Hall found it very rare in the "best society" of Philadelphia, New York and Boston, or among the planter aristocracy of Charleston. Southerners, living near ample sup-plies, consumed the most tobacco; "the farther we have come South the more universal have we found that disgusting practice" was almost every traveler's observation, although it was common enough everywhere in the United States among ordinary people.

The segar and the quid were almost entirely male appurte-nances, but as the nineteenth century began, many rural and lower-class urban women were smoking pipes or dipping snuff. During his boyhood in New Hampshire, Horace Greeley said, "it was often my filial duty to fill and light my mother's pipe." "Pray put your snuff box aside when you are working over your butter," the *Farmer's Almanack* urged New England dairy-women in 1815. Tobacco rations on some plantations went to male and female slaves alike.

But during the next decades tobacco use among women in

the North began to decline. After 1820 or so, Northern women remembered or depicted with pipe or snuff box were almost all elderly—like Margaret Jepperson of Brookfield, Massachusetts, born around 1760. Her grandson Homer Merriam recalled that she chewed snuff—greatly to the discomfort of her daughters and granddaughters—until her death in 1841. More and more, as Americans adopted genteel standards that saw tobacco use and delicate, nurturing womanliness as antithetical, young women began avoiding it as a pollutant. For them, tobacco use marked off male from female territory with increasing sharpness.

In the households of small Southern and Western farmers, however, smoking and snuff taking remained common. When women visited "among the country people" of North Carolina, an Englishwoman remarked in 1837, "the proffer of the snuffbox, and its passing from hand to hand, is the usual civility." By the late 1830s visiting New Englanders were profoundly shocked when they saw the women of Methodist congregations in Illinois, including nursing mothers, taking out their pipes for a smoke between worship services.

"A Land of Plentiful Supply"

"I could not but remark the peculiar stature of the people," noted the Englishman William Strickland while sojourning in Albany, New York, in 1795, adding that in his estimation the men were "in general little under six feet in height." The eighteenth-century French naturalist Buffon had argued that the New World inevitably produced smaller, biologically inferior plants, animals and men. But military muster rolls which systematically recorded the heights of American and European army recruits have revealed that Strickland was not far off the mark. Americans did have a "peculiar stature."

Seventeenth- and eighteenth-century Englishmen and Frenchmen were significantly shorter than they are today, between two and three inches below their present-day heights. They did not attain modern stature until the twentieth century. In the seventeenth century white American colonists were no taller than their European counterparts, but by the time of the American Revolution, they were close to their mid-twentieth-century average height, documented in World War II recruitment records, of slightly over five feet, eight inches. The citizens of the early Republic would have towered over most Europeans. Because the average adult height of a people is an index of their level of nutrition over two or even more generations, Americans' early achievement of modern stature—by a full century and a half—was a striking biological effect of the relative abundance of their lives and the prosperity of their society. Americans were taller because they were better nourished than the great majority of the world's peoples.

American settlement had begun with "starving times" at Jamestown and Plymouth, but by the early nineteenth century, wrote the Philadelphia physician John Bell, it was "natural that the Americans," with abundant land and a thinly spread population, "should be great eaters" in comparison with the peoples of the Old World. There were good harvests and bad, seasonally recurring times of shortage, and some real deprivation for the poorest. But the people of the United States, as their well-nourished heights attested, had escaped the widespread famines and crises of subsistence that had earlier devastated Europe. Their "food may well be called substantial," observed the *Universal Traveller* of 1832, "and the variety and quantity are enough to denote a land of plentiful supply."

Yet not all Americans participated equally in the "plentiful supply." Differences in stature between white and black, and between city and country dwellers, echoed those between Europeans and Americans. Enslaved blacks were a full inch shorter than whites. But they remained a full inch taller than European peasants and laborers, and were taller still than their fellow slaves eating the scanty diets afforded by the more savagely oppressive plantation system of the West Indies. And by 1820, those who lived in the United States' expanding cities—even excluding immigrants, whose heights would have reflected European, not American conditions—were noticeably shorter than the people of the countryside, suggesting an increasing concentration of poverty and poorer diets in urban places.

American "superabundance," to use Bell's word, was also a relative thing. The range and quality of the early nineteenth-century food supply was still sharply constrained by the limited techniques of preservation available to all but a few households—the underground storage of root crops, drying, smoking and salting. "Few families had regular supplies of fresh meat," Francis Underwood remembered, and saw it only "at the autumnal pig-killing or the slaughter . . . in winter of a steer." For the rest of the year, they pulled salt meat out of a barrel, cut it off a slab of bacon—or went without it.

Across the United States, almost all country households ate the two great American staples—corn, and "the eternal pork," as one surfeited traveler called it, "which makes its appearance on every American table, high and low, rich and poor." Families in the cattle-raising, dairying country of New England, New York and northern Ohio ate butter, cheese and salted beef as well as pork, and made their bread from wheat flour or rye mixed with Indian corn. In Pennsylvania, as well as Maryland, Delaware and Virginia, Americans ate the same breadstuffs as their Northern neighbors, but their consumption of cheese and beef declined every mile southward in favor of pork. Farther to the south, and in the West, corn and corn-fed pork were truly "eternal"; where reliance on them reached its peak in the Southern uplands, they were the only crops many small farmers raised. Most Southern and Western families built their diets around smoked and salted bacon rather than the Northerners' salt pork, and instead of wheat or rye bread, made corn pone or hoecake, usually described as "a coarse, strong kind of bread," and hominy, "pounded Indian corn . . . boiled together with milk."

Before 1800, game—venison, possums and raccoons, wild fowl—were for many American households "a substantial portion of the supply of food at certain seasons of the year," although only on the frontier was it a regular part of the diet. In the West and South this continued to be true, but in the Northeast game became increasingly rare as forests gave way to open farmland where wild animals could not live.

In the apple-growing North, rural Americans used most of the produce of their orchards to make cider, which they barreled for each year's drinking. They took it "hard" or alcoholic with their meals; "even children drank it at will." With the rapid growth of grain distilling from the 1790s, Southern and Western families sometimes drank whiskey at the table, while Germans drank beer. Adults and children alike occasionally drank milk from a cup or glass but more often took it in a bowl with bread sops or corn mush.

Through the first half of the eighteenth century, Americans had been primarily concerned with obtaining a sufficiency of meat and bread for their families; they paid relatively little attention to foodstuffs other than these two "staffs of life." But since that time, the daily fare of many households had grown substantially more diverse.

Known for "the hardness of the soil, the extreme severity of the climate, and the shortness of the growing season," as Harriet Beecher Stowe noted, New England was where American farmers were most crowded and their land the least fertile. As soil productivity dropped in the later half of the eighteenth century, they also faced a serious threat to their "plentiful supply." In response, Yankees changed their dietary patterns significantly from the 1750s to the early nineteenth century, making their diet more varied and less dependent on the lockstep of the seasons.

More strikingly than anywhere else in America, New Englanders had known sharp seasonal variability in their food supply, bounded by cycles of harvest, grazing and slaughtering. Households faced a yearly alternation in their daily fare, from the stored and preserved food of the cold season to the fresh diet of the warm months. Farmers began slaughtering in November and filled their meat barrels in early winter; farm women began dairying with the first fresh pasture grass of the late spring, and made butter and cheese through the early fall. Along with their bread, New Englanders consumed salt pork and beef, and dried beans, from November to May, and ate milk, cheese and butter from June until the following November.

Asa Sheldon remembered just such a traditional and seasonally monotonous diet in the poor and frugal household where he grew up before 1810. The family ate meat or cheese once a day, depending on the season, at the midday dinner. "In the summer season," he recalled, "brown bread and milk was the constant food for the whole family, morning and night." From November on, "the winter rations were beef-broth, with brown bread crumbled in, and for change, bean porridge."

Meals could become meager toward the end of either cycle. The spring was an especially difficult time because families might reach the bottom of their meat barrels before they could begin making butter and cheese to replace them. In the late fall, dairying might come to an end before slaughtering brought meat into the diet again.

Gradually, from the middle of the eighteenth century on, ordinary New England farm families struggled to overcome the effects of agricultural crowding and to free their food supply from these seasonal imbalances. They ate a little less meat than they had before, but grew more vegetables such as squash, onions, turnips and cabbages, which they had previously eaten only as "green sauce" during the growing season, and laid them up in root cellars for cold-weather eating. They added potatoes, an effective alternative to bread, and increased the size of their dairy herds so that they produced enough cheese to store for winter eating. In turn, this allowed their meat supplies to last consistently through the summer.

Changes in New Englanders' diets were part of a broader transformation. Benjamin Rush wrote in 1810 of a "revolution in diet" that he had witnessed in America over the previous fifty years, with households balancing their traditional foodstuffs with an increasing "profusion of summer and winter vegetables." Americans North and South enlarged their gardens. The greater abundance of vegetables not only added taste and variety, but protection against diseases of vitamin deficiency, particularly scurvy. As Northerners adopted "Irish potatoes," Southerners grew sweet potatoes; the growth of rice cultivation in the deep South provided both an additional cash crop and a new item in the diet.

Rush's "revolution" was in fact an ongoing one in the early nineteenth century, as Americans continued to alter their eating habits. Other sources of dietary variety appeared with the expansion of commerce in the countryside; rural storekeepers after 1800 could provide their customers with an expanding array of foodstuffs along with other consumer goods: spices, sugar, tea and coffee shared the shelves with rice, salt fish, lemons and even confectionery.

Americans were consuming the everyday stimulants, tea and coffee, in steadily increasing volume. Originally a luxury item restricted to the wealthiest households, tea gradually became an everyday beverage during the second half of the eighteenth century. By 1800, probate inventories suggest, half or more American households had the teapot, teacups and spoons that made possible the ceremonious social ritual of tea drinking. Over the next four decades, Americans continued to increase their use of tea, roughly doubling it in per capita terms; but even this sharp rise was eclipsed by the rapid acceptance of coffee, a more powerful stimulant with a stronger flavor. Household consumption of coffee grew fivefold during the same years,

The United States in 1830. Map by G. Boynton in *An Economical Atlas* by Samuel Goodrich. [Boston, 1831]. *(Old Sturbridge Village photograph by Henry E. Peach)*

This anonymous watercolor view of Taunton, Massachusetts, in 1830 depicts the center of one of the hundreds of commercial villages that had grown up in the Northern countryside. *(Old Colony Historical Society)*

A view of "Broadway, New York," between 1834 and 1836 shows the heavy vehicle traffic and busy street life of America's largest city. (Aquatint. *New-York Historical Society*)

Caleb Bingham has painted a pioneer family outside their small log house. Clothes are on the line, and the woman is working at the laundry tub: It is wash day. (*The Squatters*, 1850. *Museum of Fine Arts, Boston*)

In Samuel Gerry's New England *Farm Scene,* a man and boy are driving into the farmyard; a woman stands in the door holding a broom, and another carries a bucket across the yard. Some of the tools of farming—hay rake, ox yoke, shovel and plow—can be seen in the foreground. Oil painting, 1849. *(Old Sturbridge Village Collections photograph by Henry E. Peach)*

The Tools of Husbandry in 1790 provides a mid-nineteenth century look at the traditional farm implements in universal use during the first years of the new nation. Engraving in *Eighty Years Progress of the United States* by Charles L. Flint, C. F. McCay, J. C. Merriam, and Thomas P. Kettell [Hartford, Conn., 1867], 28. *(Old Sturbridge Village photograph by Henry E. Peach)*

Work for women as well as men, picking cotton was the American South's single most important labor of harvest. Engraving in *Eighty Years Progress of the United States* by Charles L. Flint, C. F. McCay, J. C. Merriam, and Thomas P. Kettell [Hartford, Conn., 1867], 125. *(Old Sturbridge Village photograph by Henry E. Peach)*

A young woman engaged in the graceful but highly time-consuming process of spinning wool on the great wheel. Engraving in *Eighty Years Progress of the United States* by Charles L. Flint, C. F. McCay, J. C. Merriam, and Thomas P. Kettell [Hartford, Conn., 1867], 279. *(Old Sturbridge Village photograph by Henry E. Peach)*

In this view of an early nineteenth-century printing office, one man is setting type while another man and a boy are working at the press. Woodcut in *The Panorama of Professions and Trades* by Edward Hazen [Philadelphia, 1836], 180. *(Old Sturbridge Village photograph by Henry E. Peach)*

This Bradbury stove, shown with some of its cookware, was one of many thousands produced and sold in the United States between 1820 and 1840. Stoves began to change both the work of cooking and the patterns of domestic heating. *(Old Sturbridge Village Collections photograph by Henry E. Peach)*

These workers are shown assembling and seating chairs, using standard, mass-produced parts. Woodcut in *The Panorama of Professions and Trades* by Edward Hyde [Philadelphia, 1836], 226. *(Old Sturbridge Village photograph by Henry E. Peach)*

The weaving room of a large water-powered cotton factory, one of the new environments of work in early nineteenth-century America. Engraving in *Memoir of Samuel Slater* by George S. White [Philadelphia, 1836], 385. *(Old Sturbridge Village photograph by Henry E. Peach)*

Printed or drawn by hand, family records became increasingly popular in the early nineteenth century. This New England record shows eight children born to Sally and Loa Richardson from 1797 to 1813—a relatively large family for many communities in the American North during that period, although still by no means uncommon. *(Old Sturbridge Village Collections photograph by Henry E. Peach)*

While the mother remains in childbed, another woman—neighbor or relative, perhaps the midwife—presents the new arrival to its father and older sibling. Woodcut in *Mother Goose's Rhymes for the Nursery* [Boston, 1875], 72. *(Old Sturbridge Village photograph by Henry E. Peach)*

Dr. Jesse Kittredge Smith of Mount Vernon, New Hampshire, is portrayed by Ezra Woolson with some of the tools of his trade: scalpels, a lancet for bloodletting and the paraphernalia for mixing drugs. *(Oil painting, c. 1840. Old Sturbridge Village Collections photograph by Henry E. Peach)*

Mourning pictures like Selene Livermore's *Memorial to John Flint Livermore,* became more common in American households. The death of three-and-a-half-year-old John Flint Livermore, who died in 1829, serves as a reminder that child mortality was high in the early nineteenth century. *(Watercolor, c. 1830. Old Sturbridge Village Collections photograph by Henry E. Peach)*

Carpenters are shown working on a timber-framed structure. The massive frame and roof have already been raised, and they are completing the joinery. Woodcut in *Stories About Henry and Frank* [Troy, New York, c. 1840], 6. *(Old Sturbridge Village photograph by Henry E. Peach)*

Benjamin H. Coe depicts one of the very small houses that were found throughout early nineteenth-century rural America but have not survived to the present. *At Preston, Ct.*, engraving in *A New Drawing Book of American Scenery* by Benjamin H. Coe [Hartford, 1845], 8. *(Old Sturbridge Village photograph by Henry E. Peach)*

Coe's *Ancient House in Andover, Mass.* shows a long-surviving structure built in the asymmetrical, "organic" fashion of early America, before the arrival of the Georgian style. Engraving in *A New Drawing Book of American Scenery* by Benjamin H. Coe [Hartford, 1845], 7. *(Old Sturbridge Village photograph by Henry E. Peach)*

Salem Towne, a wealthy farmer and trader in Charlton, Massachusetts, built this house in the Federal style in 1796. Now at Old Sturbridge Village, it has a completely symmetrical plan with central hallway, impressive formal entry, and paired chimneys. In 1798, Towne's house was assessed as the most valuable dwelling in Charlton and the adjoining towns of Sturbridge and Dudley. *(Old Sturbridge Village photograph by Henry E. Peach)*

Built in the 1830s, this central Massachusetts "end house" is an example of the translation of the Greek Revival style to the Northern countryside. It marked a dramatic early nineteenth-century change in house form. *(Old Sturbridge Village photograph by Richard Candee)*

This woodcut dramatically illustrates travelers' observations about the "out-of-door slovenliness" of many American farmsteads. *A Pictorial Geography of the World* [Boston, 1840] by Samuel Goodrich, p. 145. *(Old Sturbridge Village photograph by Henry E. Peach)*

August Kollner's *Pennsylvania Country Life 1840* suggests the spare interiors of many American farmhouses, with bare floors, unadorned walls and sparse furniture. *(Watercolor. Chicago Historical Society)*

Inexpensive mass-produced chairs, like this one made by J. D. Pratt of Lunenburg, Massachusetts, or those of his more famous contemporary Lambert Hitchcock, were furnishing an ever-increasing number of American homes. *(Side chair, c. 1825. Old Sturbridge Village Collections photograph by Henry E. Peach)*

The Argand lamp was one of a number of advanced lighting devices, far brighter than candles or even ordinary oil lamps, that were illuminating the homes of well-to-do American families in the early nineteenth century. *(Boston, c. 1830. Old Sturbridge Village Collections photograph by Henry E. Peach)*

The parlor of a prosperous city family, with carpets, paintings, an extensive library and an astral lamp, blazons the ideal of domestic comfort and refinement. Engraved by A. L. Dick from a painting by E. Prentiss. Frontispiece in *Christian Family Magazine* [New York, 1843]. *(Old Sturbridge Village photograph by Henry E. Peach)*

Henry Sargent's *The Tea Party* portrays the interior of a wealthy Boston family's home, possibly his own. The rooms are large, abundantly lit and sumptuously furnished. *(Oil painting, 1820–1825. Museum of Fine Arts, Boston)*

Nineteenth-century American men sometimes relieved themselves in the streets, as Lewis Miller graphically demonstrates for York, Pennsylvania. *(Watercolor. York County Historical Society, York, Pennsylvania)*

In another Miller sketch, George Heckert of York gallantly saves a woman from complete exposure as she tries to dismount and finds that her skirts and petticoat are caught on her saddle. *(Watercolor. York County Historical Society, York, Pennsylvania)*

This chamber pot was a ribald "Marrige Present" for an American couple. Polychrome transfer-printed creamware, English, late eighteenth century. *(Old Sturbridge Village Collections photograph by Henry E. Peach)*

Set in a bedchamber, this domestic scene illustrates the new early nineteenth-century world of personal hygiene. The mother is carefully brushing her child's hair. There is a mirror to aid in grooming, but most important, is a wash stand with basin, pitcher and towel for complete bathing. Engraving, *The Pleasant Journey* by Thomas Teller [New Haven, 1845], 6. *(Old Sturbridge Village photograph by Henry E. Peach)*

This pictorial attack on abolitionism and interracial sex presents a hostile caricature of black facial features. Frontispiece, Thomas Man, *A Picture of Woonsocket* [Providence, Rhode Island, 1835]. *(Rhode Island Historical Society)*

An early American stage coach makes its way down a road in western Pennsylvania. A "snake fence" encloses a recently cleared field still full of tree stumps. Engraving by T. Storer from a drawing by Isaac Weld, in *Travels Through North America and the Province of Upper and Lower Canada* by Isaac Weld, vol. 1 [3 vols.; London, 1807], following 26. *(Old Sturbridge Village photograph by Henry E. Peach)*

On one of the main roads into Boston, a driver runs afoul of a herd of cattle on its way to the Brighton Market. Such encounters were common on the roads near nineteenth-century American cities during the fall and early winter. Engraving, *Gleason's Pictorial* 2, no. 26, June 26, 1852: 409. *(Old Sturbridge Village photograph by Henry E. Peach)*

This view of the Brooklyn ferry shows one of the many steamboats that were plying Eastern as well as Western waters in the 1830s. Note the exposed location of the steam engine amidships. (c. 1840, *Old Sturbridge Village Collections photograph by Henry E. Peach*)

In William Sidney Mount's *Rustic Dance After a Sleigh Ride,* a crowd of young people dance to the music of a black fiddler—very possibly in the parlor of the artist's father's tavern in Easthampton, Long Island. (Oil painting, 1830. *Museum of Fine Arts, Boston*)

At a revival encampment in the woods, a throng of men and women stand around the outdoor pulpit to sing. One of the preachers, holding a songbook, is lining out the words of the hymn to the audience. *Camp Meeting*, frontispiece, Peter Myers, *The Zion Songster* [New York, 1834]. *(Old Sturbridge Village photograph by Henry E. Peach)*

Alvan Fisher depicts a New England corn husking with men, women and children seated on straw in the barn and other huskers outside. Having found the lucky red ear, a young man claims a kiss, but the young woman he is pursuing fends him off with a withered or "smut" one. *(Corn Husking Frolic*, oil painting, 1828. *Museum of Fine Arts, Boston)*

True to a national tradition of hard drinking, an American stands up to the bar and tosses down a glass of spirits in a rural tavern. Taverns like this one depicted by August Kollner, with walls covered with public notices and advertisements, were male social centers. *(Country Inn*, watercolor, 1840. *Chicago Historical Society)*

David Claypool Johnston captures the fabled disorderliness of the early nineteenth-century American militia in his 1819 watercolor, *A Militia Muster.* Reluctant, resentful and highly unmilitary citizen-soldiers not only are irregularly dressed and equipped but also pose a danger to one another with their bayonets. (*American Antiquarian Society*)

This woodcut reflects the strong anti-Southern bias of Northern abolitionist editors and readers; it also provides a panorama of American drink, violence and disorderly sports. Gambling, cockfighting and horse racing can be seen, as well as dueling, eye gouging, the whipping of slaves and the lynching of anti-slavery agitators. Woodcut in *Anti-Slavery Almanac for 1840* [Boston, 1839], 25. (*Old Sturbridge Village photograph by Henry E. Peach*)

The early nineteenth-century temperance campaign produced dramatic pictures as well as pamphlets. Here a reformed drinker signs a "Total Abstinence" pledge, as his wife and children rejoice. He is contrasted with the drunkard on the left, dressed in tatters and still clutching his bottle. *Lifting the Mortgage,* lithograph, c. 1840. (*Old Sturbridge Village photograph by Henry E. Peach*)

and by the 1830s it had overtaken tea in popularity nationwide. As alcohol consumption declined after 1820 with the growth of the temperance movement, hard cider, along with whiskey, rum and beer, disappeared from many American tables. Temperance households replaced these beverages with water— more Americans were drinking water in the 1830s than at any previous time—and with steadily greater reliance on caffeine. By 1833, "the use of coffee in the morning," wrote Goodrich, "and tea at night, are almost universal."

Along with tea and coffee went sugar, which Americans were also eating in vastly greater quantities than before, both in its highly refined "loaf" form and as less expensive molasses. Like tea, it had been an eighteenth-century luxury, rarely eaten by ordinary folk, and was then taken up into the everyday diet— as a sweetener for drinks, a source of quick energy, and a way of improving the taste of otherwise insipid foods like cornmeal mush. Sugar consumption grew as fast as that of coffee and tea combined; "so strongly," as the New Englander chronicler Joseph Felt observed, had sugar and sweetened beverages "become entrenched in the public appetite" that they were coming to be considered necessities of life even for the poor. When Matthew Carey estimated the dietary needs of a common laborer's family in Philadelphia in 1833, he included larger expenditures for sugar and tea than for meat.

Even in staple foodstuffs regional self-sufficiency began to break down; after the opening of the Erie Canal in 1825, southern New Englanders began to give up their traditional rye and Indian bread for wheaten loaves made from flour from New York's Genesee Valley.

American standards of eating also became increasingly disparate. Delmonico's restaurant opened in New York City in 1828, demonstrating that Parisian notions of haute cuisine were penetrating the topmost levels of urban wealth, the world of balls and formal dinners; it offered sumptuous meals to the city's wealthy. The kitchens of fashionable houses copied its cuisine to the extent the skills of their cooks permitted. At a slightly lower but still formidable level of expense, the city's successful merchants could choose among thirty different dishes of meat and fish each day at the table d'hote of the Astor House hotel, from "oyster pie" through "round of beef" to "roast wild duck"; the hotel's cellar offered over a hundred different wines.

Prosperous urban households could truly eat in "plentiful supply," and with more independence from the seasons. They could have early and late vegetables from farms near the city outskirts, and fresh poultry year-round; thanks to the growing scale of city livestock markets, those who could afford to pay for meat slaughtered out of the winter season could have frequent, if expensive, supplies of fresh beef and veal.

Urban growth also meant that city households relied for their food on increasingly long lines of supply from farms to central marketplaces, and then to shops and households. For ordinary urban dwellers, "the great cities," as Harriet Martineau maintained in 1836, were in some important ways "ill-supplied from the country." Without refrigerated transport and storage, the spoilage and contamination of milk, meat, fish and vegetables, particularly during torrid American summers, became a chronic problem. It sometimes distressed middling families but hit the poor particularly hard.

Most city dwellers, like farm families, still ate barreled salt pork and beef during most of the year, with fresh meat and early vegetables an occasional luxury. By the 1820s, the expansion and technical improvement of ice cutting and storage meant that well-to-do city households could avoid most of these problems, with iceboxes in which they could keep milk, butter, vegetables and fresh meat from spoiling in the summer heat. For those who could purchase the icebox and pay the ice bill, the refrigerator had become, the *New York Mirror* suggested, no less an "article of necessity" than a parlor carpet.

When set against the opulence of Delmonico's and the Astor House, or the abundance on the tables of households where iceboxes were necessities, the urban poor ate meagerly. Laboring families in early nineteenth-century cities relied heavily on bread, or increasingly on potatoes, which were cheaper. In periods of abundant work, good health and good luck, they could add some salt meat and cheese, and a little butter, sugar, coffee and tea. But economic fluctuations and illness frequently disturbed the precarious balance of their lives. Poor housewives spent much of their time trying to feed their families—searching for cheaper food in the markets, scavenging edible scraps from more prosperous neighborhoods, or on occasion stealing food. In difficult times, their households eliminated meat completely and cut down drastically on all condiments. Some tried to keep in pork by notching the ear of a free-roaming, garbage-eating pig and attempting to catch and slaughter it themselves. In the winter of 1837–38, the onset of financial panic and business depression threw many thousands of urban laboring men and women out of work and brought on a season of deprivation and suffering for their families; some exhausted their food supplies and their credit with neighborhood grocers and came close to starving.

Poorer rural families still remained closer to the old cycles of seasonal imbalance and spring scarcity, and enjoyed less of the variety that most of their neighbors had gradually achieved. Rural laborers' and poorer artisans' households in the North, like their urban counterparts, came to rely ever more heavily on potatoes, rather than grain.

Of all enslaved Americans, the best-fed were those few house servants or members of small planters' households who ate the same diet as their masters; "I ate at the table with my mistress and her family," recalled Lewis Bonner. Far more common was the "corn and bacon" that, Solomon Northup wrote, were "all that is allowed" the slaves on Edwin Epps's cotton plantation in St. Mary's Parish, Louisiana, "given out at the corncrib and smoke-house every Sunday morning." Their weekly allocation was "three and a half pounds of bacon, and corn enough to make a peck of meal. That is all—no tea, coffee, sugar, and with the exception of a very scanty sprinkling now and then, no salt."

Epps's "people" ate a diet little different from the fare of poorer Southern farmers—except that it lacked the beverages and condiments that provided minimal variety. Epps was a master who did not allow his slaves to work their own garden plots; those who could were able to supplement their rations and eat considerably better.

More poorly supplied were the slaves on Pierce Butler's Georgia estate who had little or no meat, "laboring hard all day upon *two* meals of Indian corn or hominy." Even if the allowances of cornmeal were substantial, slaves eating such diets risked deficiencies of iron and calcium. On the most niggardly plantations "we had a purty hard time to make out and was hungry lots of times," as the ex-slave William Moore remembered. "Marse Tom didn't feel called on to feed his hands any too much. I had a cravin' for victuals all the time. My mammy used to say, 'My belly craves something and it craves meat.'" Stealing food from the storehouses of such parsimonious masters was, some slaves found, another way to supplement their diet.

Few slaves went chronically hungry; most ate monotonous diets that were better, current estimates of their heights suggest, than those of black people in other slave societies or of some European peasants. Even in the United States, there were free but poor laboring families who ate no better and had greater daily uncertainty about their food supply—although it seems certain that the slaves would still have preferred the bread of freedom.

Abundance and expanding diversity in the diet for most Americans were countered in the 1830s by reformist attacks on what they were eating. The best-known and most influential dietary critic was the Massachusetts-born Sylvester Graham, who wrote and lectured extensively on food, health and sexual regimen throughout the North. Prosperous and middling

Americans, he argued, particularly those living in cities and villages, ate all too abundantly; they were overfed and over-stimulated. Their "superabundance of animal food," of spices and stimulants, of refined bread and pastry, was making them physically ill with "dyspepsia" or "nervously prostrated" with anxiety. Most broadly, Graham was expressing a profound unease about the consequences of commercial and industrial transformation; but his teachings had concrete, specific effects on the way some Americans ate.

Responding to the call of dietary reform the way a larger number responded to temperance, some Americans—mostly relatively young city dwellers of middling economic fortunes—became "Grahamites," and gave up the culinary abundance that most of their countrymen prized. "Many people in this place," wrote James Hartwell of Providence, Rhode Island, in 1834 to his sister in Massachusetts, "have abandoned altogether the use of tea or coffee, and the use of animal food. Their principal food is bread and water (bread made of wheat meal without sifting)."

Graham put particular symbolic and nutritive stress on bread, the most traditional of foodstuffs, but also the one whose pro-duction and distribution had most changed. In his native south-ern New England, even farm families were abandoning the heavy rye and Indian bread made of their own grains to buy wheat flour produced in New York's Genesee Valley. While country families still baked their own loaves, urban households had come, as Graham said, to "depend on public bakers for their bread." Commercial bakeries preferred highly refined and sifted white flour that was easier to work with; households with genteel tastes often did so as well, comparing its texture favorably to the coarser, heavier bread of the country. Bread made from superrefined flour, and adulterated—as it often was —with fillers and whiteners, Graham maintained with some reason, was dangerous, even poisonous. He urged city and vil-lage families to return to an idealized version of the bread of the

Northern countryside—not the "black and tough" rye and Indian, but wheaten bread, more coarsely milled, unrefined and unadulterated—what his followers came to call "Graham bread."

One of the most vivid scenes of Daniel Drake's boyhood around 1800 was mealtime at the house of one of his neighbors, "Old Billy," who "with his sons" would "frequently breakfast in common on mush and milk out of a huge buckeye bowl, each one dipping in a spoon." Old Billy and his family were less frontier savages than traditionalists; in the same decade, Governor Caleb Strong of Massachusetts stopped for the night with a country family who ate in the same way, where "each had a spoon and dipped from the same dish." These households ate as almost all American families once had, communally partaking of food from the same dish and passing around a single vessel to drink from. Such meals had often been surprisingly haphazard affairs, with household members moving in and out, eating quickly and going on to other tasks.

But by 1800 these families were already in a small and diminishing minority. Over the eighteenth century dining "in common" had given way to individualized yet social eating; as families acquired chairs and dining utensils they were able to make mealtimes more important social occasions. Most white Americans expected to eat individual portions of food at a table set with personal knives, forks, glasses, bowls and plates, preferably matching ones. Anything that smacked of the old communal ways was increasingly likely to be treated as a sin against domestic decency. Peter Cartwright was predictably shocked at the table manners of a "backward" family who ate off a "wooden trencher," improvised forks with "sharp pieces of cane" and used a single knife which they passed around the table.

"One and all, male and female," the observant Margaret Hall took note, even in New York's best society Americans ate "invariably and indefatigably with their knives." As a legacy of the fork's late arrival in the colonies, Americans were peculiar in using their "great lumbering, long, two-pronged forks," not to convey food to the mouth as their English and French contemporaries did, but merely to keep their meat from slipping off the plate while cutting it. "Feeding yourself with your right hand, armed with a steel blade," was the prevalent American custom, acknowledged Emily Farrar's elaborate *Young Lady's Friend* of 1837. She added that it was perfectly proper, despite English visitors' discomfort at the sight of "a prettily dressed, nice-looking young woman ladling rice pudding into her mouth with the point of a great knife," or a domestic help "feeding an infant of seventeen months in the same way."

There were stirrings of change among the sophisticated in the 1830s, Mrs. Farrar admitted, conceding that some of her readers might now want "to imitate the French or English . . . and put every mouthful into your mouth with your fork." Later in the nineteenth century, the American habit of eating with the knife completely lost its claims to gentility, and it became another relic of "primitive manners." Americans gradually learned to use forks more dexterously, although to this day they hold them upside down from a European point of view.

"The majority of slaves," in Northup's experience, had "no knife, much less a fork. They cut their bacon with an axe at the woodpile." Far more often than other Americans the slaves still ate communally. The pottery they used, as it has been excavated from the sites of slave cabins on plantations, consisted primarily of serving bowls and cooking pots; it contrasted sharply with the high proportion of plates found around the dwellings of white Americans. In the seventeenth and eighteenth centuries slaves often made their own pottery vessels, producing a grayish earthenware now called "Colono ware." Slaves living on the largest plantations, farthest away from extensive contact with whites, created pottery that was still remarkably African in form. After 1800 a few southern blacks were still making Colono ware, but, like white Americans, they were increasingly using English-made ceramics. Yet they continued to eat with them in traditional ways. They took their meals together from the cooking pot, ate from chipped bowls that may have been handed down from the "big house," or used "little cedar tubs" they had made themselves. Field hands often carried their midday meals with them to cook over a fire "as best they can, where they are working." Slaves whittled wooden spoons or used fragments of pottery as eating utensils. Those living near coastal waters sometimes used clamshells, and others simply ate with their hands.

The slaves' poverty in the dishes, knives and forks of their masters provided only an "example of savage feeding" to white observers. But while slaves' eating habits mirrored the material constraints of bondage, they also echoed the traditions of Africa. Squatting on the ground and using clamshells, wooden spoons or fingers were part of innumerable village mealtime scenes. Slaves ate with an alien, incomprehensible grace.

"The Dress of Both Men and Women Has Greatly Changed"

"On the whole," wrote Samuel Goodrich in surveying the changes wrought during the first decades of the nineteenth century, "the dress of both men and women has greatly changed." The years just around 1800 saw a sharp transformation of the silhouettes of both sexes, one which Americans shared with the people of Great Britain and Western Europe. For men, knee breeches, "long, broad-tailed coats," and cocked or low-crowned, broad-brimmed hats gave way to pantaloons, "short, snug, close-fitting" coats, and tall "stove-pipe" hats with narrow brims. By 1815 adherents to traditional garb had dwindled to "a few old gentlemen," who in clinging to their buckled shoes, knee breeches, cocked hats and wigs "became objects of curiosity, almost derision to the boys in the street." With a speed that must have shocked them, they came to be symbols of a seemingly ancient past.

For women, there was a shift from the full skirts, long sleeves and high necks of the late eighteenth century to the strikingly simple "classical" mode, which fit the figure much more closely and exposed far more of the arms and upper body. Younger, fashionable men and women changed first; older Americans and those in the countryside followed more slowly. Eventually all altered their clothes. As colonial voluminousness gave way to republican trimness, the new modes of dress displayed the figures of the young at the expense of the middle-aged and elderly, foreshadowing American society's gradually growing fascination with the vigor and attractiveness of youth.

Men's shorter coats and longer pants were in reality an embellished version of the working costume of sailors and laborers. As a whole society donned working dress, the new men's fashions defined a transition into commercial and industrial ways. By 1820, women's fashion had retreated from trim simplicity and turned to much more covered-up and voluminous styles that were not to be seriously challenged again until the early twentieth century. But men never returned to anything remotely like the old ways of dress.

Not only the shape of men's dress but the style of their hair spoke potently of social change. In the eighteenth century, often elaborate wigs and powdered hair were the tonsorial signs of the colonial elite, and ensured that they stood out from "men of laboring habits," as the social chronicler Joseph Felt noted. Ordinary men rarely wore either, but frequently kept their hair long, "tied up in a queue" with black ribbons or eel skins. After 1800, wig and powder went decisively out of fashion among the "better sort," spurred in part by President Jefferson's determinedly casual style—much to the dismay of city barbers. American farmers and workingmen gave up their queues, and joined the well-to-do in adopting simply kept short hair.

Customs of facial hair changed less dramatically. As they had been since late in the seventeenth century, virtually all American men were clean-shaven until the late 1820s, when "a portion of the young men," as Felt recalled, primarily city gentlemen of fashion, began to sport mustaches. David Claypool Johnston, the Boston cartoonist and social satirist, caricatured them as "young exquisites." Beards remained far less acceptable, customarily worn only by a tiny minority of Orthodox Jews. Those few men daring enough to wear beards at this time, two or three decades before their widespread adoption in the 1850s, actually suffered abuse and persecution. When Joseph Palmer of Fitchburg, Massachusetts, appeared at church with a beard in 1830 he was denied communion and later assaulted by a group of men armed with soap and razors who tried to shave him forcibly.

But although the cut of clothes had altered greatly and swiftly at the turn of the nineteenth century, deeper shifts in the materials, cost and availability of clothing were just beginning. Throughout the new nation in the years around 1800, "the families of farmers were clothed in articles of their own making," in garments of home-produced linen, wool or combinations of the two, while wealthier Americans had their clothes made of fine linens, woolen broadcloth, imported silk and cotton. Most people owned relatively few clothes, because garments were expensive, whether the cost was measured in terms of weeks of labor in the household or in dollars spent on the purchase of cloth and the services of tailors and dressmakers. An ordinary farm woman might well own no more than three dresses or "gowns," one "best" for important occasions and the others for daily work.

Between the homespun-wearing majority and those Americans whose apparel was made of much more finely finished, purchased cloth, there were sharp and immediately visible distinctions. "A man whose clothes were made at home," Francis Underwood wrote, "could be easily distinguished at a hundred yards' distance by his slouchy and baggy outlines," and the home-dyed colors and coarser textures of his cloth. Women wore dresses "shaped without much reference to elegance or fashion"; even "best Sunday" gowns followed the styles at some years' remove, while men and boys wore long homespun frocks, and donned trousers made of towcloth—coarse linen made from the shortest fibers of flax—or "butternut-colored" wool. One "tow shirt and tow trousers," a vest "such as it was" and a tow jacket made up Asa Sheldon's wardrobe for the summer as a young man working on a New England farm; in the winter he had a similar set made of striped woolen. Slaves might receive a gown or two, or a single pair of pants and a shirt. Although they were often responsible for sewing their own dresses with the cloth given them by their mistresses, slave women rarely had the time and materials to mend their own or their families' clothing. Since plantation work was hard on clothes as well as muscles, "ragged" and "miserably clothed" slaves could be seen in the fields of many plantations.

Another highly visible line separated the shod and the barefoot. "I had no shoes until the ground began to freeze," Sheldon recalled, summarizing generations of experience in the countryside; those he did wear were usually vastly oversized and had to be stuffed with rags, since they were made to last him for two or three years. Even crude footwear was costly enough so that among poor and middling families children and many adults went unshod except in cold weather. Barefoot men driving teams and shoeless women working in their gardens could be seen almost everywhere.

Underneath their trousers, most men and boys wore only their shirts, which usually extended to midthigh and sometimes went to the knee. Women and girls also wore longer shirts, often genteelly called "chemises" by 1830, with knee-length stockings, under dresses and petticoats. Although the more affluent had nightshirts and nightgowns, the majority of men and women slept in their daytime shirts. Only a small minority of men—who seem to have worn them primarily for winter warmth—wore drawers, and very few women had adopted them.

Women wore petticoats under their dresses or gowns, and some wore flexible stays to enhance their figures. Doctors continued to warn about the dangers of tight lacing, but the early nineteenth century was actually a time of moderation in this aspect of women's dress. Most stays were of cotton, without whalebone; the rigid and constricting corsets widely worn in the eighteenth century and later in the nineteenth were only adopted by a few "fashionables."

Without drawers, women were potentially vulnerable to complete and embarrassing exposure. In 1809, George Heckert of York, Pennsylvania, saved "a woman from being exposet" when she dismounted from a horse in the courthouse square; Lewis Miller's drawing shows how her dress, petticoats and shirt became caught on the horn of the saddle, leaving only her stockings. Heckert shielded her with his hat from a group of goggle-eyed youths while she struggled to extricate herself. (See illustration no. 29.)

For prosperous American families, eighteenth- and early nineteenth-century portraits reveal the changing patterns of children's dress. Infant's wear altered the least; from the seventeenth century on, mothers dressed their infants in "nappies" or diapers and long, often white, gowns. Up to the middle of the eighteenth century, young children of both sexes had worn women's gowns and petticoats, until boys put on adult male clothing around the age of seven.

Around the time of the American Revolution, children's clothing began to suggest more complicated distinctions of age and sex. Parents now put all children between infancy and three or four years old into loose-fitting muslin frocks that were clearly unlike the clothes of adult women. Between four and ten or eleven, girls stayed in frocks while boys donned "skeleton suits," tight-fitting pantaloons and jackets that were distinctively masculine but very different from the clothes of their fathers and older brothers. Older boys and girls continued to wear slightly simplified and less formal versions of adult attire. But in the 1830s, American families again blurred the distinction between the sexes up to age ten; they abandoned skeleton suits to dress boys in trousers and "surtouts" or long coats, while also giving girls trousers to wear under their frocks, perhaps to retain children longer in sexless innocence.

Many families of more modest means undoubtedly emulated the way affluent Americans dressed their children, but the majority of families surely could not afford to adopt these distinctions in full. All American children wore dresslike garments in their earliest years and put on approximations of adult clothing when they began to do serious work. In many ordinary households, young children wore only long shirts of towcloth or cotton most of the time, heavier and coarser versions of the garments which more prosperous children wore beneath their outer clothes. Miller's drawings, for instance, show young children in Pennsylvania families sitting at the supper table in shirts and bare legs. On the Maryland plantation where Frederick Douglass grew up, slave children received only two shirts each year. If children damaged their garments or wore them out, they usually went without replacements. "Children from seven to ten years old, of both sexes, almost naked, might be seen at all seasons of the year," he recalled.

In poor white families as well as slave households, children might well have to wait for dresses or jacket and pantaloons until they became old enough to work in the fields. Hiram Munger, whose father was a desperately poor itinerant sawyer in Massachusetts, remembered that he spent most of his childhood in rags, without sufficiently decent "clothes to go to school or meeting."

The continued growth of British textile manufacturing, and its rapid emergence in the American Northeast, as Goodrich noted, "greatly cheapened and multiplied almost every species of clothing worn." In steadily increasing numbers American households gave up their laboriously produced linens and woolens for factory-made cotton and woolen cloth. Their eagerness to abandon towcloth and linsey-woolsey, although not easy for those nostalgic for the days of hand textile crafts to understand, was a matter of both economic choice and genteel aspiration. Not only were they glad to be rid of time-consuming tasks, they were anxious, like the families in Mayslick, Kentucky, to go from "coarse and dirty" homespun to the "cheering influence . . . of 'boughten' clothes."

"All sorts of cotton fabrics are now so cheap," claimed Mrs. Farrar in the *Young Lady's Friend* in 1836, "that there is no excuse for any person's not being well provided." She left many poor Americans, white and black, out of her reckoning, who might dress more comfortably than in previous generations but were far from being "well provided," but testified truly to the variety and abundance in dress that mass production had made widely available. The shelves of American stores bore eloquent supporting testimony; they were weighed down with a profusion of textiles which had replaced the products of household spinning and weaving.

The state of Americans' personal hygiene depended not only on how often they bathed, but on how frequently they could wash their shirts, the garments that lay closest to their skins. Cheaper cotton fabrics also meant more and cheaper shirts, making greater cleanliness possible.

Yet Americans by the millions were still wearing homespun in the 1830s. Families in the Western states, the back-country South and far northern New England still wove most of their own cloth, like the women of Sugar Creek in southern Illinois who, Charlotte Webb Jacobs remembered, "made towels and tablecloths, sheets, and everything in the clothing line." Nathaniel Hawthorne, with his quick eye for appearances, took careful note in his journals of the homespun-wearing men and women he came across from the Vermont hills or central

Maine; they stood out distinctly against the "city-dressed" population of Massachusetts. To wear homespun became less a sign of humble status than of rusticity, of distance from the network of stores and the commercial economy it stood for.

Slaves continued to weave and wear homespun on many plantations; others had clothes made of the coarse "negro cloth" that Rhode Island mills were now producing especially for planters.

Shoelessness diminished with the rapid growth of American ready-made shoe production. The organization of New England handcraft shoe manufacture on an increasingly large scale, accelerating in the mid-1820s, provided steadily lower-priced men's, women's and children's footwear. By 1835, Yankee shoemakers were producing over fifteen million pairs of relatively inexpensive, ready-made shoes a year, and newly affordable shoes became part of Americans' ordinary wardrobes, even in summer. Plantation owners were buying "slave brogans"— shoes made especially for the Southern market—by the barrelful. Ready-made footgear did not always fit well or wear comfortably, but hundreds of thousands of white and black Americans were now able to wear shoes for the first time, or to replace old and badly broken ones more quickly.

Personal wardrobes grew larger. Women were more likely to own more than one or two dresses, men to have more than a single jacket and pair or two of pantaloons. Greater abundance brought higher standards of adequacy and "decency" in clothing; one of the principal tasks of the ladies' charitable societies widespread in the rural North was to provide clothing for poor children in the community, "sufficient to go to school and meeting."

The ascendancy of machine-made and machine-printed textiles and the expansion of the web of commerce provided entry to the world of fashion for a widening circle of American women, who in city and countryside could now buy cloth in a kaleidoscopic variety of colors and patterns along with hair combs, ribbons, buttons and other accoutrements. High style, for Americans, emerged from the fashionable houses and dressmakers' shops of what Americans recognized as "the centers of fashion"—Paris and London. Annual changes in bonnet styles and the cut of gowns traveled in a month or so to New York, and then to other American cities, via illustrated magazines, "fashion plates" or large colored engravings, private letters and stylishly dressed foreign visitors. By the 1830s, magazines like *Godey's Lady's Book,* along with increasingly widespread correspondence and travel, were making changes in fashion widely known.

New styles, and the yearly alteration and embellishment of dress that they entailed, became an ever more important part of many women's work and conversation. American city women, from the wives of the nation's wealthiest men to those of clerks and master carpenters, were well known for their displays of finery. "How the ladies dress," exclaimed Charles Dickens after walking the streets of New York and Boston, marveling at "the flutterings of ribbons and silk tassels, and displays of cloaks. . . ." The young women in Lowell boardinghouses, Lucy Larcom reported, often banded together to buy a subscription to *Godey's.* And country girls in New England towns made palm-leaf hats and braided straw for storekeepers, taking much of their wages in dressmaking materials and trim. They had been "all bewitched" by the "Boston ladies," complained the *Farmer's Almanack,* and "went and filled the house with crape and muslin."

"Laborers' dress," as Hawthorne noted, and the working clothes of craftsmen and farmers—frocks, leather aprons, heavy boots and shoes—even in store-bought fabrics, were still highly recognizable and distinct from the clothing of ministers, lawyers and merchants. Less sophisticated rural folk might only approximate or even caricature current styles; travelers in out-of-the-way parts of the United States sometimes poked fun at women "bedizened in all the wonders of country millinery." Ready-made clothing, appearing in the 1840s, would democratize American dress even further by helping to eliminate the differences between at-home sewing and the work of "city tailors." But American men and women in their Sunday clothes were already considerably harder to distinguish by their dress. Widespread engagement in fashion was part of Americans' participation in the drama of economic acquisition.

"Delicate Subjects . . .
Shameless Stories"

"On the 20th day of July" in 1830, Harriet Winter, a young woman working as a domestic in Joseph Dunham's household in Brimfield, Massachusetts, "was gathering raspberries" in a field west of the house. "Near the close of day," Charles Phelps, a farm laborer then living in the town, "came to the field where she was," and in the gathering dusk they made love—"and," Justice of the Peace Asa Lincoln added in his account, "it was the Sabbath." American communities did not usually document their inhabitants' amorous rendezvous, but such trysts were fairly commonplace events in early nineteenth-century America. It escaped historical oblivion because Harriet was unlucky, less in becoming pregnant than in Charles's refusal to marry her. Asa Lincoln did not approve of Sabbath evening indiscretions, but he was primarily concerned with who would take economic responsibility for the child. The Massachusetts law then in force encouraged women to make such confessions by immunizing them in return from prosecution for fornication. Thus Lincoln interrogated Harriet about the baby's father— while she was in labor, as the law had long prescribed—in order to force Phelps to contribute to the maintenance of the child, which was going to be "born a bastard and chargeable to the town."

The Americans they met, some foreign travelers found, were reluctant to admit that such things happened in the United States. They were remarkably strait-laced about sexual matters in public and eager to insist upon the "purity" of their manners. But to take such protestations at face value, the unusually candid Englishman Frederick Marryat thought, would be "to suppose that human nature is not the same everywhere."

"Shameless stories and indecent jokes," Lydia Maria Child noted with some pain in *The Mother's Book* of 1831, circulated widely in American oral tradition. Along with bawdy songs, they continued to thrive and occasionally saw print as broadsides. American parents, she complained, were wholly unable to provide sexual information to their children, but left them to "domestics, or immodest school-companions," who retold, each generation, "filthy anecdotes of vice and vulgarity."

The most explicitly sexual book that the majority of Americans had a chance of reading was an old one, *Aristotle's Masterpiece.* Written anonymously in seventeenth-century England but masquerading as the work of the Greek philosopher, the *Masterpiece* went through eleven eighteenth-century editions, and sixteen more between 1800 and 1831. It was pseudomedical in tone and explicit about the mechanics of intercourse and reproduction, but was not overtly pornographic—unlike John Cleland's *Fanny Hill: Or the Memoirs of a Woman of Pleasure,* which circulated widely in England and had some clandestine American readership.

Aristotle's Masterpiece was still an "underground text," one which could not be displayed openly on the bookshelves of respectable houses. Despite the number of editions the *Masterpiece* went through, no eighteenth- or nineteenth-century American has yet been found who admitted reading it. The young men who read the book—its woodcuts and descriptions focused almost entirely on the female body—probably perused it furtively in barns or behind shops and schoolhouses. It was, in all probability, the "indecent book" that a Shrewsbury, Massachusetts, schoolteacher confiscated from a group of older boys in 1840 and burned in the schoolhouse stove.

A late eighteenth-century chamber pot, made in England but bought and used in America, survives as testimony to a world of sexuality whose realities have rarely been fully acknowledged. (See illustration no. 30.) Inscribed "Marrige Present," the vessel has a green ceramic frog peeping over the rim and a grinning face on the bottom saying, "Keep me clean and keep me well and what I see I will not tell." On the outside are verses about its use. "Dear lovely wife pray rise and P. 'SS," begins one,

> Take you that handle and I'll take this.
> Let's use the present which was sent,
> To make some mirth is only meant:
> So let it be as they have said.
> We'll laugh and P. 'SS and then to bed.

At least some American couples began their married lives with such ribaldry. The well-organized birth and marriage records of a number of American communities reveal that they often anticipated their weddings as well. In late eighteenth-century America, pregnancy was frequently the prelude to marriage. The proportion of brides who were pregnant at the time of their weddings had been rising since the late seventeenth century and peaked in the turbulent decades during and after the Revolution. In the 1780s and 1790s, nearly one-third of rural New England's brides were already with child. The frequency of sexual intercourse before marriage was surely higher, since some couples would have escaped early pregnancy. For many couples, sexual relations were part of serious courtship. Premarital pregnancies in late eighteenth-century Dedham, Massachusetts, observed the local historian Erastus Worthington in 1828, were occasioned by "the custom then prevalent of females admitting young men to their beds, who sought their company in marriage." Pregnancies usually simply accelerated a marriage that would have taken place in any case, but community and parental pressure worked strongly to assure it.

Most rural communities simply tolerated the early pregnancies that marked so many marriages. New England's stern civil statutes against fornication, for example, were rarely invoked against erring couples from the early eighteenth century on. But the religious and social leadership clearly did not wholeheartedly approve. Many churches required public confessions from young members who had strayed. In Hingham, Massachusetts, tax records suggest that the families of well-to-do brides were considerably less generous to couples who had had early babies than to those who had avoided pregnancy.

Young Americans who were courting clearly took for granted a striking amount of privacy and freedom from supervision. They first came together at unchaperoned dances, singing schools, or sleighing or quilting parties and then paired off to find time alone together. In warm weather, they had the outdoors and its barns, fields and woods. And in winter, older folks often left them alone and unsupervised.

"Bundling very much abounds," wrote the anonymous author of "A New Bundling Song" still circulating in Boston in 1812, "in many parts in country towns," and bundling was a part of rural American courtship enshrouded in myth and notorious in popular history. Noah Webster's first *American Dictionary of the English Language* in 1828 defined it as the custom which allowed couples "to sleep on the same bed without undressing"—with, a later commentator added, "the shared understanding that innocent endearments should not be exceeded." Folklore and local tradition, from Maine south to New York, has American mothers tucking bundling couples into bed with special chastity-protecting garments for the young woman or a "bundling board" to separate them.

But in actuality, if bundling had been intended to allow courting couples privacy and emotional intimacy but not sexual contact, it clearly failed. Couples may have begun with bundling, but as courtship advanced they clearly pushed beyond its restraints, like the "bundling maid" in "A New Bundling Song" who would "sometimes say when she lies down/She can't be cumbered with a gown" or the young men and women in another broadside song, "In Favor of Courting," who "Let coats and gowns be laid aside/Let breeches take their flight."

Young black men and women shared American whites' freedom in courtship and sexuality and sometimes extended it. Echoing the cultural traditions of West Africa as well as the fact that their marriages were not given legal status and security, the boundaries of premarital pregnancy and illegitimacy were inevitably less clear. Slave communities were somewhat more tolerant and accepting of sex before marriage—although as the records make clear, there was no racial monopoly on sexual "virtue."

Under the conditions of plantation life some men and women had multiple sexual relationships; William Wells Brown, a slave born in Virginia around 1810, remembered that his mother had a different father for each of her seven children. But such relatively casual mating was not the common practice in the slave quarters, and probably declined as slaves took up evangelical Christianity in increasing numbers. For the mid-nineteenth century, some plantation registers survive which list household groups and name the fathers as well as the mothers of children; they show that a sizable majority of slave women had had all their children by the same father. Most of the rest had borne one child by another man before settling down to a long-term relationship.

Gradations of color and facial features among the slaves were testimony that "thousands," as Frederick Douglass wrote, were "ushered into the world annually, who, like myself, owe their existence to white fathers, and those fathers most frequently their own masters." Sex crossed the boundaries of race and servitude more often than slavery's defenders wanted to admit, if less frequently than the most outspoken abolitionists claimed. Slave women had little protection from whatever sexual demands masters or overseers might make, so that rapes, short liaisons and long-term concubinage were all potentially, and sometimes actually, part of plantation life. As a reminiscing slave put it, plantation families were sometimes riven by tensions between "a licentious master and a jealous mistress." The slaveowner Edwin Epps pursued the beautiful and athletic Patsy, Solomon Northup remembered, while her fellow slaves watched powerlessly; her repeated refusals to sleep with him earned her continually harsher treatment which eventually broke her spirit. But most plantations were not brothels. Mulattoes, and interracial sexuality, were actually far more common where black people had greater freedom: in the upper South with its small farms, larger towns and higher numbers of free blacks.

As Nathaniel Hawthorne stood talking with a group of men on the porch of a tavern in Augusta, Maine, in 1836, a young man "in a laborer's dress" came up and asked if anyone knew the whereabouts of Mary Ann Russell. "Do you want to use her?" asked one of the bystanders. Mary Ann was, in fact, the young laborer's wife, but she had left him and their child in Portland to become "one of a knot of whores." A few years earlier, the young men of York, Pennsylvania, made up a party for "overturning and pulling to the ground" Eve Geese's "shameful house" of prostitution in Queen Street. The frightened women fled out the back door as the chimney collapsed around them; the apprentices and young journeymen—many of whom had surely been previous customers—were treated by local officials "to wine, for the good work."

From relatively small towns like Augusta and York to great cities, poor American women were sometimes pulled into a darker, harsher sexual world, one of vulnerability, exploitation and commerce. Many prostitutes took up their trade out of poverty and domestic disaster. A young widow, or a country girl arrived in the city and thrown on her own resources, often faced desperate economic choices because most women's work paid too poorly to provide decent food, clothing and shelter. But others sought excitement or independence from their families, or even responded to the lure of fashionable clothes and furnishings that their earnings could provide. Young women living in New York City's poorest neighborhoods were often assumed to be sexually available. Walking on the crowded anonymous streets, or even near their own homes, they might face offhand propositions, or attempts at seduction from men who proposed an exchange of sexual favors for a "treat" or a good meal. Some of those who accepted such casual encounters went on to full-time prostitution.

As cities grew, and changes in transportation involved more men in long-distance travel, prostitution became more visible. Men of all ages, married and unmarried, from city lawyers to visiting country storekeepers to sailors on the docks, turned to brothels for sexual release, but most of the brothels' customers were young men, living away from home and increasingly unlikely to marry until their late twenties. Sexual commerce in New York City was elaborately graded by price and the economic status of clients, from the "parlor houses" situated not far from the city's best hotels on Broadway, through the more numerous and moderately priced houses that drew artisans and clerks, to the dockside grogshops in the Five Points neighborhood haunted by broken and dissipated women. The houses of the notorious Mississippi River settlement "Natchez Under the Hill" were less selective; they welcomed riverboat crews, commercial travelers and affluent passengers alike.

From New Orleans to Boston, city theaters were important sexual marketplaces. Men often bought tickets less to see the performance than to make assignations with the prostitutes, who sat by custom in the topmost gallery of seats. The women usually received free admission from theater managers, who claimed that they could not stay in business without the male theatergoers drawn by "the guilty third tier."

For Harriet Winter and women like her, who were poor and whose lovers absconded or ignored community sanctions, sex and pregnancy did not end with a wedding, however late, but with the birth of a "bastard child" and an almost indelible social stigma. Just how common her situation was is genuinely uncertain, because even those American communities known for meticulous record-keeping often failed to record illegitimate births. Frederick Marryat thought that there "were fewer illegitimate children *born*" and acknowledged in the United States than in Britain, but darkly hinted that "infanticide, or producing abortions" accounted for it.

Most Americans—and the American common law—still did not regard abortion as a crime until the fetus had "quickened" or begun to move perceptibly in the womb. Books of medical advice actually contained prescriptions for bringing on delayed menstrual periods which would also produce an abortion if the woman happened to be pregnant. They suggested heavy doses of purgatives that created violent cramps, powerful douches or extreme kinds of physical activity, like the "violent exercise, raising great weights . . . strokes on the belly . . . falls" noted in William Buchan's widely read *Domestic Medicine*. Women's folklore echoed most of these prescriptions and added others, particularly the use of two American herbal preparations— savin, or the extract of juniper berries, and "Seneca snakeroot" —as abortion-producing drugs. They were dangerous procedures, but sometimes effective.

Women "who had engaged in illegitimate love," wrote the physician James Archer in rural Harford County, Maryland, in 1802, took such abortion-producing drugs "intentionally to destroy the foetus in utero." And there were women who became desperate enough to abandon or even kill their babies. Over the years from 1800 to the mid-1840s, Lewis Miller recorded five "innocent infant[s] found in York Borough," whose unmarried mothers had abandoned them soon after birth. Only one was discovered alive.

Starting before the turn of the nineteenth century, the sexual lives of many Americans began to change, shaped by a growing insistence on control: reining in the passions in courtship, limiting family size and even redefining male and female sexual desire.

Bundling was already on the wane in rural America before 1800; by the 1820s it was discussed as a rare and antique custom. It had ceased, thought an elderly man from East Haddam, Connecticut, "as a consequence of education and refinement." Decade by decade, the proportion of young women who had conceived a child before marriage declined. In most of the towns of New England the rate had dropped from nearly one pregnant bride in three to one in five or six by 1840; in some places the rate of prenuptial pregnancy dropped to five percent. For many young Americans this marked the acceptance of new limits on sexual behavior, imposed not by their parents or other authorities in their communities but by themselves. This remarkable change in behavior drew little comment. Erastus Worthington was one of the few who noted it. "The sexes," he thought, "had learned to cultivate the proper degree of delicacy in their intercourse."

These young men and women were not more closely supervised by their parents than earlier generations had been; in fact they had more mobility and greater freedom. The couples who courted in the new style, with "the proper degree of delicacy," put a far greater emphasis on control of the passions. For some of them—young Northern merchants and professional men and their intended brides—revealing love letters have survived for the years after 1820. Their intimate correspondence reveals that they did not give up sexual expression, but gave it new boundaries. They abandoned intercourse during courtship and reserved it for marriage. Marrying later than their parents, they were often living through long engagements while the husband-to-be strove to establish his place in the world. They chose not to risk a pregnancy that would precipitate them into an early marriage.

To many early nineteenth-century Americans, an early pregnancy became a much more serious stain on a woman's character than it had previously been. In the respectable circles of Northampton, Massachusetts, in the 1820s, a rushed marriage, Susan Lyman Lesley noted, was considered "a case of seduction." She observed that "the wife always seemed under a cloud."

Many American husbands and wives were also breaking with tradition as they began to limit the size of their families. Clearly, married couples were renegotiating the terms of their sexual lives together, but they remained resolutely silent about how they did it. In the first two decades of the nineteenth century, they almost certainly set about avoiding childbirth through abstinence, coitus interruptus or male withdrawal, and perhaps sometimes abortion. These were the contraceptive techniques long traditional in preindustrial Europe, although previously little used in America. It is unlikely that more than a very few Americans were using mechanical means of birth control such as condoms or contraceptive sponges. There were virtually no references to them.

As they entered the 1830s Americans had their first opportunity to learn, at least in print, about more effective or less self-denying forms of birth control. They could read reasonably inexpensive editions of the first works on contraception published in the United States—Robert Dale Owen's *Moral Physiology* of 1831 and Dr. Charles Knowlton's *The Fruits of Philosophy* of 1832. Both authors frankly described the full range of contraceptive techniques, although they solemnly rejected physical intervention in the sexual act and recommended only douching after intercourse and coitus interruptus to their readers. Official opinion, legal and religious, was deeply hostile. Knowlton, who had trained as a physician in rural Massachusetts, was prosecuted in three different counties for obscenity, and was convicted once and imprisoned for three months.

But both works found substantial numbers of Americans eager to read them. By 1839, each book had gone through nine editions, putting a combined total of twenty thousand to thirty thousand copies in circulation. A sizeable number of men and women, most likely better off and better educated, must have learned about birth control practices from Owen or Knowlton; an American physician could write in 1850 that contraception had "been of late years so much talked of." Greater knowledge about birth control surely played a part in the continuing decline of the American birthrate after 1830, but again, couples left no direct testimony as to how they were putting this newly available advice into effect.

New ways of thinking about sexuality were emerging which also stressed control. Into the 1820s, almost all Americans would have subscribed to the commonplace notion that sex, within proper social confines, was enjoyable and healthy, and that prolonged sexual abstinence could be injurious to health. They also would have assumed that women had powerful sexual drives. But just as *Aristotle's Masterpiece,* which explicitly echoed these sentiments, was disappearing from circulation—its last American printing was in 1831—a number of Americans were turning these notions upside down. Some treated sex itself as a problem.

Starting with his "Lecture to Young Men on Chastity" in 1832, Sylvester Graham articulated very different counsels about health and sex. Sexual indulgence, he argued, was not only morally suspect, but psychologically and physiologically risky. The sexual overstimulation involved in young men's lives produced anxiety and nervous disorders, "a shocking state of debility and excessive irritability." The remedy was diet, exercise, a regular routine that pulled the mind away from animal lusts. Medical writings began to appear which discussed the evils of masturbation or "solitary vice." Popular books of advice to young men gave similar warnings. They tried to persuade them that their health could be ruined, and their prospects for success darkened, by consorting with prostitutes or becoming sexually entangled before marriage. Graham went considerably further than this, advising restraint not only in early life and courtship, but in marriage itself. It was far healthier, he maintained, for couples to have sexual relations in great moderation; for those whose diets were healthy and whose lives were truly in control, claimed Graham, intercourse would be "very seldom."

Along with these admonitions aimed at men, a new belief about women's sexual nature appeared, one which elevated them above "carnal passion." Some American men and women came to believe that females, in their true and proper nature as mothers and guardians of the home, were far less interested in sex than males. This may have worked in part to some women's advantage. Women acknowledged to be passionless were in a stronger position to control or deny men's sexual demands, whether during courtship or in limiting their childbearing within marriage. Similar notions energized the "Magdalen Societies" formed in Boston and New York in the 1820s, which attempted to reclaim prostitutes to sexual virtue and shame their clients into continence as corrupters and exploiters of women.

As a result, many young American men were newly awakened to the dangers of sensual excess, while an increasing number of couples were surely dealing with limiting sexuality in the marriage bed. Probably only a relative few—convinced and dedicated Grahamites—attempted to put Graham's stringent prescriptions into practice. A smaller minority of Americans, a few thousand in all, made even more drastic choices about their sexual lives, joining one of the Utopian religious communities that became part of the social landscape as early as the 1780s.

Most visible and numerous were the Shakers, who by 1840 were living in eighteen "societies" from Maine to Kentucky. They forsook marriage and family life for celibacy, sexual segregation, and immersion in a single communal household. Other groups—Harmonists in Economy, Pennsylvania, and Harmony, Indiana, the followers of Jemima Wilkinson at New Jerusalem in western New York—followed roughly similar practices, at least for a time. Moving completely around the circle, a tiny handful of radical "perfectionists" were asserting the primacy of "spiritual marriage" over legal wedlock and the sexual freedom of "perfect believers." In 1837, John Humphrey Noyes had begun to gather believers around him in Putney, Vermont, and to work out the doctrine of "plural marriage," or complete sexual sharing within a perfectionist community coupled with "male continence" or coitus interruptus, that would become notorious in the 1840s.

Grahamism, communal celibacy and perfectionism gave the most dramatic testimony to change in Americans' sexual ideas and practices, but they directly involved only a few. Neither contraception nor the new style of courtship had become universal by 1840. Prenuptial pregnancy rates had fallen, but they remained high enough to indicate that many couples simply continued in old and familiar ways, where serious courtship frequently led to pregnancy and then triggered marriage. American husbands and wives in the Northern cities and countryside were limiting the number of their children, but it was clear that those living on the farms of the West or in the slave quarters had not yet begun to. Although some American women restrained or renounced their sexuality, there is strong evidence that others felt far from passionless. Change was partial and uneven, yet for many people in the United States, it was profound. For them, reining in the passions or controlling the procreative act itself had become part of everyday life.

5

"THE WHOLE POPULATION

IS IN MOTION":

THE EXPERIENCE OF TRAVEL

T HERE is more travelling in the United States than in any part of the world," commented a writer in a Boston newspaper in 1828. "Here, the whole population is in motion, whereas, in old countries, there are millions who have never been beyond the sound of the parish bell." To native and foreign commentators alike, Americans were remarkably, even uniquely prone to moving about. "People travel so readily from one place to another," marveled the French traveler Moreau de St. Mery in 1794. Almost forty years later, on a steamer plying Long Island Sound in 1831, the Boston printer David Clapp wrote in his diary that traveling was a custom that had "so greatly increased as of late years, and which may almost now be considered a mode of life."

On foot and horseback, wagon and stage, steamboat and railroad, movement was an unmistakable signature of the way of life early nineteenth-century Americans were creating. One of their most striking achievements was a revolution in travel, a vast improvement and extension of the rudimentary transportation system of colonial times. The most radical changes in the speed, scale and experience of traveling came with the application of newly emerging transportation technologies—the railroad, the steamboat, the building of canals—to American conditions. Less dramatic but more important, because until well after 1840, they affected a far larger number of people, were more modest, incremental changes in the traditional modes of travel—the improvement and extension of roads, and the better design and wider distribution of wheeled vehicles. Taken together they meant that Americans born in the late eighteenth century whose active lives spanned two or more decades had experienced an unprecedented speeding-up of travel and communications. In 1786 it had taken four to six days, depending on the weather, to travel from Boston to New York. By 1830, stagecoach lines regularly made the trip in a day and a half. By 1840, the railway covered the distance in a little more than half a day. From 1820 onward, the steamboat began the conquest of the great waterways, changing travel times from months to days or a week.

As experienced in times of travel and the spread of news, the size of the United States decreased even as its territory was greatly expanding. In terms of days' traveling, the far-flung Western settlements of the 1830s were actually nearer than the relatively close-in colonial frontiers had been. It is not surprising that the early nineteenth-century United States seemed both to its spokesmen and its observers to have been a society peculiarly in motion—a characteristic enshrined in the way Americans used the word "go-ahead" both to describe and to command.

"All in Motion"—Mobility

The first of May was "moving day" in early nineteenth-century New York City, when all leases expired simultaneously. With everyone searching for a new dwelling, store or shop, the population looked to Frances Trollope be "flying from the plague," and the chaos in the streets was extraordinary: "Rich furniture and ragged furniture, carts, wagons and drays, ropes, canvas and straw, packers, porters and draymen" thronged the thoroughfares. Nowhere was the propensity of Americans to change their residences so vividly on display, yet in less dramatic forms it pervaded their lives. Contemporary Americans are used to considering themselves a highly mobile, even disturbingly rootless and restless people when compared with their ancestors, but mobility has long been characteristic of their society.

Colonial Americans had never been a static population, tied to living within "the sound of the parish bell" where they had been born, but during the late eighteenth century they were becoming more restless, less rooted to their communities of birth, and more likely to shift their residences. Early-nineteenth-century Americans became confirmed in the high rates of geographic mobility that have characterized them ever since. A great deal of this continuing wave of migration took the form of moves from one rural community to another, or from rural communities to cities. In the unremarkable agricultural community of Sturbridge in central Massachusetts, thirty-five to forty percent of the households numbered at one census moved before the next one was taken ten years later. The records of the town's Congregational and Baptist churches reveal that when church members moved, over one-half of their families went to other rural communities within twenty miles, while another one-fourth made far more dramatic moves to the city —to Boston, Providence, Hartford or the growing commercial center of Worcester, Massachusetts.

In many American cities fewer than half the households remained for the ten years between one census enumeration and the next. And even within city boundaries, there was a constant stream of internal migration; each year, close to a quarter of all Bostonians changed their residences, moving from one neighborhood to another. With the vivid exception of "moving day," the ceaseless tide of movement was comparatively invisible. It was far easier to see the other American "movers," those who took the quintessential American journey, the long trek westward. The Sturbridge churches sent the rest of their departing communicants to new congregations in western New York,

Ohio, Illinois, Michigan and Wisconsin, up to twelve hundred miles away.

"The great thoroughfares" heading west, as the *Universal Traveller* of 1831 said, were "thronged with a singular assemblage of travellers," a great wave of motion. Responding to the push of narrowing opportunities in the older parts of the countryside, and the enormously attractive pull of new land, hundreds of thousands of families headed to new homes. Families "on the great roads leading from Baltimore and Philadelphia" drove wagons in "large companies"; they slept under them at night and "cooked in the open air." "Several times during the last week the road was literally filled with movers," noted a Louisville, Kentucky, newspaper in 1825. The families passing through from Georgia, Virginia and the Carolinas had their household goods "packed on horses, or in carts drawn by calves, cows and horses." When an entire plantation's households, sometimes numbering a hundred people or more, moved to the richer lands of Alabama and Mississippi, a few of the slaves teamed wagonloads of goods or drove livestock. Most blacks, however, traveled westward shackled together, crammed into wagons or carts or even walking much of the way. New Yorkers heading for "the Ohio" took their farm wagons to Buffalo or Cincinnati, where "the whole caravan, consisting of family, horses, dog, wagon, and furniture, are put on the steamboats."

Moving family and household goods, to say nothing of farm implements and livestock, any great distance was a formidable feat. Westward-moving families risked the same hazards of road and weather as other travelers; but journeying with infants, children, often pregnant women and the elderly, they were uniquely vulnerable to illness and misfortune. A vehicle upset that might only inconvenience stagecoach travelers could destroy all a household's furniture and crockery. Unanticipated expenses along the way sometimes exhausted slender reserves of cash. After a difficult and unhealthy traveling season in 1829, noted the Reverend Timothy Flint, many poor migrants were stranded in Cincinnati—whole families down to their last dollar, sick with fever or "wretchedly furnished with . . . the comforts almost indispensable to a long journey." By 1830, the best-off Northern migrants could avoid some of these perils; they were able to sell off their vehicles and livestock near home, ship their household goods out separately, and take stage and steamboat to the point nearest their destination, where they bought new wagons and horses for the last leg of the journey. Carrying their possessions on their backs or pushing handcarts, poorer Americans walked "to the land of promise," Goodrich observed, in family groups: "the aged grandsire leaning on his staff, his son in the prime of manhood, and his grandchildren . . . the youngest often strapped to the back of the eldest." But in the long route over the Alleghenies, many of these families "suffered from want," and the "old and feeble sometimes perish among the mountains."

Once they arrived, movers were even less likely to stay in their new communities than were Americans in the East. In the Illinois settlement of Sugar Creek, nearly two-thirds of the families listed on one census had moved away by the time of the next.

The most mobile of all Americans were the truly rootless, itinerants whose numbers on the roads were expanding dramatically in the early nineteenth century. Peddlers, showmen and tinkers roamed the roads. Itinerant singing masters, dancing teachers, portrait painters, handwriting instructors, silhouette cutters and phrenologists brought their unfamiliar talents into rural communities often avid for instruction and novelty.

Over the course of four or five years, James Guild of Tunbridge, Vermont, lived not one but several American lives of the road. At age nineteen, in 1821, a discontented "farmer boy who had been confined to the hoe or the axe," he took a trunk of goods, nerved himself up to "put on a peddler's face," and walked west to Rochester, New York, asking at each house on the way, "Do you wish to buy some hare combs, needles, buttons, button molds, sewing silk, beads?" Meeting with little success, Guild then took up a traveling tinker's leather apron and soldering iron, "so mean that none would notice me," and made his way repairing pots and spoons. Then, in succession, he helped exhibit a traveling bison, played the tambourine in a show, became a "profile cutter" who traced sitters' silhouettes, and learned the rudiments of portrait painting from another itinerant. Guild finally became a traveling painter of miniature portraits and teacher of penmanship, trades he pursued from Cleveland, Ohio, to Charleston, South Carolina. Peddlers by the thousands were the advance guard of American commerce, helping both to create and supply growing rural markets for consumer goods. Visiting "every inhabited part of the United States," men—mostly young and disproportionately from New England—traveled door to door over the back roads of the American countryside. They drove wagons loaded with tinware, books, hats or dry goods, or went on foot with lighter loads of essences and perfumes and sewing notions.

Itinerant entrepreneurs of popular culture were part of the expanding life of the American road. Hundreds of "traveling exhibitions"—circuses with musical and gymnastic performances, menageries, puppet shows, displays of exotic scenes, freaks and strange relics—could be found traveling through the United States by the 1820s. They ranged from single individuals traveling with their exhibits in a shabby wagon to companies of a dozen or more performers. They brought brief glimpses of the unfamiliar, the exotic, the grotesque into thousands of rural communities, often oddly and offhandedly expanding Americans' knowledge of the world beyond their localities. Nathaniel Hawthorne encountered an "old Dutchman" at a roadside tavern in 1838 who "travel[ed] the country with his diorama," and charged "respectable farmers" a few pennies each to see his exhibition: "There were views of cities and edifices in Europe, and ruins,—and of Napoleon's battles and Nelson's sea fights; in the midst of which would be seen a gigantic, brown, hairy hand

—the Hand of Destiny—pointing at the principal points of the conflict, while the old Dutchman explained."

Hawthorne was disdainful of the diorama's quality, calling it "a succession of the very worst scratchings and daubings that can be imagined," but it had its attentive audience. Strange apparitions in jars went on the circuit, along with human oddities such as the preternaturally thin Calvin Edson, "the living skeleton." Menageries exhibited exotic animals such as lions, elephants, anacondas and monkeys, even the "stuffed whale on a wagon" that traveled through eastern Pennsylvania in 1818. In the eighteenth century all of these beasts would have been mere rumors, or at most a few crude images in woodcuts.

P. T. Barnum began his career as an itinerant showman in 1836, with one of the largest American traveling shows. Barnum and his partner Aron Turner directed a circus company consisting of "thirty-five men and boys," including singers, a "band of music," trick riders, a clown and a celebrated Italian acrobat. Traveling in a cavalcade of "wagons, carriages, tents, horses and ponies," they performed in hundreds of communities from Connecticut to North Carolina in the course of six months, giving one or two shows a day. Barnum then took half the company and spent the winter touring South Carolina, Georgia, Alabama, Kentucky and Tennessee. Life on the road was frequently precarious, but most of the county seats and country villages where Barnum and his troupe stopped were "swarming with country people who came 'to see the show.' "

Some few Americans, the most marginal of all, wandered the roads aimlessly. Esther Bernon Carpenter remembered the "odd estrays going about" in the Narragansett country of Rhode Island—several deluded, self-ordained preachers, "wanderers over the face of the earth," who looked for any audiences they could gather, a blind beggar woman who turned up every year on her annual pilgrimage across southern New England, men scattered in their wits who stopped to work in haying season. Hawthorne even crossed paths with a wandering opium addict in Orange, Massachusetts, in 1838. American roads showed fewer of such people than those of Europe, yet they could be seen by anyone looking closely enough.

"The Common Roads"

In the years between 1790 and 1840, Americans built thousands of miles of new roads, and improved and repaired their old ones. In the Northeast, from 1790 to 1820, private turnpike companies built roads in the hope of profiting from the increased flow of commerce; they rarely succeeded but left an improved "turnpike manner" of road building behind. Later, local governments sped up the pace of road construction in the 1820s and 1830s. Across the United States, the editor of a farmer's periodical thought in 1839, people had displayed a "passion for improving roads" which had improved them "to an extent beyond . . . what settlers fifty or sixty years ago would have anticipated." The expansion of stage and wagon travel and the expanded movement of goods, livestock and settlers heading West would have been impossible without great efforts in building crowned roads that allowed water to drain to the sides, smoothing out ruts and potholes, bridging streams. In the 1830s, the best roads in the United States were the major county roads and turnpikes of southern New England, the lower Hudson Valley and southeastern Pennsylvania. Travelers could go with the greatest ease on the ways that fanned out from the seaboard cities to nearby communities, and the thoroughfares that connected the cities to each other.

Elsewhere the American landscape continued to present impressive obstacles to travel. From the viewpoint of contemporary Europe or critical American experts, American roadbuilding achievements were still modest. "The common roads of the United States," William Gillespie wrote in his 1847 *Manual on the Principles and Practices of Road-making,* were still "inferior to those of any other civilized country." Americans' extraordinary mobility, their character as a "go-ahead" people, pushed them to travel as far and as fast as they could on roads that remained difficult.

Passing through western New York in 1822, the Englishman Henry Addington several times saw "the wreck of a coach or wagon, sticking in picturesque attitudes in some hole in the low road. . . . How any vehicle can get through such fearful breakers as those routes present sometimes for four or five miles continuously it is difficult for those who have experienced their ferocity to comprehend." Travelers in the early United States spent a good deal of ink on describing and lamenting the conditions of the roads they traversed; it was natural enough, since they usually spent more time on the highways than they did at their stopovers and destinations. Legally, American roads were defined as very wide rights of way—10, 20, even 40 rods wide, or from 160 to over 600 feet. But in reality most highways were narrow tracks within those bounds. Roads began as single-tracked bridle paths, usually later widened to accommodate carts and wagons, but off the largest thoroughfares there was often not enough space for two vehicles to pass abreast. The remainder of the right of way was often left in woodland or, if the timber had been cleared, allowed to grow up in brush or used for grazing livestock.

Northern hill roads, reminisced a Massachusetts man, were "strewn with loose stones of assorted sizes, over which horses stumbled." In the "rich mud roads of Ohio" that Harriet Martineau encountered, the slow-going sandy thoroughfares or "clayey roads cut into deep ruts" of the coastal South, teamsters often mired their wagons to the hubs. Farther west, or in newly settled northern New England, travelers saw nothing for hundreds of miles but newly cleared tracks still encumbered with tree stumps. Worst of all were the "corduroy" roads built of transversely placed logs, which Americans sometimes used to bridge swampy areas; to Henry Addington in 1823, traveling on them seemed "an uninterrupted series of plunges from one hole to another."

A foreign traveler's readiness to be critical of American manners, social order and domestic arrangements usually increased as his ride became bumpier. But the reasons for the state of the early Republic's roads were not mysterious. Building and maintaining relatively comfortable and moderately safe roads took enormous amounts of labor. Gangs of men and teams of oxen or horses were required to remove rocks, fill in holes, dig ditches for drainage, grade surfaces with shovels, cart and spread stone and gravel. Thinly stretched town and county governments were primarily responsible for their construction and upkeep. Americans made the immense effort of building good roads only where population, commerce and traffic were dense enough to promise a return on the investment to the company or the community. In the Northeast and the more densely settled parts of the West, roads steadily improved in construction techniques, materials used and maintenance. Bringing Western or Southern roads up to the standards of Connecticut or eastern Pennsylvania, let alone the macadamized standards of England near London, was both beyond the resources of society and economically irrational. Thus American roads declined in speed, comfort and safety south of Baltimore and west of the Appalachians.

Foot and Horseback, Wagon and Chaise

Local travel, like local population movement, was less noteworthy and harder to see. For most Americans around 1800, country neighborhoods of a few dozen farms or less constituted the normal boundaries of everyday movement, on visits that intertwined socializing, neighborly help and economic exchange. Beyond their neighborhoods they made less frequent trips to artisans' shops, stores, taverns and churches at villages or crossroads settlements. In a New England town families even on the most outlying farms could make these journeys every week since they were rarely more than a few hours' walk or an hour's ride away. In frontier Kentucky families might go a month or more between such trips. Although goods sometimes moved long distances by sea in pre-Revolutionary America, and settlers continuously pushed into the interiors of the seaboard states, few people traveled routinely outside their daily and weekly circles of neighborhood. By 1830 gradually improving local roads and more vehicles meant that ordinary folk could move about more often and more easily within their communities.

Hundreds of thousands of people—their numbers seriously underestimated by observers chiefly impressed with the more dramatic traffic of horses and vehicles—still traveled primarily on foot. In early nineteenth-century landscape paintings which showed Americans on the road, there were sometimes pedestrian figures in the background, occasionally pictured giving directions to mounted travelers or families riding in carriages. "Without thinking it a trouble," as Alonzo Lewis of Lynn, Massachusetts, recalled, many poorer Americans were accustomed to walking "from three to six miles on Sabbath to meeting," or to visit stores and taverns.

Children ranked lowest on the scale of access to horses and vehicles and walked everywhere. In the towns of New England, the number and location of neighborhood district schools reflected a social consensus about just how far the younger scholars, four- or five-year olds, should walk—usually a distance of up to two miles one way. The New England clergyman William Ellery Channing recalled starting school before he was three years old; when he tired on the mile-long journey he was carried on his older brother's back. Youths and young men in particular were accustomed to covering long distances on foot. As a fourteen-year-old, P. T. Barnum was sent for a summer's higher schooling to an "Academy" three miles away. He "marched and countermarched" the distance "six times per week." Young New Englanders "working out" during the week in other communities as farm laborers or schoolteachers sometimes walked eight to ten miles to be home on Sunday. Anxious to see a ship launched in Salem harbor, Asa Sheldon and a group of twelve- and thirteen-year-old farm boys walked fifteen miles from their town of Wilmington, Massachusetts, to the city overnight, spent the day and walked back, exhausted, the next evening.

In between "shank's pony," as walking was called, and the steam-powered railroad was the horse—the prime mover of early nineteenth-century travel. Reliable figures are difficult to come by, but the number of horses in the United States probably grew faster than the population between 1790 and 1840 as their use as draft animals in place of oxen expanded and the number of horse-drawn vehicles increased. In the United States of 1840 there was on the average about one horse for every four or five people. After that time the ratio of horses to people ceased to increase and then slowly declined, as city-dwelling families, who were much less likely to own horses, became an ever greater proportion of the population. The evidence of tax assessments and household inventories makes it clear that they were far from universal possessions. They were distributed less equally than are automobiles among the American population today. The great majority of urban families owned no horses, as did close to half the farm families in many New England towns, where oxen remained the primary draft animals. Even in regions where horses were almost universally used for farm work, there were many rural Americans who exchanged labor or farm produce with better-endowed neighbors for the use of horses in plowing, hauling, or traveling.

Through the eighteenth century, vehicles other than crude, slow and uncomfortable two-wheeled carts were rare: Americans undertook most of their nonpedestrian travel on horseback. The number of conveyances and work vehicles greatly increased after 1790, although in many places it was still common to see two or even three family members riding an overburdened farm horse to crossroads churches or village stores. "Within a few years past," wrote the Connecticut clergyman, Samuel Goodrich, in 1800, four-wheeled "waggons drawn by horses have been greatly multiplied." Within a couple of decades they had become the most common of American road vehicles—used for farm work, hauling goods and produce, and family transportation.

By 1830, Samuel Goodrich the younger testified, Americans were driving a "multitudinous generation of travelling vehicles" that had been "totally unknown" in his father's time. Where once "pleasure vehicles," comfortable conveyances intended solely for personal transportation, were the exclusive possession of the very rich, many more families now owned them. Two-wheeled, one-horse "chaises" and "gigs" or four-wheeled, two-horse carriages became increasingly common sights in both Northern cities and countryside. Traffic counts on the Norfolk and Bristol turnpike in Massachusetts in 1824, for instance, revealed that chaise drivers outnumbered horsemen four to one. But pleasure equipages were still the possession of a highly visible minority. In most country towns of Massachusetts, no more than one household in seven owned a carriage or chaise.

It was "the custom of the country," James Stuart observed, "in New York and New England . . . for all to ride in some sort of carriage," but he was counting farm vehicles as well. Owning a farm wagon and horse was the mark of middling economic status; wagons, the same turnpike records revealed, were almost four times as numerous on the road as chaises. Farm wagons sometimes had removable seats, but their owners more commonly turned them into passenger vehicles with a few rough adaptations. Boarding with an Ohio family in the 1830s, Homer Merriam rode to Cincinnati in a "market wagon"; the parents sat in front on "two old-fashioned kitchen chairs placed side by side," while "back of this the wagon was spread with straw, and on this myself and the children sat, having no seats." In the South carts and horseback travel remained more common than wagons and chaises. Southern planters took deep pride in their horsemanship and traveled long distances on horseback, although some kept carriages for major family journeys. They continued to raise fine riding horses, while Northern horse breeders came to concentrate on vehicle-pulling trotters.

"My horse came like a bird," Elizabeth Ward wrote to her sister in 1822 about an exhilarating twenty-eight-mile chaise journey she took on her own. Writing in a way totally different from men's laconic references to such trips, she was clearly surprised at her own skill and freedom: "Well, thought I, this is pretty well . . . and never so much as took the whip in my hand all the way." American women were able to travel farther, more frequently and more freely than their counterparts in Europe. Yet their opportunities for movement continued to be limited by custom, economic dependence and the ties of their domestic obligations. They continued to have less freedom than men to travel independently outside their neighborhoods; it would have been inconceivable for a group of girls, or even adult young women, to have undertaken the all-night walking trip that Sheldon made with his companions. They were also less likely to have those skills of horsemanship, and even less free to use them. A minority of women could ride, often skillfully, and others, like Elizabeth Ward, could drive vehicles. But powerful conventions of posture and costume ensured that they did not ride astride, as men did, but sidesaddle, which offered both more danger of falling and less control of the horse.

Slaves were the only Americans whose travel was explicitly restricted. During the weekday, most plantation field hands walked only from the quarters to the fields and back again, although their routine could be punctuated with evening visits, hunting and raiding expeditions. On Sunday, "immense numbers of blacks," as Margaret Hall noted, could be seen "everywhere along the roads" in the plantation South. The Sabbath was the slaves' closest approximation to freedom, when they could walk the roads to visit friends and family in separated quarters or on other plantations. Some slaves were able to travel because they worked as teamsters or drovers on their masters' business; others journeyed with them as servants. Beyond these circles of restriction, independent travel by slaves was tantamount to escape. In most parts of the plantation South quasi-official patrols oversaw movement on the roads; they stopped slaves to ask them for passes from their masters and apprehended those who could not account for themselves. Restrictions became increasingly tight after Nat Turner's insurrection of 1831 fueled fears of slave uprisings. Unauthorized slave travel was a clandestine and off-the-highway affair.

On the Roads

American farmers had often traveled long distances to take their goods to market. Around 1800 many New England farmers were making long winter journeys, sledding their butter and cheese on horseback or even carrying it on foot to Boston or New York. Kentuckians and Ohioans poled flatboats down the Mississippi for hundreds of miles to bring the produce of the Ohio Valley to market at New Orleans. Yet by the 1830s Americans thought of these strenuous adventures as part of a heroic and primitive past. Drovers, teamsters and "market men," and improved roads and steamboats had created a system of commercial transportation. The densest crowds of travelers—a continuous procession throughout the day in most weather—could be found on the roads linking Boston, New York, and Philadelphia. Dominating the road in sheer tonnage were heavy freight wagons, pulled by four, six and even eight horses. Sometimes canvas-covered to protect their cargo from the weather, they were piled high with boxes, crates, barrels and bales. Stagecoaches, chaises, riders on horseback, all intent on making fast time, wove around them. Farmers plodded along in their "market wagons"; pedestrians kept to the roads' wide margins. At the busiest times of the year there were immense traffic jams caused by cattle, sheep, hogs, even flocks of turkeys, on their way to city butchers.

There were wagons in "endless procession," Ralph Waldo Emerson wrote from his Concord study in 1836, "which from Boston creep by my gate to all the towns of New Hampshire and Vermont." Teamsters moved slowly—a good day's teaming was twenty-five or thirty miles, with a six-horse team pulling a four-ton load. In rain or snow, traveling in what teamsters remembered as "Southern mud" or the stretch of "Jersey swamp" between New York and Philadelphia, progress could be much slower still. With many vehicles moving at two to four miles per hour, roads could easily become crowded with relatively small volumes of traffic. Even on the road leading from the thinly settled Carolina back country to Charleston, noted John Lambert, "fifteen or twenty" wagons were "often to be seen, following each other in the same track," as they carried goods and produce in and out of the city.

The growth of road-borne commerce made driving freight wagons, the work of the teamster, a rapidly expanding occupation in the early nineteenth century. By 1840 close to fifteen thousand American men worked as full-time teamsters, spending most of their days and nights on the road behind their horses, along with many more who combined farming or a trade with hauling over shorter distances. They were coarse and hard-featured men, toughened by constant exposure to the weather and, a New Hampshire man observed, "profane if the travelling was not good." The farthest-traveling teamsters were true citizens of the road. Lambert found them "rude and insolent" to other travelers who got in their way, with an "invincible antipathy" to more settled folk. Southern members of this "gentry of the whip" were, Thomas Hamilton thought, "familiarly called 'crackers' " due to the characteristic sound of that indispensable tool of their trade. Northern teamsters, who perched on a bench at the front of their wagons, angrily disputed the art of driving with Southerners, who rode one of the rear or shaft horses, guiding the team from their saddleless mounts. On major thoroughfares, teamsters stopped at taverns that specialized in providing strong drink and rough-and-ready hospitality—and which stage passengers and other more genteel travelers avoided.

At certain times of the year, the animal traffic along major Eastern roads exceeded the number of human travelers. But it was one-way traffic, which drovers—the men who collected livestock and herded them to their destination—moved off the farms into city livestock markets and butchers' stalls. From January to June, the roads saw only a trickle of cattle. Sheep began to be driven to market after shearing in July. Between October and December, enormous droves of cattle and pigs "fairly choked the roads" into the cities and created massive traffic jams.

Drovers used herding dogs—"barking at strays who straggle on the flanks of the line of march," Hawthorne noted, "then scampering to the other side and barking there"—as well as their own voices and stout staffs to keep the animals in line, but they had hard and slow going. "Thirteen miles [was] about a day's journey" for a pig drover he met in western Massachusetts, "in the course of which the drover has to run about thirty." A hundred miles' travel from farm to city market might take more than a week. The best-equipped, like the turkey drovers of New Hampshire, worked in groups of two or three, "walking alongside a wagon which carried a bed and a small stove." Others, like Hawthorne's pig drover, slept on barroom floors or crammed three to a bed in tavern chambers. At night, exhausted men turned their animals into the "strongly enclosed pastures" which tavern keepers and nearby farmers rented to them. Buying and selling livestock along the way, they arrived at the market with its rows of animal pens to make the final bargain for their herds, and then began the long trip home.

Traditionally, wherever it was cold enough to freeze hard, "winter was the time . . . for making journeys." The hazards of cold and storm were outweighed by leisure from farm work and greater speed; sleighs and sleds moved faster over snow than wagons over rutted or muddy roads. Most rural Americans were still too heavily involved with farm work to journey far during the growing season. But as urban and commercial life disengaged itself from the rhythms of agriculture, the season of travel for many began to shift to the summer, when, as the editor of the *Boston Traveller* noted in 1828, "the travelling world are all in motion."

Most of the members of the new American "travelling world" were commercial men in a hurry, the merchants and men of varied business interests who had orders to fill, sales to make, land to buy, promissory notes to collect on or money-making opportunities to look over. "Nearly one half of the trading population," it was estimated in 1836, "is constantly engaged in travelling." As roads improved they sought greater speed and comfort and more predictable schedules by traveling in the warmer months.

Traveling for pleasure—a great rarity under eighteenth-century conditions—was becoming, in Francis Grund's words, "a favorite amusement" among affluent Americans in the years after 1820. Newly married couples—if the husband was a young merchant or professional—went on "nuptial journeys." Families left the city for cooler or more bucolic places. Wealthy Southern planters came North for part of the summer months; sometimes they chose New York City, but there were seasonal colonies of Virginians and Carolinians in towns like Northampton, Massachusetts, and Litchfield, Connecticut. And the decreasing cost of steamboat travel by the 1830s put one-day steamboat excursions on the Hudson or the Connecticut rivers within the reach of city artisans and their families.

For those who could afford them, doctors began to prescribe

journeys to cure or alleviate illness through a change of climate, change of scenery or active exercise. In his search for health in the mid-1830s Homer Merriam took train, stage and steamboat from Massachusetts to Ohio, rode horseback every day for six months, returned to his home on horseback, and then went on a five-week fishing voyage! Resort communities like Ballston Spa and Saratoga, in New York, and Stafford Springs in Connecticut sprang up around medicinal springs, attracting pilgrims in search of health. Traveling not in search of health but of stimulation and fresh experience, young Nathaniel Hawthorne, who had leisure and adequate although not ample means in the 1830s, took yearly summer excursions in New England and New York, once going as far west as Niagara and Detroit.

European observers were struck by the rough democracy of American public conveyances, their absence of clear patterns of class separation or subordination. Stage drivers were notoriously unwilling to see themselves as respectful servants of their passengers' convenience. Early nineteenth-century steamboats had ladies' compartments, there were sometimes separate ladies' railway cars, and free black travelers were often forced to the outside of the coach or the deck of the boat. But accommodations were rarely partitioned by class or amount of fare paid. No private compartments allowed small groups to travel in seclusion.

The new Republic's transportation system, even as it expanded dramatically, was also chronically crowded. Although there are occasional accounts of traveling in near-empty vehicles, coaches, boats and railway cars seem usually to have been full, and often packed to bursting.

On stagecoach, steamboat and rail, American women traveled less often than men, but with an expanding freedom. Where men traveled primarily on business, women usually traced out the paths of kinship, traveling to aid ailing parents, to meet husbands at new homes, to pay long visits to sisters.

Sometimes they found it difficult. Journeying from Worcester, Massachusetts, to Middletown, Connecticut, in 1816, Maria Ward Tracy found it frightening "to take the stage all alone at so late an hour and no alternative I must ride all night. . . . I felt as I never did before." On arriving home, she continued, "all were surprised that I should come alone. All my friends and neighbors appear very happy to see me and think I had more courage than they should." Many women clearly felt that they needed protective male companions while traveling. The letters of the women of the Ward family of Shrewsbury, Massachusetts, make frequent references to finding male escorts for travel out of the state. Yet some American women had broken away from these traditional constraints. Foreign travelers were surprised by the number of women they saw on American conveyances. Women on their own were common on heavily traveled Northern stagecoaches and rail lines by the 1830s; Dickens was struck by the numbers of Lowell mill girls who were taking "the cars" back and forth to Boston in 1841.

With the remarkable developments in transportation of the last forty years, thought Goodrich in 1835, there was "scarcely an individual so reduced in circumstances, as to be unable to afford . . . to travel a couple of hundred miles from home." Four or five decades before, Goodrich knew, long-distance travel had been one-third as fast and three times as expensive. Yet although much easier than it once had been, traveling remained a relatively expensive activity. By the 1820s, for example, stage fare for a short trip like the run between Boston and Providence was two dollars and fifty cents, the equivalent of two days' wages for a skilled journeyman artisan in most trades. To take the stage between Boston and New York cost from ten to eleven dollars, or eight days' wages. The expense of an overland stage journey from New York City to western Ohio ran from seventy to eighty dollars, well over two months' wages. Because travel by water was cheaper and more efficient, the long voyage up the Mississippi from New Orleans to Cincinnati cost less, around thirty dollars. At these rates, most Americans could not travel widely or often. A relatively short stage trip was expensive enough that an ordinary craftsman or cash-poor farmer would have felt the pinch, and a long journey was a major cash outlay. But if travel was not routine, it was now part of the horizon of possibility for many ordinary individuals.

Road, River and Rail

Cold and dark or hot and dusty, the crowded stagecoach was the most common way, although not the most glamorous, Americans traveled long distances. There were a few scattered stage lines connecting Northern cities in the late eighteenth century, but their real growth began after 1790. A dense network of stage routes was built up through eastern Pennsylvania, southern New York, Massachusetts, Connecticut and Rhode Island, and was then extended over the much greater distances west and south. By the mid-1820s, stage connections could be made from Boston through to New Orleans, or from New York City as far west as St. Louis. Boston travelers in 1825 could choose from over sixty different stage routes, and over two hundred fifty coaches left the city each week. Ten years later, just before the arrival of the railroad, stage travel was at its peak; Boston had over one hundred stage lines which dispatched nearly six hundred coaches a week. Operating with continual relays of fresh horses, the stage was much faster than private conveyances and spared its passengers the driver's fatigue and exposure.

The American stages of the 1790s were simply large freight wagons, with boxes built on top to accommodate passengers, and neither springs nor braces to damp down their jolting. Seated on backless benches, the passengers all faced forward, and entered from the front by scrambling over the seats.

Over the next three decades, "stage waggons" became considerably more comfortable. By the 1830s they were suspended from their frames by strong leather straps or "thorough braces," which gave riders protection from the jolting of the roads. Passengers could enter, more decorously and with less effort, through a door in the side. The front passenger seat was turned to face rearwards, so that travelers could converse.

Nine passengers rode inside the coach on three seats. The middle seat, customarily the last occupied, often had only a leather band for back support. A tenth passenger—who, indignant travelers pointed out, also paid full fare—sat outside with the driver on the box and took the weather as it came. Unless they were all of slight build, the nine were usually tightly packed, although if the passengers agreed another traveler was sometimes squeezed in.

At all seasons, stagecoaches were highly permeable to the weather. The upper half of the coach's body was an open framework, covered by thin leather curtains which buttoned down to the solid panels below. This arrangement allowed for "free ventilation," and gave passengers an excellent, if dusty, view of the passing landscape in fair weather. "In the winter, however," as Thomas Hamilton summed up his two years of stagecoach traveling, "the advantages of this contrivance are more than apocryphal." The leather curtains kept out only part of the weather; the "wind whistled through a hundred small crevices," bringing cold, rain and snow right into the passenger compartment. The interior of a buttoned-up stage was also ordinarily very dark, for only a few vehicles had even small windows. As stages rocked along on their leather thorough braces, passengers felt, in Frederick Marryat's words, as if they were "being tossed in a blanket, often throwing you up to the top of the coach, as to flatten your hat, if not your head." On steep hills, passengers frequently had to get out to walk to lighten the load for the horses. If the stage broke down, they were recruited by the driver to make emergency repairs.

Coach travelers were thrown together on a footing of great intimacy. Fellow passengers' habits with respect to tobacco chewing, segar smoking and personal cleanliness were only too apparent after a short time, as they endured together what the abolitionist William Lloyd Garrison, a deeply experienced rider of stages, called a "prodigious sacrifice of bodily ease." Travelers frequently tried to divine their companions' individual biographies and errands before opening conversation, Garrison said, "stealthily reconnoitering each other's person for the purpose of discovering 'who and what are you?' " But when the ice was broken—it took longest among the more cautious inhabitants of the Northeastern states—the vehicle could become a forum for full-fledged masculine debate on politics or theology, an arena for bargaining, or a theater for imposture, when travelers assumed new identities or tried to shed old ones.

Steamboat travel—on the Hudson, the Connecticut or the great Western rivers—was less confining, and often far more comfortable. In 1828, Peter Cartwright and two other Methodist ministers boarded the steamboat *Velocepede* at St. Louis en route to Pittsburgh. Steamboats had been successfully operating on the Western rivers for only a little over a decade. "They were then," Cartwright said, "a new thing among us." Like other Western steamers, the *Velocepede* was a long, low, shallow-bottomed boat with a massive, clanking engine amidships and two tiers of rickety enclosed decks above. Aboard the boat Cartwright and his companions, like other Western travelers, found "a crowded cabin . . . a mixed multitude."

On most of the close to four hundred vessels that plied the Mississippi and Ohio rivers in 1830 there was a rough democracy of accommodations. There were no staterooms, and passengers bedded down on berths that folded down from the walls of the cabin. Female travelers simply slept behind a curtain. When boats became overcrowded passengers "took part in a sort of lottery" every night to determine who got the berths and who would be allotted "chairs, benches and tables" to sleep on in descending order of their desirability. On Thomas Hamilton's first night on a Mississippi steamboat, "fortune fixed me on the table, and there I lay with the knee of one man thrust directly into my stomach, and with my feet resting on the head of another."

Once on board the *Velocepede* the ministers looked at the crowd of "profane swearers, drunkards, gamblers, fiddlers, and dancers" with discomfort and revulsion. Steamboats thrust their passengers into close and often disagreeable proximity, and often painfully juxtaposed the pious with the profane. Faced with this fallen and sinful world in microcosm, Cartwright, a remarkably charismatic and powerful man, worked unceasingly to turn his fellow passengers away from their incessant card playing to discussions of history or astronomy. He debated the merits of Christianity with an unbelieving Army officer, and on Sunday, he even managed to stop the dancing and fiddling and organized a full-blown evangelical Sabbath, complete with three sermons. But this was a virtually unique attempt at reforming steamboat life, which on the majority of Western vessels remained heterogeneous and disorderly. The boats that plied the Hudson and Connecticut rivers and Long Island Sound were sometimes more orderly and sober, but their passenger arrangements were much the same.

The canal boats pulled by horse teams along the Erie Canal offered even more cramped accommodations. Passengers found themselves "lying packed like herrings in a barrel," sometimes on "repulsively filthy" berths. On a canal-boat journey between Albany and Utica, New York, a company of sixteen Presbyterian ministers outdid Cartwright and outraged their fellow travelers with excessive piety; they monopolized the passenger cabin day and night for religious services, missionary conferences and prayer meetings.

"I saw today for the first time a Rail Way Car," wrote Christopher Columbus Baldwin in 1835. "What an object of wonder! How marvellous it is in every particular. It appears like a thing of life. . . . I cannot describe the strange sensation produced on seeing the train of cars come up. And when I started in them

. . . it seemed like a dream." In the ten years after 1830, Americans saw the "Rail Way" as the most striking sign of change in a time filled with changes. With no more than seven hundred miles of track laid down in 1835 and only three thousand in 1840, only a small fraction of the American people had traveled on a railroad. Yet it became a reference point of modernity, against which other aspects of life could be measured, and the future prognosticated. Its unprecedented speed made it the "go-ahead" vehicle for a people "all in motion." Under the most favorable possible conditions—good weather, a good road, and strong, rested horses—a stagecoach might manage eight or nine miles an hour. The small locomotives of the 1830s, pulling a handful of cars over uneven track, could travel at fifteen to twenty miles an hour—twice as fast, over long distances, as anything passengers had previously experienced. It was, the eighteen-year-old Caroline Fitch of Boston wrote after her journey to Worcester on the Western Railroad, "the lightning flash" set against the stagecoach's slow "dawning of day." Just as unprecedented was the noise. Like other passengers, Miss Fitch felt "doomed to my own reflections" when she rode "the cars," since the roaring of the engine and the grating and squealing of iron wheels on iron rails "prevented me enjoying conversation." Ash and cinders from the wood-burning engine showered on the passengers; many railway cars were as open as stagecoaches, and the soot seemed to find its way in everywhere. Early American "Rail Way" passengers disembarked dirty and half-deafened by the noise, but deeply impressed by the speed. "It was 'whew!' and we were there, and 'whew!' and we were back again."

Upsettings and Explosions: The Hazards of Travel

Chaises and wagons, stages, steamboats and railways offered Americans not only greater opportunities to travel long distances, but increased danger. Although horse-drawn vehicles moved relatively slowly, their low speeds did not make traveling on them safe. The materials they were made of—wood, leather and small amounts of iron—were fragile even at early nineteenth-century speeds. Collisions sometimes caused serious accidents, but "upsettings," the overturning of vehicles on the road, were far more frequent and dangerous. Boulders, potholes, runaway horses, steep grades, broken axles or suddenly shattering wheels could all cause upsets, sometimes disastrous ones. Stagecoaches were built substantially enough so that upsettings were not often fatal, although passengers could be hurt. On any long journey, an experienced traveler would expect to be upset once or twice, but it was often much worse; a New Yorker reported in 1829 that his stage had overturned nine times in the course of a single journey to Cincinnati and back. Heavy stages sometimes broke through flimsy bridges or fell through the ice crossing a frozen river, but the most terrifying misadventure of all for stage passengers was to plummet down a steep mountain road with the horses out of control.

In more lightly built sleighs and chaises, drivers and passengers were exposed to much greater risks from overturning. They were thrown out of careening vehicles onto the road, or injured by broken pieces of the frame. Teamsters, riding alone up on their unenclosed seats, sometimes fell asleep and pitched off their wagons, or as the *Massachusetts Spy* reported in 1801, fatally entangled themselves when "the skirts of an outside coat caught in a wheel."

Drink caused many accidents. Two sailors rented a horse and chaise in Newburyport, Massachusetts, in 1818, took it on the road, and began to pass a bottle back and forth. They overturned the vehicle twice on their way out of the city, damaged it badly and decided to return. As they made their drunken way back, the Boston *Columbian Centinel* reported, "they again upset, a splinter entered the side of one of them, and penetrating to the heart, instantly put a period to his existence." Inebriated men ran children over in the streets and drunken stage drivers risked their passengers' lives. Temperance reform almost surely made American roads safer.

The new technologies of travel, particularly as developed and operated by Americans, were even riskier. The steamboat *Helen McGregor* was leaving the Memphis docks in February of 1830 when the head of the starboard boiler cracked, and the ensuing explosion blew fifty men into the river. They were flayed alive or killed by inhaling live steam. Such explosions were almost a routine hazard of steamboat travel. Southworth Allen Howland's *Steamboat Disasters and Railroad Accidents in the United States*, published in 1840, provided short accounts of the better-known catastrophes, including this one. It was a popular book, and a fairly thick one. Charles Dickens reported that American friends advised him to find a steamboat berth toward the back of the boat, because it was the safest place in the event a boiler burst. All Western steamboats used inexpensive but fragile and unpredictable high-pressure engines, and even the inherently safer low-pressure engines of Eastern steamboats could explode if poorly maintained. Hot fireboxes, sparks and cinders were constant sources of danger to wooden decks and flammable cargo. Nearly a third of all the steamboats that ran on the Mississippi before 1850 were lost in accidents.

Railway engines rarely exploded, but passengers on the trains of the 1830s took their chances with derailments and collisions, or with axles and vehicle frames breaking. Negligence and inexperience, rather than the failure of materials, contributed most to the dangers. There was little consciousness of safety anywhere in early nineteenth-century American travel. "The running of machinery as long as it will last," noted Howland, with no regard for its condition until it actually broke down, was a common practice among his countrymen. Steamboat and railway crews, "that class of men to whose charge we often commit our lives and property," often knew relatively little about the machines in their charge and took risks which they poorly understood, exhibiting "gross carelessness, or what is equally as bad, reckless daring." American passengers accepted these risks with seeming equanimity as the price of rapid motion.

Before 1800, any trip outside the familiar bounds of locality was likely to be slow, difficult, an uncertain adventure and a physical challenge. Even after decades of remarkable change in the speed and scale of transportation, travel in the United States was still often an uncomfortable and hazardous enterprise. But the dangers and discomforts of traveling were less important to Americans than the opportunities that it presented. Hundreds of thousands of them took to the roads in wagons and chaises, thronged stagecoaches, boarded steamboats, eagerly waited for the railroad—where many of their eighteenth-century counterparts would have trudged on foot. The breaking up of age-old constraints on human movement was exhilarating.

6

I N NO country in the world," boasted a Philadelphian in 1810, "is the practice of music more universally extended." His proud claim would have been hard to assess, but music making and dancing were widely shared by Americans of all social classes and both races. Music is usually discussed in specialized separation from other parts of American life, but that is not the way in which it was experienced by a people who depended on their own resources for entertainment after long and laborious days of work. The American "practice of music," aside from the relatively sophisticated concert life of a small urban minority, was an affair of participant performers and small, informal audiences—in dwellings and schoolhouses, churches and taverns, and the streets of cities and of slave quarters. Their musical world was still shaped by the oldest instruments of all, singing voices and rhythmically moving feet.

"Old Ditties" and "Sentimental Songs"

> It came upon a Martinmas day
> When the green leaves were a falling
> Sir James the Graham of the West Country
> Fell in love with Barbara Allen.

The homes of the New Hampshire countryside where Horace Greeley was growing up before 1820 resounded with already-ancient ballads. "When neighbors and neighbors' wives drew together at the house of one of their number for an evening visit," he remembered, his mother and her friends frequently sang "old ditties . . . such as 'Barbara Allen' " from British oral tradition. This was hardly unusual; as the nineteenth century began many American families, North, South and West, were singing around their hearthsides the unwritten traditional songs that folklorists were later to collect. "Aunt Lois Wax-worthy," an archetypal farm wife in the *Farmer's Almanack* in 1838, still could not churn her butter "without her accustomed twang of Chevy Chase," another traditional ballad whose roots in narrative went back to a fourteenth-century battle on the Scottish border.

Along with farming practices, dietary preferences and religious beliefs, settlers from the British Isles had brought their songs with them from their home communities. From the seventeenth century on, Americans sang them—usually unaccompanied—in chimney corners, haymows and tobacco fields, and only rarely wrote them down. In a chain of oral transmission across the generations, men and women passed their songs along from one singer to another. This most deeply rooted American music was in some ways the most evanescent. Some of the great ballads have continued in living use in Appalachia, but the slow mutation of tunes over the years has made it difficult to reconstruct precisely what early nineteenth-century versions sounded like.

"On Friday morning he did go," went a verse to the song "Springfield Mountain,"

> Down to the mountain for to mow
> He mowed, he mowed all around the field
> With a poisonous serpent at his heel

Americans also sang some ballads that had originated in the New World, often based on a striking local occurrence. "Springfield Mountain" was probably based on the story of Timothy Myrick of Wilbraham, Massachusetts, who was fatally bitten by a rattlesnake while mowing hay in 1761. But most of their songs belonged to the British Isles, and English-speaking Americans were never closer to their cousins across the Atlantic than when they sang them. With their narrative origins in the distant past, the British ballads' stories were usually compressed, sparing of detail, unsentimental, even grim—tales of tragic death, jealousy, loss, violence, the blighting of love, the murder of illegitimate children. They reflected the words and ways of an ancient countryside, sometimes transforming the prosaic concerns of everyday life into stark poetry.

Men and women clung longest and most faithfully to the old songs in the deepest, most isolated parts of the countryside. To know and sing nothing else was to be stamped a rustic, like the "country girl in the heart of Massachusetts" at whose rural isolation Benjamin Franklin had poked fun in the eighteenth century—"who has never heard any other than psalm tunes or 'Chevy Chase,' 'The Children in the Wood,' and other such old, simple ditties." But most ordinary Americans' music making encompassed more than these traditional songs. They sang many others which had their origins in print and urban commerce, but which they brought into oral tradition.

"Songs, ballads, etc. . . . purchased from a ballad printer and seller in Boston . . . to show what articles of this kind are in vogue with the vulgar at this time, 1814," the renowned New England printer and publisher Isaiah Thomas scrawled on the top leaf of a collection of broadside song sheets. In the bundle were almost three hundred songs or ballads printed in Boston between 1810 and 1814, which Thomas had the rare foresight to imagine might be of interest to later generations. The songs were of both English and American origin; their anonymous authors sometimes wrote down what they heard in the streets but usually composed them. Such ballads were the songs ordinary city folk sang; in New York as well as Boston they bought sheets for a penny or two from small printing offices. They then fitted the broadsides' words to well-known tunes and sang them in homes, streets and taverns, just as Londoners did. The same songs were sometimes published, just as ephemerally, in newspapers as well.

The broadside ballads also had audiences and performers in the countryside. Travelers passing through, farmers returning from market, teamsters and stage drivers brought copies of the broadsides themselves or remembered versions to pass along to other singers. They "caught a new melody by attentively listening to it, and learned the words by assiduous repetition," as Francis Underwood remembered of country singers in New England. Sometimes a broadside song, written by an unknown scribbler in New York or London, became so popular that it was incorporated into a community's oral tradition, its urban, printed origins forgotten, and endured to the present to be collected as a folk song. Some American singers acquired an extraordinary oral repertoire of ancient ballads and broadside songs. A man in early nineteenth-century Enfield, Massachusetts, "knew the words and music of above two hundred songs."

The songs "in vogue with the vulgar" offer a virtually unique glimpse of what ordinary Americans in New England were singing about in the years around the War of 1812. The most popular themes were those of American public life; almost a third of the songs dealt with political and military events. Most in demand were narratives of the ongoing war's battles, such as Commander Oliver Hazard Perry's victory against the British on Lake Erie, or the epic naval duel of the *Constitution* and the *Guerrière*. But the people of New England were also still listening to songs about events and issues decades old—accounts of colonial struggles with Britain, the Revolutionary War and the political affairs of the new nation's first decade. The lengthy narrative song "American Taxation" was one of them. It had first appeared in print in Boston before the Revolution; singers in the New England countryside were still singing it from memory well into the 1820s.

Fully one-fourth of the ballads that street hawkers and small shops sold were dramatically heightened versions of everyday life. They told a rich variety of English and American stories, loosely based on fact and folklore, about courtship, seduction and sexual misbehavior, domestic trickery and conflict, and tales of outrageously good or bad luck: "The Lawyer Outwitted," "The Old Maid's Last Prayer," "The Deceitful Young Man." Next came songs dealing with extreme and sensational events—"The Dreadful Hurricane at New Orleans," "Shocking Earthquakes at Charleston," floods, shipwrecks and comets, murders and executions, piracy and Indian warfare. Only a very few were religious songs.

None of Thomas' ballads were wholeheartedly obscene, but many of the courtship songs, like "The Farmer's Daughter," "A New Song in Favor of Courting" or "The Female Haymakers" were bawdy or at least suggestive, more likely to be sung at taverns, shops or in the fields away from disapproving ears. A verse of "Corydon and Phyllis" told how

> Ten thousand times he kiss'd her
> While sporting on the green
> And as he fondly press'd her
> Her pretty leg was seen

with the refrain

> And something else
> And something else
> What I do know
> But dare not tell.

Some singers undoubtedly passed along bawdier versions of these songs that were not committed to writing.

But some of the broadside pieces that the "vulgar" sang were originally part of a more sophisticated musical world—songs by identifiable composers like the prolific Irishman Thomas Moore, in which words were set to self-consciously composed tunes—and had originally been published in much more expensive form in songbooks or sheet music. These songs began as the music sung in the polished households of the city's most prosperous families. The humble printers who published broadside sheets pirated their words, and poorer folk picked them up from the song sheets and either caught the tunes by ear or substituted more familiar melodies.

Such music was emerging to great social importance in the early nineteenth century in the form of "parlor songs." They were modest vocal compositions, sung by young women accompanying themselves on the pianoforte in fashionable parlors throughout the United States.

Like traditional ballads and broadside songs, they too were part of a shared British-American musical culture; British lyricists and composers dominated the American market until after 1840. But parlor songs created for a prosperous public a world of the tender emotions, far more sentimental and idealized than anything in the music of poorer Americans.

> O share my cottage, gentle maid
> It only waits for thee
> To give a sweetness to its shade
> And happiness to me

contrasted sharply with the explicit sexuality of "Corydon and Phyllis" or the spare lyrics of "Barbara Allen." Well-to-do households on both sides of the Atlantic throbbed with highly conventionalized lyrics on romantic love, familial affection and grief over the loss of loved ones.

Parlor songs were gradually democratized in the nineteenth century, eventually becoming the secular music most often sung in American households. Americans who never saw sheet music learned them from broadsides, occasionally newspapers, and other singers; over a period of several years, a highly popular parlor song would become incorporated into the oral tradition. Ordinary folk displayed a striking eagerness to take up genteel music, but in the early nineteenth century they sang parlor songs alongside older ones. "Uncle Peter," a New Hampshire country singer of the 1830s, performed traditional ballads, broadside songs of various dates—and parlor tunes that had first appeared in Boston ten or fifteen years earlier. The Stevens family of Wyoming County, New York, sang a similar mix of old songs and new ones as they recorded them in their unique manuscript songbook begun around 1840.

The genteel and affluent were far less interested in the music their poorer or more rustic Americans sang. John Pendleton Kennedy rendered a clash between two musical worlds in *Swallow Barn,* a portrait of Virginia plantation life in the 1820s. When a group of well-to-do young people asked an elderly white musician to oblige them with a song, he responded with a broadside tune, "American Taxation":

> While I rehearse my story, Americans give ear
> Of Britain's fading glory, you presently will hear
> I'll give a true relation, attend to what I say
> Concerning the taxation of North America.

They rejected it disdainfully after two verses. It was not "sentimental and pitiful" enough. After they discovered that the old singer hadn't learned any "touching, sorrowful" parlor songs, they told him "stop there; we don't want to hear the music." Later, they asked him to pick up his fiddle and play a dance tune. Searching for the "sentimental and pitiful," such Americans left broadside narratives to the "vulgar," and had little interest in the ancient ballads, whose unsentimental narratives, repetitive refrains and rough melodies spoke of a world they had abandoned.

Over several decades, the new songs took up an increasingly larger share of what people listened to. Country families in the

Northeast were quickest to take up parlor songs, just as they were to accept other commercially produced goods—brooms, stoves, factory-made chairs and looking glasses—for their households. By the 1830s, broadside publication had declined substantially. The bawdy courting songs, the recitals of executions and battles, "The Lawyer Outwitted" and "The Old Maid's Last Prayer," were less often printed although they were still being sung from memory. Traditional balladry had not disappeared from the Northern countryside, but it was flourishing far more vigorously among the people of the mountain South. Yet in 1840 the old ballads and broadside songs could still be heard not only around country firesides but at the heart of the American Industrial Revolution, in the factories of Lowell. "In the long winter evenings" while tending machines in the Boston Manufacturing Company's mills, Harriet Hanson Robinson and her friends from northern New England sang "the old-time songs our mothers had sung, such as 'Barbara Allen,' 'Lord Lovell,' 'Captain Kid,' 'Hull's Victory.' "

"Had a Violin and Commenced Dancing"

Margaret Hall was in danger of being "danced to death in this grave country . . . where the very Professors of the colleges join in the amusement," during her journey through the United States with her husband in 1827 and 1828. The Halls socialized extensively with the new nation's small elite of wealth and fashion, attending a seemingly endless succession of balls in Boston, New York, Philadelphia, Baltimore, Washington, Richmond and Charleston. The great planters, merchants, successful professional men and their wives that made up the best society of early nineteenth-century America were notably devoted to dancing. But throughout the country, farm girls and apprentice boys as well as "grave professors," Louisiana slaves as well as fashionable ladies, found recreation, exercise and emotional release in the dance.

The gamut of occasions for the dance was wide in American

life. Most informally, small groups gathered in houses or at taverns to scrape up impromptu dances. "There were about 30 attended," wrote the twenty-two-year-old Sally Brown in her diary for September 17, 1833, about a dance at her cousin Asa's house in Plymouth, Vermont, where they "had a violin and commenced dancing at candle lighting time and continued until three in the morning when the party broke up." William Sidney Mount's painting of 1830, *A Rustic Dance,* depicts such a gathering in a country house crowded with couples, where "dancing commenced in the parlor, 'tough and tight,' " as Miriam Green described it, with the dancers' "feet flying like drumsticks on the floor." (See illustration no. 36.)

Raisings, huskings, apple-paring bees, sleighing parties, weddings often ended with neighborhood dances; John Lewis Krimmel painted a *Quilting Party* in 1813 that shows the quilting frame dismantled and a dance just getting under way. Courting couples in New England "went jingling away" in their sleighs, Harriet Beecher Stowe recalled, and "a supper and a dance awaited them at a village tavern ten miles off." Christmas, Thanksgiving or Election Day occasioned village or plantation balls, with more elaborate arrangements. "In all the large towns dancing assemblies used to be stately held," said Stowe, when a large and prosperous house was thrown "all open and lighted with the best of tallow candles." In Worcester, Massachusetts, the yearly Cattle Show Balls included, noted Christopher Columbus Baldwin in his diary, "more than an hundred ladies and gentlemen," an elaborate catered supper and a six-piece orchestra. Most formal and impressive were the dances like those which the Halls attended—expensive and elaborately arranged balls, lit by chandeliers in which burned enough candles to light most farmhouses through the winter. Here professional musicians played, French dancing teachers might call the figures, and the latest steps and tunes could be seen and heard.

At the end of the eighteenth century, most white Americans danced to steps and music which would have been easily recognized by any British traveler—the reel and the contradance, earlier sometimes called the "longways, for as many as will," which put men and women in two opposing lines. Like the ballads, English and Scots-Irish settlers had brought them over in their "cultural baggage." Contradances were as communal in their form as one-room houses or one-pot meals. They were group performances, in which couples moved in predetermined patterns up and down the long lines of dancers. Just around 1800, the cotillion, or quadrille—a four-couple dance directly ancestral to the modern square dance—arrived in the United States from France. Dancing the cotillion or not was at first a sign of partisan political allegiance. Pro-French Jeffersonian Republicans embraced the new dance while Anglophile Federalists spurned it. But as political passions cooled, cotillion dancing rapidly gained popularity throughout the fashionable urban world, and then began to spread more gradually through rural America, where dance tunes and steps became complicated mixes of the old and new.

Americans performing the cotillion danced in small groups, moving in synchrony with three other couples. They had moved at least part of the way between the long communal lines of the contradance and the freely moving pairs of later ballroom dancing. Many young people came to see the contradance as emblematic of outmoded and rustic ways. "The elder prigs," Baldwin complained, forced the younger company at the Worcester Cattle Show Ball in 1833 into "dancing alternately a cotillion and a contradance." Showing their discomfort, many of the dancers went "wrong on purpose, lest it appear by going right, they had been accustomed to country company."

New dance tunes and cotillion figures were most often introduced to the United States in a New York or Philadelphia ballroom, often under the eyes of a French or Italian dancing master. Traveling dancing teachers studied the most popular new steps and music before they undertook their next journeys into the country. Young women visiting from smaller towns memorized dances to teach their friends at home. Within a year or two, a publisher might incorporate them into a new edition of an American dance book. Along any one of these channels new dances were learned and passed along repeatedly until they could be found, a few years later, in farmhouse parlors and rural taverns.

Dancing—as it does today—most deeply engaged young people in their courting years, the late teens and early twenties. Mount's numerous dance scenes were overwhelmingly populated by young couples. Outside of the fashionable world a smaller number of married people danced regularly, although once or twice a year the festivities would "commence with the young people" and "creep gradually upwards among the elders . . . till the music finally subdued them, and into the dance they went."

In the earliest decades of the nineteenth century, Stowe reminded her readers, there were country balls "at which the minister and his lady, though never uniting in the dance, always gave an approving attendance, and where all the decorous, respectable old church-members brought their children." Her father, Lyman Beecher, the redoubtable champion of New England religious orthodoxy, had been an inveterate fiddle player as a young minister in Easthampton, Long Island, in the 1800s. But things were to change.

In 1817 the English Lieutenant Francis Hall entered a tavern in Lexington, Virginia, to find that a party of young people "had met to have a dance" in one of its public rooms. In the other a black-coated minister was "pacing up and down," and groaning aloud at the revelry next door. A member of the dancing company looked in to cajole him, pleading that to "jump about to the cat" was as harmless as to "sit still with our hands before us." He responded that "the difference is that the one can be done to the glory of God and the other cannot," and resumed his pacing. This nameless Virginia preacher was one of an increasing number of Americans who saw dancing as a moral problem—no longer an unremarkable part of everyday life but an exercise in display and sensuality.

Evangelical ministers, North and South, came to attack dancing and other secular recreations ever more vigorously in the course of revival campaigns and regular preaching. By the 1830s, American clergymen outside Unitarian and Episcopalian circles were far more likely to condemn dancing than to give it even grudging tolerance, and the proportion of Americans who danced was actually declining. Like drinking, dancing began to sharply differentiate Americans' styles of life, and to split communities. The line of respectability in the Massachusetts hill town of Enfield was "drawn at dancing," said Underwood, once Evangelical sentiment became powerful in the 1830s; "the country balls" still given there "were attended only by the worldly and irreligious." Many Americans' interest in dancing waxed and waned alternately with waves of religious enthusiasm; the itinerant dancing master Nelson Mount wrote his brother William Sidney in 1837 that his dancing school in Monticello, Georgia, was "principally made up with back sliding Methodists," but that prospects were much poorer in Macon, where "a great revival has been going on." Large numbers of Americans continued to dance, but with the awareness that many of their countrymen and countrywomen had come to consider it sinful.

Increasing hostility to dancing coincided with the appearance of another, radically different dance form. The "valse"— later waltz—reached the United States by way of Paris in the 1820s, introducing an entirely different language of bodily movement. Valsers completely abandoned the corporate or small-group form of earlier dances and danced as couples, whirling around the ballroom on their own. Partners clasped each other face to face in a stylized embrace. Even when performed with the utmost propriety, the valse provoked numerous accusations of licentiousness from Americans disturbed by its challenges to the social and sexual symbolism of dancing. But valsing stayed within the fashionable ballrooms of Charleston, Baltimore, Philadelphia and New York, as dancers in the countryside and smaller towns proved much slower to adopt it than they had the cotillion. Evangelical opposition may have been galvanized by the valse, but for the most part ministers were condemning as sensual the contradances and cotillions—dances whose side-by-side pairings and minimal body contact seem remarkably chaste to modern eyes.

Yet while some Americans abandoned their dances as sinful, others strove to learn new ones and become more polished performers. Instruction in the social graces and the latest cotillion figures became increasingly popular outside the fashionable circles of city life. Writing in his diary in the early 1840s "I think I shall go if I have to go alone," the eighteen-year-old carpenter's apprentice Edward Jenner Carpenter saved up a month's "overwork" payments to subscribe to a dancing school offered by a traveling master. He and two dozen other apprentices and young journeymen took lessons for two months, and finished up with a ball in frank imitation of the town's wealthy citizens or "big bugs." Young citizens of commercial villages and market towns, intent on adopting genteel ways, were increasingly eager to take up the dance styles of the fashionable world—barring the valse. Itinerant dancing masters found patronage from aspiring men and women from Greenfield to Milledgeville, Georgia, and Decatur, Illinois.

"Among the Blacks"

In her extensive catalog of what she disliked about the United States, Frances Trollope included most everyday music, asserting in 1832 that she "scarcely ever heard a white American, male or female, go through an air without being out of tune before the end of it." Yet "among the blacks," she admitted, there were "good voices, singing in tune." Those who gave enslaved Americans credit for little else could not deny their rich, vigorous and distinctive musical life.

Slaves walking from the fields to the great house of the Maryland plantation on which Frederick Douglass was born "would make the dense old woods, for miles around, reverberate with their wild songs, revealing at once the highest joy and the deepest sadness." The song and dance of American slaves was a complex hybrid of African and English styles. There were performances in some places, relatively isolated from whites or with more slaves of the first or second generation, that would not have been strange in West African villages. As succeeding slave generations' links with their African origins grew more distant, they incorporated English words, melodies, instruments and steps into their music, transforming them in the process. Blacks sang with multiple and complicated rhythms, far more powerful and propulsive than any whites could manage. Where white Americans usually performed ballads or parlor songs solo before silent audiences, slaves created group songs in which all participated, responding antiphonally to the leader's call. "The chorus strikes in with the burden," observed Frances Kemble Butler, "between each phase of the melody chanted by a single voice." She added that they sang "in admirable time and true accent." Black singers were also far freer, as Douglass said, to "compose and sing as they went along," improvising a song or adding wholly new verses to a familiar one on the spot.

Wherever black men and women worked together in large groups, they sang antiphonal songs that marked the rhythms of their labor. Songs helped black rowers time their strokes, woodsmen mark their blows as they felled trees, or cotton pickers, cane cutters and rice harvesters keep pace with their work. "We would pick cotton and sing, pick and sing all day," wrote a black autobiographer. Occasionally masters required slaves to sing in the fields, presumably to make the work go faster; a few others attempted to prohibit leisure-time singing in the cabins. Most appear to have let the slaves' music alone.

Afro-American songs spoke more often and more directly of everyday reality than did the words of white music. Many were songs of love and courtship, far franker and more realistic than the parlor songs. Slaves sang about recent plantation events, often in ways not easily decoded by white hearers, or poured out the trials of bondage. At times they expressed, even if obliquely, a deep longing for freedom, like this one sung in Louisiana:

> Harper's creek and roarin' ribber,
> Thar, my dear, we'll live forebber
> Den we'll go to Ingin nation,
> All I want in dis creation,
> Is pretty little wife and big plantation.

Others songs—clearly not intended to be overheard—dealt more directly with master-slave relationships, like the complaint Douglass recorded,

> We raise de wheat
> Dey gib us de corn . . .
> We peal de meat
> Dey gib us de skin
> And dat's de way
> Dey takes us in.

Slaves often created their own instruments—particularly African banjos made from hollowed-out gourds and covered with coonskin. They used "the bones"—a pair of shank bones or jawbones from a slaughtered animal—to beat out rhythms. Even without instruments of any kind, slave musicians could still create complex and driving rhythms for dancing by "patting juba," as Solomon Northup described it, "striking the hands on the knees, then striking the hands together, then striking the right shoulder with one hand, the left with the other—all the while keeping time with the feet, and singing." While visiting a South Carolina plantation in 1836, Caroline Howard Gilman noticed how the fiddler Diggory had used "his quick eye and ear" during a few visits to Charleston to learn "the tunes and figures of some newly-introduced cotillions." Many slave musicians, like Diggory, mastered the European violin, picking the bowings and fingerings up by ear as did the great majority of whites.

Diggory played the new dances first for his master's dancing parties, and later in the quarters, but blacks and whites danced the same measures in very different ways. Plantation dances in Louisiana often lasted "until broad daylight." Dancers competed in "tearing down," trying to exhaust each other, Northup said, with "he or she remaining longest on the floor receiving the most uproarious commendation." At a slave ball on a Georgia plantation, Frances Kemble Butler could see only chaos in "all the contortions, and springs, and flings, and kicks, and capers" of the dancers. Slaves danced their own versions of the reels and cotillions of their masters, but with a propulsive energy, and an uninhibited sensuality, that ethnocentric white observers could not understand or approve. Black Americans were most African in how they moved their bodies in the dance. They held themselves fluidly and flexibly, and rotated rhythmically from the hips. Blacks, in turn, were far from complimentary about the stiff and rigid way in which white men and women danced. "Listless and snail-like" white people, Northup thought, danced "the slow-winding cotillion . . . with measured step."

In the years after 1800, powerful religious emotion more and more pervaded the world of American slaves. As evangelical religion progressed among them they came under the same pressures as whites to abandon dancing, and many did. Methodist preachers had been so successful in a Georgia plantation neighborhood in the late 1830s that they had silenced "above twenty violins," a visiting Englishman reported. But even those Afro-Americans who gave up the joys of the dance could not abandon the rhythms of bodily movement so ingrained in their daily life. In their worship services they participated with the same "ecstasy of motion, clapping of hands, tossing of heads," the ex-slave James Smith of Virginia remembered, that they had devoted to dancing. On the South Carolina coast slaves gave up "worldly" dance but drew on African precedent to create the "shout"—a sacred dance in which participants linked arms and shuffled slowly in a circle while chanting rhythmically.

They also began to create the spirituals. Sung at camp meetings and worship in the quarters, these "catches and hallelujah-songs of their own composing," in the words of a disapproving white minister, fused the powerful rhythms and call-and-response antiphony of other Afro-American music with extraordinary religious intensity. Each spiritual, as Levi Coffin recalled of North Carolina in the 1820s, was "a sort of prayer in rhyme, in which the same words occurred again and again," and Caroline Howard Gilman wrote down the words of one sung by South Carolina slaves in the 1830s:

> Master Jesus is my captain
> He is my all in all
> He give me grace to conquer
> And take me home to rest
>
> I'm walking on to Jesus
> Hallelujah!
> I'm walking on to Jesus
> Hallelujah!

Over the rest of the nineteenth century slave spirituals come to have a powerful impact on the religious music of white as well as black southerners, helping to shape their words and melodies. Still composing and singing "as they went along," slaves were making some of the most powerful music that America was ever to know.

Pianofortes and Fiddles

After a long trip through sparsely settled Southern countryside, Margaret Hall walked into the house of a merchant in the still raw and rough-hewn port town of Mobile, Alabama, in 1827.

She was surprised to find a pianoforte being played by his young daughter, who "strummed her lesson . . . under the guidance of a foreign teacher." Nothing could have been farther from the unlettered, immensely powerful music making of the slaves than the parlor accomplishments of young white women of prosperous families—of all Americans the most likely to have some training in the "science of music." In the eighteenth century a few cultivated American ladies had learned to play the harpsichord or the Spanish guitar; from 1800 on affluent women in much larger numbers were taking up the new pianoforte, which came to have great social as well as musical power.

"In almost every mansion" in Boston, a Swedish visitor had observed in 1823, "it was customary to have music in the evening"; on one summer night he took a leisurely stroll among the city's most prosperous homes to enjoy the "melodious sounds" of the pianofortes within. This domestic music making was customarily an occasion for display of daughters' talents, and it became part of the ritual of courtship in many households. Parlor music was not simply an affectation—many young women learned to play skillfully, and came to a genuine love of music. But both for those who played well and those who played poorly, it had another significance.

Well-to-do city families placed pianofortes prominently in their parlors along with other expensive items of furniture. To exhibit this "badge of gentility" was a matter of conspicuous consumption, needing considerable wealth. A relatively cheap pianoforte, at two hundred dollars, would have cost a city carpenter or cabinetmaker nearly half a year's wages; at six hundred dollars or more, the most expensive ran as much as a small house, or a country minister's annual salary. Pianofortes were prominently displayed in the backgrounds of portraits commissioned by affluent American families, unmistakable symbols of homes which could afford to cultivate the arts as well as the domestic virtues. The pianoforte in the parlor, the sentimental parlor song and the cultivated young woman became a virtually inseparable trio in the early nineteenth century—a powerful image of refined domesticity.

The arrival of the first pianoforte in a rural community brought the power of city ways into the countryside in the most dramatic possible way. "It is impossible to exaggerate the sensation that was produced in the village," wrote Francis Underwood of his boyhood community, "when that instrument was first heard. It was a clear, moon-lit evening in summer, and the windows were open. Passers-by lingered in the street, and an admiring row of boys appeared to be impaling themselves on the fence pickets as they leaned forward to listen." The pianoforte's range of tones and harmonies deeply impressed its new hearers, who were used to the sound of country fiddles, militia fifes and drums, and twanging mouth harps. The great majority of American households were never graced by a pianoforte. Yet it came to symbolize the material and social ambitions of many families. Half in envy, half in admiration, they expanded their range of aspiration.

If the pianoforte was primarily a woman's instrument, most others were reserved for men. Music making in the open air was particularly a male preserve. Boys and young men played fifes and drums, the instruments of martial music, for the military exercises of militia detachments. In larger commercial towns, there were some amateur players of brasses and woodwinds who made up larger military bands or came together informally to play on civil occasions. In the cities a comparative handful of professional instrumentalists could be found who gave lessons, and played for theaters, concerts and formal balls.

By far the commonest of American instruments was the fiddle, but it had an ambiguous social status. Fiddlers, almost universal in paintings and drawings of dance scenes, accompanied most contradances and cotillions. In the countryside, a young man with a musical bent often supplied the music for his neighborhood's dances, only to give it up on reaching maturer years. Christopher Columbus Baldwin met an old friend with whom he had grown up in the rural community of Templeton, Massachusetts; now a serious and sedate Congregational minister, he had been "our standard fiddler at all the junkets." Middle-aged men may often have passed their instruments on to their sons, once they judged that their dancing and fiddling years were over; no owners of fiddles older than thirty could be found in Worcester County probate inventories. To the evangelical opponents of dancing, the fiddle was the devil's own instrument, particularly associated with drink and sensuality.

Away from country neighborhoods—on the plantation or in the city—playing the fiddle for dancing was often considered a servile activity. Slaves in the South and free black men in the North made up a disproportionately large number of the fiddlers who played at balls, assemblies and tavern parties. William Sidney Mount's frequent paintings of dance scenes usually portray black fiddlers; and his brother Nelson complained from Illinois that although he could have "found profitable business at drawing the bow" for dances, his self-esteem would not allow him to work alongside the "two black men at the same business."

There were other, simpler ways of providing accompaniment for dancing. One was "mouth music." "We never had a fiddler at such times," wrote Miriam Green of her New Hampshire neighborhood, "but we often had Uncle Peter, aided by other voices, to sing for us, which was about as good." Some accompanists surely also played the small iron music makers called mouth harps or Jew's harps, widely found in eighteenth- and nineteenth-century archaeological sites.

"The Performance of Church Music"

"All who have a voice, both young and old, male and female," wrote the New Hampshire printer and politician Isaac Hill, "can unite in the performance of church music." Many Americans turned the hymns and psalm tunes learned at Sabbath worship into everyday music for work and social occasions and "the farmer's evening fireside." Pious workingmen sang sacred songs at the plow or in the shop, like Deacon Cooley, who, according to the *Farmer's Almanack*, "always drives his team to the tune of [the well-known hymn] Old Canterbury." Women's charitable and missionary societies customarily closed their meetings with hymns. Harriet Beadle's family sang "old hymns" after meeting, "on Sunday afternoons toward twilight."

The "ultra-pious," in Underwood's phrase, exclusively sang hymns at home as a way of keeping secular music at bay; others, like Harriet Hanson Robinson and her friends at Lowell, or the Stevens family of New York, sang hyms comfortably along with more worldly songs.

The Sabbath itself was not a day of silence, but of widely shared music. Some city churches had well-trained choirs and elaborate organs; their congregations were primarily audiences. But participatory congregational singing—central to most American religious traditions—was dominant in the churches of the countryside. From backwoods Tennessee chapels to New England meetinghouses, in what was for many of them their most deeply expressive action of the week, hundreds of thousands of Americans sang hymns and psalms together on Sunday.

Written texts and tunes were the ultimate basis of Protestant congregational singing, but many congregations were only partially literate, and hymn books were expensive and usually far fewer than the number of singers. The actual "practice of music" in most American churches remained oral, and without instrumental accompaniment. Worshipers sang a handful of tunes from memory, and fitted a wide variety of psalm and hymn texts to the music. They memorized some of the most familiar, often-sung words as well, but well into the nineteenth century American congregations continued in the practice of "lining out"—in which a leader, holding his hymn book, read a line or two at a time to the congregation, who then sang it in response. "Still, to this day," wrote George Hood, an early historian of religious music, in 1845, lining out in some form was common in country churches "over three-fourths of the territory of the United States." Lining out created a strange and disorderly world of sound. "In one of the western states," Hood attended a worship service around 1840 "where the clerk, a lawyer of some note, used to dole out the hymn two lines at a time—with a nasal twang that Ichabod Crane might have envied but never have obtained." Without instrumental accompaniment, the pace of singing was very slow. Members of the congregation might sing the same text to two or three different tunes. Some singers added their own idiosyncratic quavers and trills on long notes. Most striking of all was the constant interruption of the music with the repetitive alternation of speech and song: the "broken and retarded sense and spoiled melody" that hostile observers noted. Lining-out congregations often ran, in Hood's words, "out of the tune into the words, and from the words into the tune, without stopping or changing either the pitch or the time."

Some lining-out congregations began to sing with greater unity and discipline. In the 1830's Warren Burton attended a Methodist service where the "officiating minister gave out the hymn in portions of two lines," and the worshippers "rose simultaneously from their seats," and "joined all together in some simple air." When a thousand or more singers were assembled for a camp meeting, the lined-out music could be shattering; the grandson of the famous revivalist Francis Asbury remembered that "the immediate din was tremendous; at a hundred yards it was beautiful, and at a distance of half a mile it was magnificent." But whether outsiders overheard it with pleasure or with pain, lining out was not intended for them. It was purely participatory music, aimed at no audience outside its own performers, members of a congregation wholly engaged in worship.

Lining out first disappeared, and the religious music of rural

America first was transformed, in New England during the eighteenth and early nineteenth centuries. Discontent with lining out in country meetinghouses built gradually during the eighteenth century, when rural ministers and community leaders began to hear with new ears. Their congregations' singing started to impress them as discordant and unmusical, and they struggled to introduce "regular singing"—often beginning by persuading their churches to sing according to a single uniform beat marked out by a hand-waving leader. These campaigns against the older ways produced conflict and bitterness within churches and towns, but after 1770 they succeeded in creating three new musical institutions in the countryside: the "select choir" to lead the congregation in singing, the singing school where rural folk were instructed in the rudiments of reading music and part singing, and a homegrown literature of four-part vocal music.

A new figure appeared, the New England–bred singing master who traveled from town to town to conduct singing schools or begin choirs and frequently wrote the music for them as well. William Billings, the Boston tanner and musician, was the best known of these men, but all the rest lived and worked in the countryside. Between the American Revolution and 1820, the self-taught singing masters created a distinctive rural church music. They wrote energetic hymns and four-part anthems with harmonies that European-schooled musicians later found laughably incorrect. New England meetinghouses rang with "fuging tunes," compositions in which each of the four parts— bass, tenor, counter and treble—entered separately, and, as Harriet Beecher Stowe described the music of her childhood, "ran, and skipped, and hopped, and chased each other round." Their "grand, wild freedom" and "energy of motion" was in a very real sense halfway between the learned, "correct" music of Boston or London and rural traditions of lining out and ballad and broadside singing. They were, as she observed, "the battle-cries of a transition period of society."

Rural New Englanders abandoned the collective music making of lining out for the leadership of the singers. Sometimes— as the reformers had intended—congregations followed the lead of the men and women in "the singers' seats" and sang the simply structured hymns along with them, while sitting back to listen to the more difficult anthem; but in many churches the mass of the people ceased singing altogether. At first the select choirs followed long Protestant tradition in singing unaccompanied, but the singing masters were eventually successful in bringing instruments—usually a bass viol, predecessor of today's cello—for use in accompanying the singers.

A later generation of country singers abandoned the singing masters and their music just as their predecessors had given up lining out. Criticism of "country hymnody" began in New England's cities in the 1790s but met little rural response for another twenty years. Eventually, however, the leaders of country churches began again to hear with different ears. They judged the singing masters' melodies, harmonies and standards of performance "rude and primitive"; the fuging tunes came to seem not stirring but undignified, with too much "shrieking and growling" because their vocal ranges were too great for ordinary voices to sing genteelly. When New Englanders went to church after 1820, they increasingly sang or heard music— composed by Englishmen or well-trained American musicians —that was much more restrained and genteel. The harmonies were correct, the melodies took no sudden dips or jumps, the vocal ranges were smaller and there was no fuging.

Church music became easier to sing. From a modern musician's point of view, it also lost most of its complexity and aesthetic interest. New Englanders in many larger communities found partial compensation in the development of "choral societies," modeled after Boston's Handel and Haydn Society founded in 1815, which performed European sacred music in concert. But the music they were singing in church was increasingly insipid. Ironically, one of the effects of this second wave of change was probably to restore congregational participation in singing, which at least in some churches had declined during the reign of the singing school. Country congregations—and individual families—began to buy hymn books; some of the more affluent churches installed small organs in their meeting-houses. Together, hymn books and organ—as they do in most Protestant churches today—guided an increasing number of worshipers through the shoals of "correct" singing.

While Yankees were giving up their distinctively transitional, rural church music in the cause of gentility, other Americans were beginning to take it up as they moved away from lining out. Congregations in New York, New Jersey and Pennsylvania adopted New England country hymnody over the next two decades; by the 1830s, they were followed by others in Ohio, Kentucky and Virginia and then by churches farther west and south. Because Southerners remained closer than other Americans to traditional oral music making, they adopted rural hymnody with a difference; Southern singing masters, rather than writing their own tunes, harmonized widely sung folk melodies. North of Virginia, the music of the singing masters flourished for no more than a few decades, to be replaced with more "correct" singing as it had been in New England. Among Southerners, it endured throughout the nineteenth century as "shape note" and "Sacred Harp" singing.

During the early nineteenth century, the American "practice of music" became an increasingly variegated patchwork of written and unwritten, rustic and genteel forms. Even in the same community there might be men and women singing ancient ballads around the fireside, while others clustered around a new pianoforte to hear a young lady play the latest piece of parlor music. Some Americans made immense and repeated efforts to perfect music in their churches while others still sang bawdy or irreverent broadside songs in nearby taverns. Danc-

ing both declined under the impact of the revivals and flourished where the attraction of city ways was stronger than religious prohibitions. Traditional and communal forms of dance
and song were losing their dominance in many places. But in
this "transition period of society" old and new were intricately
intertwined.

7 "OCCASIONS TO MEET TOGETHER":

THE SOCIAL WORLD

N O ONE has ever longed for a return to the stark limits of early nineteenth-century medicine and mortality. But many Americans have yearned for a lost social world—of songs and stories exchanged around the hearth, husking frolics and barn raisings, of Thanksgiving feasts, country-store socializing and apple bees. They are thinking of orderly families and joyous communal rituals when they imagine that somewhere back in time, in a predominantly rural America, there was a better and simpler life. Looking back, they see early nineteenth-century America as materially poor but communally rich.

Early nineteenth-century social life was still predominantly small-scale and face-to-face. Households, neighborhoods and church communities were central because there were fewer institutions and organizations calling on people's allegiance and participation. Yet neighborliness, cooperation in work and play and the social rhythms of the agricultural year, attractive as they still are, were only a part of the American social world. Many American gatherings were rough and crude in a way that paralleled the gritty and disorderly texture of the landscape. There was loneliness and isolation, drink and drunkenness in astonishing amounts, violence and social ways that were painfully coarse, even bizarre.

There were also the facts of change. By the middle of the

nineteenth century, some Americans were already nostalgic for vanishing ways of social life. In the rural communities of his boyhood, thought Horace Greeley, there had been "more humor, more fun, more play, more merriment . . . than can be found anywhere in this anxious, plodding age." The United States he knew had passed through a great social transition. Many men and women looked back on the early nineteenth century with a sense of profound change in customs, manners and social tone, of what Daniel Drake called "important revolutions in the state of society."

"Social Enjoyments"

Just beyond the limits of each family's house or farmstead was the neighborhood, the little community whose boundaries encompassed the settings of most daily social experience. Throughout America, as the New Englander Lyndon Freeman recalled, families "found occasions to meet together . . . to have a social chat." But neighbors and neighboring were not the same throughout the United States. Americans in the cities, in the villages and established rural settlements of the North, or on the widely scattered farms and plantations of the West and South had widely different "occasions to meet together."

The villages and neighborhoods of the northeastern countryside had intricate social webs. "It was a uniform custom," wrote Freeman of his boyhood, "for the women to visit . . . from house to house, to take tea and enjoy a social afternoon." In New England's country towns neighborhoods were often roughly defined by the boundaries of rural school districts—areas of two to four square miles, and twenty to fifty families. Americans everywhere were so mobile that a sizable minority of families never stayed long enough in any community to become deeply enmeshed in its life. But those who remained for any length of time in well-established settlements visited and traded with their neighbors weekly, if not daily.

On the morning of April 28, 1836, "Mr. Ball and his sons" stopped in at the house of Aaron and Mary White in Boylston, Massachusetts, before getting to work in the Whites' fields. "Mrs. Bush called here this afternoon," Mary White noted in her voluminous diary, and a little later, while her daughters Eliza and Catherine went visiting themselves, she "called at William Hastings' to get Miss Goodenow" and brought her back to the house for tea. After supper, "Mrs. Loring, Mrs. Sanford, and Miss Cotton called here in the evening." The wife of a storekeeper and farmer, Mary White left behind a detailed account of her comings and goings for almost three decades.

Visitors came to Mary White's house to pay visits nine or ten times a week on the average, while she herself called on other families three or four times—in addition to her never-failing attendance at Sunday meetings, funerals, journeys with her husband and the meetings of sewing circles and female benevolent societies. Several times a year, neighbors sent for her nursing help in cases of serious illness. Women came in the afternoon, singly or in groups, to take tea. Entire families arrived in the evening and sometimes "tarried" overnight. Married children, nephews and elderly aunts visited, the minister and deacons of the Congregational church came by, or men stopped to pay an account or borrow a vehicle and lingered to talk.

Pamela Brown of Plymouth, Vermont, was nineteen and unmarried when she began keeping her journal in 1835. Her range of social contact was different from Mary White's, but almost as impressive. Pamela went to church no more than once or twice a month, but she attended every funeral in Plymouth and spent many nights sitting up with the sick. Most important to her were the four or five visits a week she exchanged with young male and female friends; she would often "tarry" with them for two or three days away from home, and sometimes visit relatives in other towns. After Thanksgiving signaled the end of the harvest season, she went almost weekly to dances, singing schools and "quilting frolics," all without her elders supervision.

Mary White was an unusually active and vigorous woman; she no longer had young children to care for and shared household work with her daughters. Pamela Brown was a young woman of courting age who assisted her mother but had not yet acquired heavy domestic responsibilities of her own. Their diaries reveal life at the centers of their communities' social webs.

The "conflicting claims of society and of children," Ann Jean Lyman wrote in 1824, had pressed her to curtail her visiting. Mothers with young children and demanding household duties had less time and opportunity to socialize—or to keep diaries— than Mary White or Pamela Brown. But most country women found some time for visiting even in the midst of difficult work routines.

In moving from New Jersey to carve a farm out of the immense wilderness of the Kentucky forest, Daniel Drake's family had "left the village and public roadside, with its cavalcade of travellers, for the loneliness of the wood, a solitude which was deeply felt by all of us." The social isolation of families in the most thinly settled parts of America bore most heavily on women, for the sexes had very different opportunities to move beyond the limits of the farmstead or even the farmyard. Drake's mother "felt the solitude in which we were entombed, more severely than any other member of the family." Tied to endless domestic tasks, women "could not go much from home," while their husbands, "whom business would frequently call away" from their solitary labor in the fields, could travel and socialize while hunting, trading and attending public gatherings.

In pioneer settlements they might go several months without seeing someone outside their immediate circle: " 'Tis strange to us to see company," a farmer's wife told Frances Trollope in 1828 "in a partial clearing in the very heart of the forest" in southern Ohio. "I expect the sun may rise and set a hundred times before I shall see another *human* that does not belong to the family."

Some mistresses of plantations, particularly in the new cotton country of Alabama and Mississippi, felt similarly "entombed," although they were hardly alone. They were responsible for managing the domestic life of dozens, sometimes hundreds of others, white and black. Yet confined by childbearing and their heavy daily responsibilities, they too visited far less often than their husbands. Plantation life was punctuated by dances and open-air barbecues, elaborate christenings and weddings, but they were occasional events, not weekly ones. There was too much work to do and too much distance to cover.

But even widely scattered families sought to create a web of "private and family visiting with abundance of small talk" across the distances that separated them; their "desire for society," a Kentuckian recalled, was like "the desire of a hungry family for food." Frequent isolation also made them "social and hospitable," remarkably generous to acquaintances and passing travelers: "their insulation makes them glad to see each other." Less frequent sociability was often more intense. Southerners and Westerners defined their neighborhoods more widely in space than closer settled Northerners, and they built their social networks on more intermittent contact. A Southern planter's "notions of space" were "so liberal," a Northerner noted in the 1830s, "that he will readily ride a dozen miles to dine." Crossroads churches or stores were often the centers of social interaction for areas several miles around.

Greeley remembered how his parents passed the nights in singing ballads and exchanging old stories with their New Hampshire neighbors. In the most pious of American households visitors may have confined their conversation to the most recent Sabbath sermon, or the prospects for a religious revival. More often, thought a Massachusetts man, visits were "sometimes made an occasion for gossip and tattle"; more charitably put, they dealt with the tangible and prosaic concerns of everyday life. Eighteen-year-old Zeloda Barrett of New Hartford, Connecticut, took down "the heads of the discourse" when Eliphalet Ensign and his family visited the Barretts on a January evening in 1804. "1st was about Swine," she wrote, noting a conversation about livestock. "2nd Demicrat pigs" indicated lamentation in Federalist New Hartford about the recent success of Jefferson's party. The next topic of discussion was "about Mr. Spencer and Mr. Smith's arbitration," the settlement of a local property dispute. As the "discourse" ranged further, Zeloda kept track of it with at least an inward smile, from "Mrs. Ensign's sore finger" to "Colonel Kellogg's commission for a general" in the state militia. The evening concluded with heated talk "about the meetinghouse being seated," an important issue in the community as it concerned how families were to be assigned their pews in the Congregational meetinghouse.

The times of social gathering in the American countryside moved against the season-driven swings of agricultural work. Between the spring plowing and fall harvest, visits were shorter and gatherings less frequent. In July, during the rushed, exhausting and anxious labor of getting in the Northern hay crop, most other activities were suspended. Stores and shops shuttered their doors or stood almost empty, visits sharply declined, few couples married and few children were conceived.

"On a late autumn day" after the crops had been brought in, recalled Ellen Rollins, the store in Wakefield, New Hampshire, "was like a miniature fair. . . . Incoming and outgoing wagons kept up a constant procession." The stores of rural America were more than their communities' crucial economic link to wider markets and manufactured goods. They were central gathering places that linked households and neighborhoods, community forums and information centers. Particularly just before planting or past harvest they were lively and crowded places. While "loafers . . . smoked and gossiped on the bench outside," men and women talked at country stores "of stock and produce; of sickness and mortality," and discussed the most recent births and marriages.

Economic exchanges and social relationships were deeply intertwined; business transactions proceeded at a leisurely, conversational pace. Husbands and wives headed for different parts of the store; "men made their coarser purchases" of tools, tobacco, hardware, while "women pulled over" the storekeeper's bolts of cloth, shoes, dishes, ribbons, combs and buttons, "and what they were too poor to buy talked over with admiring neighbors."

Winter in the Northern states was a contradictory season, a time of growing discomfort and greater leisure. Family life contracted into a room or two, and even routine outdoor chores grew increasingly difficult as the temperature dropped. In severe cold and storm, households could spend weeks in isolation. But when traveling was good "in the winter season"—on sleighs over frozen roads—"alternating visiting through a neighborhood in the evening was quite common," as Lyndon Freeman remembered. Winter was also the courting season, a time young people would later pleasantly remember for its parties, sleigh rides, singing schools and dances. Stores did less business in the winter, but often stayed open as men gathered there, sometimes late into the evening, and "compared the girths of cattle; made note of prices, forestalled the weather; praised the work of wives and daughters."

Urban Americans lived closer to one another than did those anywhere in the countryside. Some city neighborhoods had a closely knit social life centered around workshops and stores, the taverns and groceries where artisans and laborers gathered. Their wives walked in and out of each other's dwellings several times a day and could sit together outside on the steps. But cities were not necessarily places of social intimacy. Many, perhaps most, American city dwellers did not stay put long enough to develop long-enduring social connections. Poor and transient city neighborhoods created a real if always changing community life that depended on quickly integrating newcomers into the social web.

But once residents of the larger American cities left the small worlds of their neighborhoods, they plunged into a "world of strangers"—a sea of people, few of whom even residents of long standing could identify. By the 1830s, New York had already become the quintessential world of strangers to many Americans; they saw the hurrying and unknowable throngs on Broadway as a stunning contrast to the communities of village and countryside.

Far freer than other women from household work, the wives and daughters of "the wealthier members of the community" in American cities, as the visiting Thomas Hamilton observed, spent much of their time in elaborate and very different networks of social exchange. In the evenings they "opened their houses to the reception of company," giving and attending dinner parties, dances and formal balls. They turned neighborly visiting into formal "morning calls," adopting "calling cards" and an increasingly complex etiquette which determined the length and frequency of calls, whether a call should be returned or not and the sorts of people to whom a family was, or was not, "at home." Families connected by kinship, business and politics interchanged calls and invitations, but ranked and classified their acquaintances in ever more precise grades of social acceptability. Etiquette books, which articulated the rules of such social interchanges, sold increasingly well. Wealthy and fashionable families in Philadelphia, Hamilton thought, barricaded themselves behind "a system of exclusion" as rigorous as any in aristocratic England.

In the small, closely packed villages of the slave quarters, blacks led a communal life that was only poorly known to their masters. After their day's work they sat "up half the night, and over a fire in all seasons," Isaac Weld observed. Slaves passed their evening hours visiting, moving freely in and out of each other's cabins on the street, or talking and singing outdoors. On many plantations owners allowed them occasional Saturday night parties, with donated whiskey to drink and chickens to roast. The most adventurous or determined—young men going courting, those bent on seeing separated kinfolk or attending a neighboring plantation's Saturday barbecue—would take to the roads to visit quarters away from their own plantations.

Some masters tried to impose eight o'clock or nine o'clock curfews to curtail slave socializing, but they primarily wanted to discourage their off-plantation travel. They found it frustratingly difficult, because black Americans showed great tenacity in maintaining an autonomous social life. "The strictest watching," opined a South Carolina judge, "could not at times prevent them from visiting their acquaintance." Even when cabins were locked to keep out late-night callers and patrols guarded the roads, young black men traveled cross-country and climbed down chimneys, often risking severe punishment.

"An Affair of Mutual Assistance"

Corn was the universal American crop, and the husking frolic was rural America's distinctive harvest ritual. From Louisiana north to Maine and west past the Mississippi, huskings signaled the close of the agricultural year. Stripping the leaves from harvested ears of corn was not strenuous work, merely a slow and tedious chore. Households could come together to accomplish a single family's work in an evening, leaving enough energy for vigorous sociability and celebration afterwards. "Neighbors were notified rather than invited," noted Daniel Drake, "for it was an affair of mutual assistance."

Westerners and Southern uplanders husked in a competitive, male-dominated style; while men and older boys husked, women were "busily employed . . . on the supper." Husking frolics in southwestern Pennsylvania began, recalled a Green County chronicler, when "the neighbors were invited in on a moonlit night," and "the corn was hauled to the barn floor and thrown in a long ridge about four feet high." Two young men were "nominated as captains," and chose their teams who lined up on opposite sides of the pile and "set in to husking with all their might, each making as much noise as he possibly could."

The contest between two husking teams was ferocious; "I have never seen a more anxious rivalry or a fiercer struggle," wrote Drake of huskings where "corn might be thrown over unhusked. . . . Your feet might push corn to the other side of the rail. . . . if charged with any of these tricks you of course denied it." Men often embellished their competition on the husking floor with ritualized drunkenness and physical combat. Among Kentuckians, the "green quart whiskey bottle" was "often replenished, and circulated freely." After a late supper, "the fighting took place and by midnight the sober were found assisting the drunken home."

The white farmers of the seaboard South and New England gave huskings a different physical and social shape. Men and women, and sometimes children, usually sat alternately in a circle around the pile of corn and husked it together. Drink was often part of the ritual for the men, who imbibed rum or hard cider, but Eastern huskings emphasized relationships between men and women more than male competition. Finding a lucky red ear or a withered "smut" one was a talisman of courtship. "The laws of husking," the Connecticut poet Joel Barlow wrote in 1792,

> every wight can tell—
> And sure no laws he ever kept so well;
> For each red ear a general kiss he gains,
> With each smut ear she smites the luckless swains.

American slaves, too, participated in "corn-shuckings," both on their own plantations and often traveling to others nearby.

> I know that supper will be big
> Shuck that corn before you eat,
> I think I smell a fine roast pig

Shuck that corn before you eat
I hope they'll have some whiskey dar
Shuck that corn before you eat
I think I'll fill my pockets full
Shuck that corn before you eat.

So ran the first verses of a well-known refrain slaves often sang while stripping the ears. Masters provided a corn-shucking feast with whiskey and cider and the slaves made it a festival, as other Americans did—with the one crucial difference that they husked their masters' corn, not their own in "an affair of mutual assistance" between families.

Americans came together not only in huskings, but on many other occasions of cooperative labor. "Log-rollings" for clearing timber, "stone bees" for ridding fields of rocks, even "dunging frolics" for spreading manure on the fields were common in most parts of the United States. Farm families kept these gatherings outside the overtly economic web of rural life; even farmers and artisans who carefully recorded the most minute transactions with neighbors in their account books almost never charged the time spent in "mutual assistance."

Americans' most dramatic rituals of cooperative work were house and barn raisings. Timber-frame building necessarily brought large numbers of men together, and an air of genuine risk as well as of masculine display of strength hung over the united efforts of men struggling to erect a massive frame. Workers could be killed if a two-story broadside slipped away from their hands and raising poles and fell on them. There was unfeigned relief when the crew put up the fourth and last section of the frame and locked it into place. The ridgepole—in New England sometimes called the rum-pole—capped the frame at the peak of the roof. When it was set in place, the raisers began a series of athletic contests and drinking bouts. Intrepid men volunteered to climb up the frame to the ridgepole while carrying a bottle of rum or whiskey, or even to perch on it as it was lifted into place. As the crowd looked on, one of the men at the top drank a toast, christened the structure with the contents of his bottle, and proceeded to "name the frame" as if it were a ship, sometimes even in verse. The frame standers then raced to scramble down from the top or demonstrated their daring by "jumping ten feet at a leap on the plates and cross-timbers, thirty feet above the ground," as they did when a meetinghouse was raised in Warren, New Hampshire, in 1818, or performing headstands atop the ridgepole. Eating, wrestling and more drinking usually concluded the day.

Cooperative raisings played a very minor role in the building of cities, where large groups of paid workers labored together to put up buildings much more unceremoniously. But in the rural United States they remained important occasions for many decades. House raisings did not disappear until the widespread adoption of balloon framing made them technologically unnecessary, and barns continued to be framed and raised in the older way for considerably longer.

Smaller in scale and less dramatic, but just as pervasive, were the "gatherings . . . composed of females only," which usually involved textile production or work with cloth and needles— archetypally female tasks that could be accomplished in company. Just as in husking corn or raising a frame, collaborative quilting, sewing or spinning allowed women to accomplish a large task quickly and then to reciprocate the help. Quiltings, raisings and huskings and all other "affairs of mutual assistance" gave American rural life a distinctive texture; everywhere they mixed cooperation, competition and courtship.

Sometime before 1830, in Francis Underwood's extraordinary evocation of his mother's social world, a dozen farm wives from her New England country neighborhood, dressed in their "best gowns, cambric collars, and lace caps," arrived for a "quiltin." They took their places in a small farmhouse's sitting room and arranged themselves around the four sides of a quilting frame "that so nearly filled the room that there was little space behind the chairs."

They began to stitch pieces of patchwork to a padded lining

in intricate patterns. While their experienced fingers flew through stitches that needed little conscious attention, they "exchanged information in regard to measles and whooping cough," and the relative merits of bleeding and botanic dosing. Later they argued over the reported sighting of a black bear in the woods, and vigorously discussed the veracity of absent neighbors and the marriage prospects of girls in the vicinity. The quilting women did not fight, wrestle or broad-jump like men, but contested instead with pointed gossip and verbal duels. They adjourned for "tea," a sizable late-afternoon meal, with the story of the just-deceased tavern keeper, whose old clock "that hedn't ben runnin' for a year suddenly broke out a strikin'. They caounted, an' it struck forty-four! Jest the dyin' man's age."

When young unmarried women quilted together, they ended their work with the arrival of young men for a dance or games; in Kentucky, the young men stayed outside the house while the women worked, making noise and "plaguing the gals" until they were finished, then came in to eat.

A completed quilt not only adorned a bed but implicitly embodied the work and skills of an entire neighborhood's women. In the early 1840s farm women in Pennsylvania, New Jersey and Delaware were making the web of neighborhood explicit with "friendship quilts" in which each square was actually signed with its contributor's name.

Outdoors and indoors, fields and house, separately defined the primary work gatherings of men and women. Raisings and other outdoor work parties "were composed of boys and men only," and women were onlookers and servers of meals. Men came into work parties indoors only in the way of courtship— either, as in Kentucky, "plaguing" them by interrupting, or working alongside them in New England apple-paring bees where girls tried to read their future husbands' initials in the shapes of the peels they tossed behind them. Huskings, conducted in the barn or the barnyard, spaces transitional between the field and the house, sometimes "brought the two sexes together." The lines of separation were sharper to the west; men and women mixed more easily in New England than in Illinois or Kentucky.

"They Have Few Holidays"

The people of the United States "have few holidays," sniffed a disapproving Margaret Hall, "and the few they do have are going rapidly out of use." Americans were not really abandoning their holidays, but they observed a calendar that was remarkably simple and austere compared with those of England or Western Europe, where the weeks were studded thickly with saints' days, feasts and fasts, and the time-hallowed festivals of specific villages and occupations. Few days of special observance had survived transplantation in the New World. The Puritan founders of New England and the Quaker settlers of Pennsylvania had deliberately abolished them as unscriptural, and even elsewhere in America most had been unable to take root without ancient traditions of place and craft.

Except for a small minority of Catholics, Americans did not observe Easter with great ceremony, and many ignored it completely. The feasts of the Anglican church were noted in the *Book of Common Prayer,* and in some almanacs, but most were rarely observed even by American Episcopalians. Halloween had not yet arrived from Catholic Ireland; instead, boys in many seaport towns made great bonfires every 5th of November to mark "Pope's Night," or "Guy Fawkes' Night," a militantly Protestant English holiday which marked the discovery of the Gunpowder Plot against the Houses of Parliament. The Irish in Baltimore, New York and Philadelphia celebrated the feast of St. Patrick on March 17th; their Protestant adversaries countered by hanging a "Pad" or "Paddy" in effigy.

Most Americans observed Christmas—their modern descendants' most lavish and commercialized holiday season—on a smaller scale, or not at all. Presbyterians, Baptists and Congregationalists, whose Calvinist heritage remained strong, traditionally ignored Christmas completely. It was a day when farmers slaughtered hogs and farm wives dipped their candles. "It was remembered," wrote Samuel Goodrich, that the cellar of his family's house in Connecticut "had been dug in a single day, and that day was Christmas."

Many Southerners, in contrast, celebrated Christmas week in the tradition of the Church of England, and gathered their kinfolk, often down to distant cousins, around the holiday table. On many plantations, as Solomon Northup said, "the Christmas holidays" were "the time of feasting, and frolicking and fiddling —the carnival season of the children of bondage." At Christmas slaves were given their longest holiday from labor, often a week or more, "according to the measure" of each master's generosity. In St. Mary's Parish in southern Louisiana, each planter took a yearly turn in providing an outdoor Christmas feast "for three to five hundred . . . inviting the slaves from neighboring plantations to join his own on the occasion."

But the majority of Americans who "kept Christmas" neither exchanged gifts nor decorated their homes. They left more elaborate celebrations to the Lutheran Germans of Pennsylvania, who marked Christmas by decorating a tree after the fashion of the old country, and particularly to the people of New York City. With their dual Dutch and English heritage, New Yorkers made the most of Christmas. They burned Yule logs, told their children the story of St. Nicholas—New York's Reverend Clement Moore wrote the poem now known as " 'Twas The Night Before Christmas" for his own family in 1822—and often took the week between Christmas and New Year's as a holiday. Well-to-do New Yorkers also marked the holidays by giving presents; the days before Christmas were a time of heavy shopping in "confectionery stores and toy shops."

By 1830, some Americans were beginning to find Christmas observance in the expansive New York style contagious. Prosperous urban families, even a few in New England, took up gift exchange, evergreen boughs and St. Nicholas. Christmas celebration became a mark of wealth and gentility.

For New Englanders, "the autumn Thanksgiving" usually celebrated in early December had long been "the king and high priest of all festivals," in Harriet Beecher Stowe's words. "The good and ancient custom of New England," was "fast extending over the other parts of the country," the *Massachusetts Spy* observed in 1819. Although not yet a national holiday, it was proclaimed by the governors of New York, New Jersey, Pennsylvania and Ohio as well as those of the six New England states; in subsequent years Thanksgiving spread farther south and west, but Yankees thought that "south of Connecticut such holidays scarcely deserve the name."

The earliest leaders of New England had declared special "days of thanksgiving" without reference to the seasons, for particular acts of divine favor or deliverance. But during the eighteenth century a people increasingly preoccupied with agriculture had transformed it into a ritual celebration of abundance "in the Fall, after the harvests, when the garners are full." By the early years of the nineteenth century, Thanksgiving was still in part a day of holy remembrance, but also a time of harvest festival and homecoming. Families attended church services in the morning, but "accumulated mountains of edibles" over the course of a month's preparation for the year's greatest feast in the afternoon. Every year it was an occasion for the renewal of the ties of kinship, and grew in importance as Americans in New England and elsewhere became more and more a dispersed people, migrating West and cityward. City "apprentices . . . who are not permitted to visit their parental and rural homes more than twice in a year," remarked the *Universal Traveller,* came home on Thanksgiving, and family members sometimes traveled "hundreds of miles to meet again, to renew the bonds of affinity and affection under the paternal roof."

Yankees also observed Fast Day in April, when work ceased and citizens were supposed to abstain from food. Fast Day was only a pale reflection of their early ancestors' days of public repentance and humiliation, but together with Thanksgiving it still allowed them to begin the agricultural year with repentance in preparation for plowing and planting, and to end it with celebration once the harvest had been assured.

The calendar that mattered to many Americans was civil and secular, not sacred. It punctuated the year with seasonal militia musters, the cycle of state and local elections—almost all were yearly—and the periodic sessions of circuit-riding courts. On these days large crowds flocked to township centers and county courthouses, as much to socialize as to do public business. "With Americans," Thomas Hamilton discovered, "court time . . . implies frolicking time." The citizens of the United States more or less accomplished their public purposes of electing officials, recording deeds and attending court, but these civil concerns were often "quite eclipsed," as Daniel Drake described it, "by a heterogeneous drama of foot races, pony races, wrestling, fighting, and general uproar."

Some men came to certain public gatherings reluctantly. The militia laws of each state called out all able-bodied men for military drill two or three times a year, usually in the spring and fall. The satirist David Claypool Johnston's 1819 watercolor *The Militia Muster* portrays a ragged company of Massachusetts men who have just assembled for military training. (see illustration no. 40.) Some are evidently the worse for drink and others lack guns or essential pieces of their uniforms; one of the militiamen has absentmindedly bayoneted his neighbor in the posterior. Across the United States, militia training was frequently perfunctory or worse. Many men had come to resent training bitterly, both for the time it took away from their work and the subordination to commanding officers it presupposed. Most enrollees cared little for their martial responsibilities and some made deliberate travesties of military discipline. Early nineteenth-century "training days" were a byword for disorder.

The only holiday of midsummer was an unavoidable one. "The Fourth of July," wrote Frederick Marryat in his travel diary in 1837, "the sixty-first anniversary of American independence!" In each American community, he went on, "the Declaration of Independence has been read; in all one, and in some two or three orations have been delivered, with as much gunpowder in them as in the squibs and crackers." Despite its notably awkward timing for a nation so agricultural—it came in the midst of haying in the North, corn and cotton cultivation elsewhere—Americans made the Fourth their most universal holiday. In "fifty thousand cities, towns, villages and hamlets, spread over the surface of America" citizens observed rituals that varied little, firing cannons, watching parades of prominent citizens and listening to endless orations in town commons and courthouse squares. Americans probably seized their national day with particular relish because it was the only sanctioned way of taking a break from the intensive labor of midsummer. "The Americans may have great reason to be proud of this day," Marryat concluded, "but why do they get so confoundedly drunk?"

"A Day Set Apart"

Every Sunday morning, at the crossroads Baptist church in Mayslick, Kentucky, around 1810, there were "horses hitched along the fence, and men and women on foot or horse back, arriving from all quarters." Around the small structure Daniel Drake remembered "neighbors shaking hands and inquiring after each other's families; a little group leaning against the fence in conversation; another seated on a bench talking it over; another little party strolling among the graves and squads of children sitting or lying on the grass to rest themselves."

For a steadily growing number of Americans, Sabbath services were the most important social encounter of each week.

Whether they sat "on backless benches" at the Mayslick meeting, on plush seats in a New York City Presbyterian church, in the pine pews of a Connecticut meetinghouse or on the bare ground at a "praise meeting" in the slave quarters, it was the week's crucial event, the hub on which the world turned. Once inside, worshipers prepared for a lengthy encounter with the word of God: a morning service that lasted up to three hours, and usually a second in the afternoon. Congregations stood or knelt through prayers that might be half an hour long, and were accustomed to sit through one or even two turns of the preacher's hourglass.

American houses of worship were only occasionally places of comfort or of what later came to seem churchly decorum. Many churches had broken windows "stuffed with hats and old rags," travelers observed, and unrepentant spitters kept sections of their floors covered with tobacco juice. Members of congregations would bring "nuts and fruits" to sustain them during services, and "strew the refuse about the premises," complained Connecticut's Reverend Fosdick Harrison in a sermon around 1820. Many Northern congregations still endured bitter winter cold in their unheated structures, sometimes seeing the wine freeze in the communion cups.

Worshipers came to church with their family dogs, who followed them into their pews or darted in and out, "chasing one another round and round the church," as Artemas Williams of Massachusetts remembered. Sketching the interior of a Lutheran church in Pennsylvania, Lewis Miller portrayed an angry sexton in hot pursuit of canine intruders. In warm weather, chickens and turkeys walked in through the open doors; sometimes one would "by degrees fly to the pulpit" and perch on the open Bible. Ministers intent on their preaching managed to ignore them.

As to how the Sabbath should be spent, Americans were a divided people. Unchurched folk liked to pass their Sunday leisure "lounging and smoking around the house," as Sylvester

Judd put it, or finding a neighbor with whom to share a drink. For the rougher sort in Logan County, Kentucky, remembered Peter Cartwright, "Sunday was a day set apart for hunting, fishing, horse-racing, card-playing, balls, dances, and all kinds of jollity and mirth." The people of New Orleans and the Louisiana countryside long adhered, as Francis Grund noted, "to their original French manner of considering Sunday as a day of amusement." New Orleans Sabbaths featured not only dances and drinking, but promenading prostitutes, frequent duels and hours-long slave dances to African drums and rhythms in the public squares. Their thoroughgoing substitution of holiday release for churchgoing decorum fascinated and shocked other Americans.

The most pious households kept the Sabbath strictly. Francis Underwood's family, like many others, attended morning and afternoon worship services, took a decorous noontime dinner in the pews and avoided all "secular amusements." Toys were put away, and only religious reading was allowed; play, laughter, even loud voices were forbidden. Some of those whose families observed the Sabbath with such rigor remembered its peace fondly; a Connecticut women called it "part of the happiest dreams of . . . childhood." Others agreed with Underwood that it had been a day of sacred repression, "the most fatiguing and most wearisome in the week."

Some Americans kept to a middle ground. German Lutherans and Episcopalians observed Sunday less austerely. Kentucky Baptists felt that "suspension of labor and attendance at worship were required, but social enjoyments were not forbidden." They often visited around the neighborhood after worship, but "with more propriety" than during the week.

As the American postal system grew rapidly after 1800, there were bitter battles in Congress about the transportation and delivery of mail on the Sabbath. The proponents of "public convenience" were strong enough to keep the mails moving on Sunday, but legislators struggled over whether postmasters should be required by law to keep their offices open if mail arrived on the Sabbath. Despite periodic floods of protesting petitions, most of the time they were.

Worship was the one important public occasion in which women sometimes outnumbered men as enthusiastic participants. In most of America's Protestant churches the majority of those who had testified to their religious experience, signed church covenants and become full members were female. Unconverted men often accompanied their converted wives to church and were faithful members of the congregation, but a minister scanning the pews from his pulpit would often notice the disparity.

"In a wild district on the confines of Indiana" in 1832, Frances Trollope arrived at the site of a camp meeting, where "a space of about twenty acres had been cleared." She found a multitude of tents pitched "in a circle round the cleared space," surrounded by another circle of wagons with horses hitched to them.

Camp meetings, the great open-air gatherings of the revival, took worship outdoors and extended it to thousands at once. No other American gathering was more notorious, or more spectacular. Particularly as Methodism spread, outdoor religious meetings became commonplace across the United States, but they remained largest and most dramatic west of the Appalachians. By and large, they were assemblies of humble, often unlettered people. The members of most other religious denominations in the East, and the more prosperous and genteel everywhere, kept their religion indoors.

Camp meetings created densely packed temporary communities which ranged in size from a middling village to a small city. Eastern meeting-goers drove out to camp from their farms and villages for a day or two or, by the 1830s, could even arrive on an excursion steamboat. Westerners gathered from "a district of country fifty miles in extent," wrote the transplanted

New England minister Timothy Flint, to stay for a week. Meetings were most prolonged and ecstatic where community was thinnest.

A large camp meeting's "congregation consisting of thousands" was both a religious exercise and a major social gathering; they were often as well attended as "court times" or a militia musters. In the gatherings of Tennessee, noted Flint in 1827, large numbers of believers anxious for an encounter with saving grace mingled with "aspirants for office" who planned "to electioneer, and gain popularity," and "vast numbers who were there from simple curiosity, and merely to enjoy the spectacle." Families ate and slept in their wagons or in the small canvas tents they brought with them. Serious meeting-goers often visited around the camp during the morning and spent the afternoon at the prayer-meeting tents in preparation for the outdoor services, which often began at dusk or sometimes later at night. Under the glare of "lamps hung in line upon the branches," or "immense fires of blazing pine-wood," the preachers mounted a crude wooden rostrum to take turns exhorting their hearers, who stood throughout the service or sat on rough benches.

The voices of the revivalists—men who could reach an audience of thousands without amplification—and the massed singing and shouting of the crowd generated powerful tides of emotion. "Amen, Amen! Jesus, Jesus! Glory, Glory!" responded the crowds, Trollope recounted, as ministers called "anxious sinners . . . to come forth into the pen, immediately below the preacher's stand." Even some who had come to observe or to scoff fell under their spell. "The combined voices of such a multitude, heard at the dead of night," admitted even the skeptical Trollope, with "the dark figures of the officials in the middle of the circle" and "the lurid glare thrown by the altar fires in the woods beyond," had an extraordinary effect.

Giving themselves up to religious ecstasy or "a conviction of sin," women and men by the hundreds would burst into tears and wailing, throw themselves prostrate on the ground or be taken by even more "powerful exercises." Camp meeting congregations sometimes yielded to "strange and wild" religious transports, like the uncontrollable bodily movements called "the jerks." It "was overwhelming in its effects," said Peter Cartwright, who had preached at hundreds of camp meetings, "upon the bodies and minds of the people. No matter whether they were saints or sinners, they would be taken under a warm song or sermon, and seized with a convulsive jerking all over, which they could not by any possibility avoid, and the more they resisted against it, the more they jerked." Cartwright had seen many anxious sinners as well as some unwilling scoffers taken with the jerks. Especially in his early days before 1820, he had witnessed even stranger and wilder things—men and women "running, jumping and barking," going on all fours and vocalizing like dogs.

Many meetings had a shadowy mirror image nearby—a gathering of irreligious "roughs" or "rowdies," usually fueled by liquor, who assembled to break up the meeting, knock over the tents and disperse the preachers. Cartwright was a physically powerful man who personally fought innumerable pitched battles with "Satan's crew"; most other revivalists sought out lay protectors. Hiram Munger was one of them, who spent much of his life in holy fisticuffs as a "regulator," an untitled but effective sergeant at arms for Methodist meetings all through the North. At hundreds of camp meetings, Munger led groups of defenders, using his courage and great strength to maintain the physical boundaries between the godly and the ungodly. Munger's own career also showed that the boundaries between rowdies and camp-meeting believers could be easily crossed. He had been a scoffer in his youth who did his share of breaking up meetings, but after his conversion he put his strength at the Lord's service.

The "howlings and groans" and "convulsive movements" of camp-meeting worshipers fascinated onlookers and horrified the most fastidious, who saw not grace at work but uncouth emotional excess, even sensuality. For many participants, camp meetings were like "standing at the gate of heaven," they said, the high points of hard-pressed and often lonely lives, times of true religious transformation.

"Tavern Haunting, Tippling and Gaming"

In sight of "the village church" in most American communities, observed an Ohioan, stood "the village tavern," and the two structures "did in fact represent two great opposing principles." The tavern was the most important gateway to the primarily male world of drink and disorder, one that encompassed much that was rough-edged and riotous, sometimes cruel and violent.

In the United States before 1830, taverns were surely the most widely accessible local institution of all. The great majority of American men in every region were tavern-goers. The printed street directories of American cities listed tavern keepers in staggering numbers, and even the best-churched parts of New England could show more licensed houses than meeting-houses. In 1827 the fast-building city of Rochester, New York, with a population of approximately eight thousand, had nearly one hundred establishments licensed to sell liquor, or one for every eighty inhabitants.

Taverns were Americans' most important centers of male sociability. They were often the scenes of excited gaming and vicious fights, and always of hard drinking, heavy smoking and an enormous amount of alcohol-stimulated talk. City men came to their neighborhood taverns daily, and "tavern haunting, tippling, and gaming," as Goodrich remembered, "were the chief resources of men in the dead and dreary winter months" in the countryside.

City taverns catered to clienteles of different classes: sordid sailors' grogshops near the waterfront universally connected with brawling and prostitution, neighborhood taverns and liquor-selling groceries visited by craftsmen and clerks, well-appointed and relatively decorous places favored by substantial merchants. Taverns on busy highways often specialized in teamsters or stage passengers, while country inns took their patrons as they came.

For their communities and neighborhoods, taverns were also crucial places for acquiring information. Men came not only to drink but to to hear the latest news from teamsters and travelers or to read the latest newspaper. On the taproom's walls they could see a profusion of messages, advertisements and legal notices: the "placards of stage-routes, woodcuts of enormous stallions in prancing attitudes, and notices of sheriff's sales," that Nathaniel Hawthorne recorded, or announcements of town meetings and sessions of county courts, warnings about runaway apprentices or escaped slaves, and handwritten notes offering cotton and corn, livestock and land, houses and shops for sale. The "excessive and impertinent curiosity" for which foreign travelers often criticized Americans was probably rooted in the fact that so much of their contact with ordinary folk inevitably occurred in taverns along the road. Men at taverns were eager for information and felt licensed to inquire.

Taverns accommodated women as travelers, and let out rooms for dances, but their barroom clienteles were almost exclusively male. Outside the dockside dives, or the liquor-selling groceries of poor city neighborhoods, women were rarely seen drinking in them. Although widows sometimes operated urban taverns in the eighteenth century, their number had shrunk markedly after 1800. Laws forbidding taverns to serve servants, apprentices and minors were on the books throughout the states, but in most places they were not rigidly enforced. The unwritten consensus of many communities was that liquor would not be denied to those youths who did a man's work or were accepted in the company of drinking men.

Gambling was another continuing preoccupation for many

male citizens of the early Republic. Men played billiards at tavern tables for money stakes. They threw dice in "hazard," slamming the dice boxes down so hard and so often that tavern tables wore the characteristic scars of their play. Even more often Americans sat down to cards, often playing brag, similar to modern-day poker, or an elaborate table game called faro.

"Gaming, especially the playing at cards," the country lawyer George Davis recalled, had been widespread in the New England countryside since the post-Revolutionary turmoil of the 1780s. Most rural taverns "had their recesses for gamblers" and some of the rural communities' most eminent citizens, men who "claimed an elevated standing," gambled in their "private retreats" along with far more ordinary folk. Lawyers and physicians would hazard their fees at the card table, and judges gambled after court had adjourned. The planter gentry of the South had a much longer tradition of devotion to dice, cards and horse racing as part of their often furious competition with each other. Humbler white Southerners shared their tastes as far as their means permitted. Gambling ways spread widely to the new states of the West as well. Wagering in the tavern brought all classes together as few other activities did.

Outdoors, they wagered with each other on horse races, or bet on cockfights and wrestling matches. Earlier, gentlemen in the South had jealously guarded horse racing as their exclusive prerogative, but they had allowed it to become democratically widespread by 1800. North and South, there were racecourses on the outskirts of most large towns and many in smaller communities. The "old race ground" in York, Pennsylvania, was on the Lancaster Road, and even as small a community as Enfield, Massachusetts, had a regularly used racecourse two miles down on the river road from the town center.

Demonstrating a still widely prevalent indifference to the suffering of animals, men gathered at taverns and racecourses to savor blood sports, dog and cock fights in which dogs savaged each other and roosters were matched to tear each other to pieces with long steel spurs tied to their legs. Cockfights were "indulged in with avidity at the South," as travelers reported, but there were many Northerners like John Micklefield, with a "most pertinaceous habit for his favorite amusement," who even as an old man had been willing to walk forty miles from Salem to Roxbury, Massachusetts, in 1815 to see a particularly good match. The "kindred sports of bull- and bear-baiting"— setting packs of dogs against their larger but chained adversaries—also attracted wide audiences. Almost everything that gamblers and gamesters did was illegal practically everywhere and punishable by stiff fines, but the laws were enforced erratically, if at all.

American taverns were also windows on the exotic, the places where traveling exhibitions, menageries and circuses stopped and put on their shows. The earliest American circus audiences were not, as they became much later, gatherings of families with excited children in tow, but adult and primarily male. The shows were clearly part of a masculine world whose boundaries were defined by liquor and the possibility of violence. Men attending an animal exhibition in Shelburne Falls, Massachusetts, Hawthorne observed, walked around, often "getting within the barriers and venturing too near the cages." Many were "drunk, swearing and fighting." A few women had come to the show, but they sat separately on a tier of benches on one side of the tent, carefully walled off from the throng of men.

Drink was everywhere in the social world of early nineteenth-century America—first as a taken-for-granted presence and only later as a serious and divisive problem. "Liquor at that time," recalled the carpenter Elbridge Boyden, "was used as commonly as the food we ate." Drinking at taverns, although the most visible, may have accounted for no more than a quarter of what Americans consumed. Before 1820, the vast majority of Americans firmly considered alcohol a crucial part of their sociability as well as an essential stimulant to exertion. Like the Kentuckians Daniel Drake grew up with, they "regarded it as a duty to their families and visitors . . . to keep the bottle well replenished." To lack liquor was a breach of hospitality: "for a friend to call and find it empty was a real mortification to one party, and quite a disappointment to the other." Weddings, funerals, frolics, even a casual "gathering of two or three neighbors for an evening's social chat," were almost unthinkable without "spirituous liquor"—rum, whiskey or gin, "at all seasons and on all occasions." While visiting on winter evenings in Sturbridge, remembered Lyndon Freeman, "the women became silly and the men foolish" on "toddy," or sweetened rum and water.

Northern households made hard cider their common table beverage and all ages drank it freely. "Dramming"—taking a fortifying glass in the forenoon and again in the afternoon—was part of the daily regimen of many men. Clergymen took sustaining libations between services, lawyers before going to court and physicians at their patients' bedsides. To raise a barn or get through a long day's haying without fortifying drink was thought a virtual impossibility. Slaves enjoyed hard drinking at festival times and at Saturday-night barbecues as much as any of their countrymen. But of all Americans they probably drank the least on a daily basis, because their masters could usually control their access to liquor.

In Parma, Ohio, in the mid-1820s, Lyndon Freeman and his brothers were used to seeing men "in their cups" and passed them by without comment. But one "dark and rainy night" they discovered something far more shocking, "nothing less than a *woman beastly drunk* . . . with a flask of whiskey by her side." American women drank as well as men, but usually much less heavily. They were more likely to make themselves tipsy with hard cider and alcohol-containing patent medicines than to become inebriated with rum or whiskey. Temperance advocates in the late 1820s estimated that men consumed fifteen times the volume of distilled spirits that women did; this may have been a considerable exaggeration, but there was a great difference in drinking habits between the sexes. Americans traditionally found drunkenness tolerable and forgivable in men but deeply shameful in women.

By almost any standard, Americans drank not only near-universally but in enormous quantities. Their yearly consumption at the time of the Revolution has been estimated at the equivalent of three-and-a-half gallons of pure, two-hundred-proof alcohol for each person. Since the mid-nineteenth century, per capita consumption in the United States has never been much over two gallons a year—a contrast that is even more remarkable because the proportion of the population old enough to be serious drinkers was then much smaller.

After 1790, probably in response to anxieties generated by rapid and unsettling social and economic change, American men began to drink even more. By the late 1820s their imbibing had risen to an all-time high of almost four gallons per capita. "Beastly intoxication" in public became ever more widespread, and many men went from dramming and regular "tavern haunting" to spending whole days intoxicated on alcoholic binges.

"All of Them Had a Knock Down"

York, Pennsylvania, was a peaceable place as American communities went, but the Miller and Weaver families had a long-running quarrel. It had begun in 1800 when the Millers had found young George Weaver "stealing apples" in their yard and punished him by "throwing him over the fence," injuring him painfully. Over the years hostilities broke out periodically. Lewis Miller remembered walking down the street as a teen-aged boy and meeting Mrs. Weaver, who drenched him with the bucket of water she was carrying. He retaliated by "turning about and giving her a kick, laughing at her, this is for your politeness." Other York households had their quarrels too; in "a general fight on Beaver Street," Mistress Henck and Mistress

Forsch tore each other's caps from their heads. Their husbands and then the neighbors interfered, and "all of them had a knock down."

When Peter Lung's wife refused to dig some potatoes for supper from the yard of their small house, the Hartford, Connecticut, laborer recalled in his confession, he "kicked her on the side . . . then gave her a violent push," and went out to dig the potatoes himself. He returned and "again kicked her against the shoulder and neck." Both had been drinking, and loud arguments and blows within the Lung household, as in many others, were routine. But this time the outcome was not. Mrs. Lung was dead the next day, and Peter Lung was arrested, tried and hung for murder in 1815.

Casual violence was part of the daily fabric of American life. Fighting often arose from daily friction or long-standing grievances between families or individuals. For some Americans violence was a means of self-assertion, or even a recreation, a way of spending leisure time. Slaves experienced it intimately and daily, as part of the structure of their subordination.

Across the Northern countryside, wrestling was a common test of strength and sometimes a way to settle a grudge. Men grappled outdoors within a ring of spectators, often in "last man" competitions, whose rules required that a new opponent be sent into the ring each time a man was pinned, until the eventual victor emerged. Long matches, which onlookers watched "with the keenest vigilance for every motion of the competitors," usually concluded raisings, militia musters or stints of work at road building. Although striking blows was forbidden, wrestling could still be dangerous, even deadly. In New England, Goodrich noted, "several fatal accidents occurred" when the champions of different towns strove together, "to try their superiority by matches." More commonly, wrestling was governed by stricter limits on physical harm; the reigning champion of the Enfield, Massachusetts, area, for example, retired after breaking an opponent's leg.

Although many American children were indulgently raised, harsh corporal punishment was commonplace and some were unluckily caught within the pervasive violence of their households. There were "whole families," claimed William Alcott, "whose mental faculties are dull, as the consequence—I believe—of a perpetual boxing and striking of the head." Alcott had seen parents strike their children with "pieces of wood . . . a common-sized tailor's press board . . . or the heavy end of a wooden whip-handle." Minerva Mayo of Orange, Massachusetts, was tied to her mother's loom for hours as a young child and severely beaten for breaking away; when in 1818 at age eleven she disturbed her father while he was haying, "he caught me by the arm, and gave me a toss into the air, and I came down upon the head of his rake. . . . I yelled so loud that I was heard near a mile, he then took me and carried me to a heap of stone, and laid me down upon the ground, and placed a large flat stone on my back, here I laid in this position until I became very submissive." Many Americans, like Susan Blunt, matter-of-factly remembered "very severe whippings" at what seem today strikingly young ages.

Christopher Columbus Baldwin was not a brutal man, yet he confided to his diary in 1836 that after teaching school "four winters in succession" in Massachusetts he had "never looked upon a child that I have not felt for the moment as tho' I wanted to fall to whipping it—so hardened does the heart become by keeping school." Harsh corporal punishment was traditional in the instruction of the young. Although many teachers used gentler means, the "liberal application of birch and ferrule," along with blows to the head and slaps in the face, were most commonly used to punish misbehavior or slowness to learn. For untrained teachers without a natural gift for instruction, they may have seemed the only way to keep order.

New teachers in country schools often had to prove their manliness in combat with the neighborhood's "big boys," who might be still coming to school in their late teens. Parents and school committees simply assumed that a schoolmaster worth his pay would overcome any challenges to his authority on his own. If a teacher was defeated and "barred out" of his schoolhouse by his pupils, his school was "broken up" before the end of the term and he ignominiously lost his position.

Just as the style of houses or husking frolics varied from region to region in the United States, so did the shape of combat. When considering whether to take pistols with him while traveling in America in 1796, William Strickland was told that it was "customary and sometimes necessary to the Southward," but that "it was entirely useless to the Northward" in New England, "where it would be . . . by no means well received." The states of the South and southwest were the strongholds not only of open-handed hospitality but of dueling and no holds barred hand-to-hand combat.

Dueling had been rare everywhere before the Revolutionary War. Early-eighteenth-century Southern gentlemen were sometimes known to settle their differences with wrestling or hand-to-hand fighting. But many American military officers acquired the practice from the aristocratic example of their French allies and British enemies. After the war they brought the custom into civilian life. Although it never got a foothold in New England, by 1800 it was "rapidly progressing" among upper-class American men, in Lyman Beecher's words, and "stalking with bolder front as you pass onward to the South." But when Aaron Burr killed his old political enemy Alexander Hamilton in a duel outside New York City in 1804, the resultant shock and outrage made dueling untenable in the Middle States and drove it below the Potomac. Outside the professional army and navy, where it continued in use to settle quarrels between officers, dueling flourished as a distinctively Southern practice, taking secure root among a planter gentry who valued competitive self-assertion and skill with weapons, and attached enormous importance to maintaining personal honor.

Secluded dueling grounds were set off on the outskirts of most

Southern towns; St. Louis had its "Bloody Island" in the middle of the Mississippi, and New Orleans's "The Oaks" was occasionally known to see several duels in a single day. Technically, dueling was no more legal "to the Southward" than it was in Pennsylvania or Massachusetts. Legislatures and courts—themselves filled with duelists—turned a blind eye; it was "but too well established by custom," as one observer put it. Most Southerners eminent in state or national politics had fought at least one duel; they ran the greatest risk of insult because in America's free-swinging politics public officeholders were subjected to a wide range of verbal and printed attacks.

Men who followed the dueling code remained constantly ready to defend their reputations and status as gentlemen. Slighted or insulted by a social equal, a man would write the offender a note asking for an explanation or retraction. A man who refused to explain or apologize provoked a challenge to combat and set in motion the choosing of seconds, who arranged the "affair of honor," summoning physicians and a referee to supervise the dueling ground. All of this was conducted in language of exquisite politeness; by 1838 there was even a duelist's book of etiquette, John L. Wilson's *The Code of Honor*, published in Charleston. But Southern dueling, although a hazardous enterprise, was not a uniformly bloodthirsty one. Most dueling encounters never got past the initial stages; seconds usually worked hard to reconcile the parties and provide an acceptable explanation of the offending conduct.

Customarily, dueling ritual required that the combatants stand a fixed distance apart, face off with pistols and fire on a predetermined signal. Yet only a minority of duels—probably no more than one out of seven—ended in death or serious injury. The display of courage and graceful behavior in defense of honor, not their antagonist's death, were the aim of most duelists. Men frequently reconciled on the field of combat or deliberately shot wide of the mark. Wounded combatants often forgave their opponents, and men who killed rarely exulted and sometimes wept. The duel was less a form of polite murder than a dangerous and very serious game.

"Whenever these people come to blows," wrote Isaac Weld of the poor farmers of the South in 1796, "they fight just like wild beasts, biting, kicking, and endeavouring to tear each other's eyes out with their nails." "Rough-and-tumble" fighting was unarmed conflict completely without rules, except that either party could end the fight by crying "enough" and admitting himself defeated. Maine lumbermen fought with no holds barred in their camps, viciously marking their adversaries with their hobnailed boots, and tavern brawlers across America sometimes fought savagely with intent to maim. But during the early nineteenth century, rough-and-tumble combat was the specialty of Mississippi River boatmen, frontier hunters and ordinary farmers in the communities of the Southern back country. In the most isolated and least literate and commercialized parts of the United States, it was "by no means uncommon," continued Weld, "to meet with those who have lost an eye in a combat, and there are men who pride themselves upon the dexterity with which they can scoop one out. This is called *gouging.*"

For these hard-bitten men, a hasty word, a trading disagreement, a lost bet or a drunken challenge could light the fuse of a desperate confrontation, where combatants would gouge or even "endeavour to their utmost to tear out each other's testicles." Unable to contest the power of the slaveowners or imitate their style, gougers roared and screamed. They asserted their manhood against each other by creating an inverted parody of dueling. Where duelists displayed punctilio and self-control, rough-and-tumble fighters demonstrated and admired unrestrained aggression, raw physical strength and courage in the face of pain. As he left Ohio and began traveling in the backcountry South in 1816, wrote Timothy Flint, he "saw more than one man who wanted an eye, and ascertained that I was now in the region of 'gouging.'"

Slaves wrestled among themselves, sometimes fought each other bitterly over quarrels in the quarters and even at times stood up to the vastly superior force of masters and overseers. They rarely if ever gave way to the ferocity of gouging. White Southerners lived with a pervasive fear of the violent potential of their slaves; every incident, from the slave revolts in Haiti in 1790's to the Nat Turner uprising in Virginia in 1831, when a party of slaves rebelled and killed whites before being overcome, gave rise to tighter and harsher controls. But in daily reality, slaves had far more to fear from them.

Margaret Hall was no proponent of abolition, and had little sympathy for black Americans. Yet in her travels South she confronted incidents of what she ironically called "the good treatment of slaves" that were impossible to ignore because they took place before her eyes. At a country tavern in Georgia, she summoned the slave chambermaid but "she could not come" because "the mistress had been whipping her and she was not fit to be seen. Next morning she made her appearance with her face marked in several places by the cuts of the cowskin and her neck handkerchief covered with spots of blood."

Southern stores were very much like Northern ones, visitors noted—except that they stocked "negro-whips" and "man-traps" on their shelves. A few slaves were never beaten at all, and for most, whippings were not a daily or weekly occurrence. But slaves were of all Americans by far the most vulnerable to violence. In public places or along the road blacks were subject to casual kicks, shoves and cuffs for which they could retaliate only at great peril. All slaves had, as William Wells Brown said, often "heard the crack of the whip, and the screams of the slave," and knew that they were never more than a white man's or woman's whim away from a beating. With masters' unchecked power came the possibility of worse than whipping, the mutilating punishments of the old penal law—branding, ear cropping, and, although rarely, even castration and burning alive as penalties for severe offenses. The negro-whip, for sale in most Southern stores and brandished by masters and overseers in the fields, stood for a pervasive climate of force and intimidation. Many white Southerners had little sympathy with gougers, duelists or beaters of slaves, but the ever-present possibility of violence hung heavily in the air "to the Southward."

The penal codes of the American states were far less bloodthirsty than that of England. Capital punishment, for example, was not often imposed on whites for crimes other than murder. Yet at the beginning of the nineteenth century many criminal offenses were punished by the public infliction of pain and suffering. Whipping posts and stocks stood on the common near the meetinghouse in most of the towns of New England, and in front of county courthouses everywhere. In Massachusetts before 1805, a counterfeiter was liable to have an ear cut off and a forger to have one "cropped" or partially amputated, after sitting an hour on the pillory. A criminal convicted of manslaughter was set up on the gallows to have his forehead branded with a letter *M.* In most jurisdictions, petty theft was punished with flogging and those living nearby could hear "now and then fearful screams in the week-time." While in New Haven, Connecticut, around 1810, Charles Fowler recalled seeing the "admiring students of [Yale] college" gathered around to watch minor criminals receive "five or ten lashes . . . with a rawhide whip."

Public executions were the ultimately violent gatherings of American life. As the Reverend Jonathan Fisher described the hanging of Ebenezer Ball in Castine, Maine, in 1811, "light infantry and artillery companies" formed a hollow square to escort the public procession. The sheriff of the county rode ahead of "a cart containing the prisoner's coffin," which was followed by a "platoon of deputy sheriffs with drawn swords," and then the condemned man himself, pinioned with ropes and already wearing his burial shroud, "with four or five ministers on each hand." Bringing up the rear were more troops, and a "drum and fife playing the death march."

Throughout the United States, hangings were irregularly occurring gathering days that brought enormous crowds to the seats of justice. Each execution, with its formal reading of the judgment and sentence, the prayers of the ministers and the last statement of the condemned, was a highly charged piece of public theater, whose intention was to confirm the power of the law and the solidarity of society against the offender.

However, executions were not only solemn spectacles but days of brutal festivity. Thousands of spectators arrived to pack the streets of courthouse towns. On the day of a hanging near Mount Holly, New Jersey, in the 1820s, the scene was that of a holiday: "around the place in every direction were the assembled multitudes—some in tents, and by-wagons, engaged in gambling and other vices of the sort, in open day." In order to accommodate the throngs, hangings were usually held not in the public square but on the outskirts of town. The gallows was erected on a hill, or at the bottom of a natural amphitheater, so that the onlookers could have an unobstructed view.

When a man named Loechler was to be hanged in Lancaster, Pennsylvania, in 1824, Lewis Miller and several friends made up a party to travel twenty-five miles to witness the execution. Miller later sketched the crowd streaming from Lancaster center out to the place of execution, and noted, "Oh! What a crowd of people to see a poor sinner of a creature hung at the gallows!" Execution crowds were primarily male, although Miller showed a handful of women assembling to watch Loechler's final minutes; fathers sometimes took their young sons along and held them up to see.

Tavern keepers were even known to hire watchers to keep a careful eye on the condemned prisoner in the weeks before, "so that the culprit should not, by suicide, cheat them out of the day's gains." A reprieve or stay of execution might disappoint a crowd intent on witnessing the deadly drama and provoke a riot, as it did in Pembroke, New Hampshire, in 1834.

"An Advance in Civilization"

At a drunkard's funeral in Enfield, Massachusetts, in the 1830s
—the man had strayed out of the road while walking home and
fallen over a cliff, "his stiffened fingers still grasping the handle
of the jug," wrote Francis Underwood—the Reverend Sumner
G. Clapp mounted "a log by the woodpile" and preached the
town's first temperance sermon before a crowd of hardened
drinkers. In this way Clapp began a campaign to "civilize" the
manners of his parishioners, and "before many years there was
a great change in the town; the incorrigible were removed by
death, and others took warning." Drinking declined sharply,
and along with temperance came "a general reform in conduct."

Although it remained a powerful force in many parts of the
United States, the American way of drunkenness began to lose
ground as early as the mid-1820s. The decades since the Revolution had witnessed a striking upsurge in liquor consumption,
but it provoked a potent reaction—an unprecedented attack on
all forms of drink that first gathered momentum in the northeast. Some New England clergymen had been campaigning in
their own communities as early as 1810, but their concerns took
an organized impetus with the founding of the American Temperance Society in 1826. Energized in part by a concern for
social order, in part by evangelical piety, temperance reformers
popularized a radically new way of looking at alcohol. The
"good creature" became "demon rum"; prominent physicians
and writers on physiology, like Benjamin Rush, told Americans
that the beverages they had traditionally considered healthy
and fortifying were actually bodily and moral poisons. National
and state societies generated an enormous output of antiliquor
tracts, and hundreds of local temperance societies were
founded to press the cause, first of moderation in drink but
increasingly of total abstinence from liquor.

Americans responded to this barrage of persuasion by drastically decreasing their consumption of alcohol. By 1840 it had declined by more than two-thirds for the nation as a whole, from close to four gallons per person each year to less than one and a half. Country storekeepers gave up the sale of spirits, local authorities cut down the number of tavern licenses, and farmers even abandoned hard cider and cut down their orchards. The shift to temperance was a striking transformation in the everyday habits of an enormous number of Americans. "A great, though silent change," in Horace Greeley's words, had been "wrought in public sentiment."

But although the "great change" affected some Americans everywhere, it had an uneven impact. Organized temperance reform was sharply delimited by geography. Temperance societies were enormously powerful in New England and western New York, and numerous in eastern New York, New Jersey and Pennsylvania. More than three-quarters of all recorded temperance pledges came from these states. In the South and the West, and in the laborers' and artisans' neighborhoods of the cities, the campaign against drink was much weaker, and rarely reshaped community life. In many places, drinking ways survived and even flourished; but as individuals and families came under the influence of militant evangelical piety, their "men of business and sobriety" increased gradually in number.

Where the temperance movement was most successful it redefined social boundaries. "Our consumers of strong drink" had diminished to "a class" of Americans by the 1840s, wrote Greeley, where previously "they were the whole people." Without moving physically, taverns lost their place near the center of community life. A few taverns became citadels of a newly defined respectability. They gave up their rum and whiskey selling to be transformed into "Temperance Hotels" where water, coffee and tea were the only beverages obtainable, and patrons restricted themselves to conversation and reading the newspapers. Many taverns disappeared; most became gathering places for the otherwise minded, "the exchange for rustic wit, the focus of hate for parsons and deacons, and of ridicule for the new-fangled temperance society," as they did in Francis Underwood's New England. Temperance newly defined another boundary as well. As liquor grew "unfashionable in the country," Greeley noted, Americans who wanted to drink and carouse turned increasingly to the cities, "where no one's deeds or ways are observed or much regarded."

Gambling, racing and blood sports, closely linked as they were to drink, also fell to the same forces of change. In the central Massachusetts region that George Davis knew well, until 1820 or so gaming had "continued to prevail, more and more extensively." After that, "a blessed change had succeeded," overturning the scene of high-stakes dice and card games that he knew in his young manhood. Impelled by a new perception of its "pernicious effects," local leaders gave it up and placed "men of respectable standing" firmly in opposition. Racecourses were abandoned and "planted to corn." "Bearbaiting, cock-fighting, and other cruel amusements" likewise began to dwindle in the countryside. In many places outside the Northeast, the rude life of the tavern and "cruel amusements" remained widespread, but some of their excesses of "sin and shame" did diminish more gradually. Much—although clearly not all—of rural Kentucky had seen "a delightful increase in refinement and piety" during his lifetime, Daniel Drake believed.

Far from declining, traveling shows and exhibitions increased greatly with the expansion of travel and improvement of roads. In many communities men turned to them for entertainment as rougher public spectacles like cockfights and horse races disappeared or became too disreputable. Everywhere his shows traveled in the late 1830s, P. T. Barnum noted the opposition of the clergy and the leaders of local churches. Shows found their audiences among those for whom the lyceum lecture, the prayer meeting and the temperance hotel still had little appeal.

"If you love fun, and frolic, and waste, and slovenliness more than economy and profit," wrote Robert B. Thomas, the editor of the *Farmer's Almanack* in 1833, "then make a husking." He and other Northern agricultural reformers had been waging a campaign against cooperative work and its rituals for decades. Pressing farmers to become commercial and efficient, they subjected traditional exchanges of hospitality for labor to stringent economic analysis. Too many workers, they argued, came "more for the sport than to do any real good," and farmers seriously concerned about improving their corn yields had to watch out continually for those "who will not husk clean," or did not do enough work to make them worth feeding.

A rising number of farmers began to take this advice, along with other recommendations for making land and labor more productive, and turned away from mutual assistance to more complete reliance on themselves and their immediate families. As farmers gave up traditional patterns of diversified, semisubsistence agriculture to produce much more exclusively for city and village markets, they gradually but completely abandoned frolics and bees. In Concord, Massachusetts, whose farms began early to specialize in supplying the markets of nearby Boston, work rituals were already waning by 1825. Across New England, huskings were in decline by 1836, thought Goodrich; they were substantially "more frequent formerly than at present."

House and barn raisings fit too well with timber-frame technology to be dismissed as wasteful or irrational. But in the 1830s, some Northern raisings began to be scenes of serious contest about drink and disorderliness. Impelled by concerns both for temperance and the efficient organization of work, some master carpenters joined with church-building committees and prospective house or barn owners to erect buildings without liquor. The Petersham, Massachusetts, country builder Elbridge Boyden undertook his first raising in the new style while building a church in 1836. Knowing that strong opposition had defeated such plans before, Boyden and his allies secured what he calculated would be the minimum number of nondrinkers needed to raise the heavy "ledgements" of the structure. A large number of angry traditionalists also arrived on the appointed day, planning to refuse to lift unless they were given their accustomed rum and a chance to and climb the ridgepole. They expected that the frame would stay on the ground until the old ways were restored. But Boyden had reckoned correctly. The traditionalists watched as he and his orderly crew put up the first side of the frame, and then they left in disgust.

Traditional forms of women's sociability came under challenge as well. Farm women gave up spinning frolics when they gave up spinning, as the widening availability of machine-made fabrics gradually made it obsolete. But new, more consciously purposeful and organized forms of social activity emerged to compete with quiltings and other "social chats." Especially in the years after 1820, Northern women by the tens of thousands in cities and villages and on prosperous farms joined "Female Charitable Societies," "Sewing Circles" and "Missionary Societies," that were based on traditional gatherings for cooperative work or visiting. Women continued to sew, quilt or embroider. But they shaped their meetings into quite different "occasions to meet together."

The members of these societies did not work cooperatively for each other's households but for communitywide or nationwide aims—clothing the town's poor or raising money to equip missionaries. "Feeling the worth of our time," the bylaws of many societies strictly regulated the conduct of meetings; they forbade the gossip and storytelling of "social chats" and quiltings in favor of "conversation as becomes the Gospel." Tales of bears and mysteriously striking clocks gave way to the reading aloud of religious tracts and books of advice. Even the bountiful

refreshments that often ended women's gatherings were sometimes called into question as members struggled with proposals
to the effect that there "be *no tea* but all attention to business."

In 1823, a just-installed young minister in Shrewsbury, Massachusetts, stunned his congregation by ordering the dogs banned
from the meetinghouse after they had run free there from time
immemorial. Thousands of other early nineteenth-century
churches saw the same changes, as dogs, turkeys and geese
were banished from worship, and more exacting standards both
physical and social, of churchly decorum were enforced. Congregations voted to repair broken windows, cushion pews and
install stoves to make winter services more bearable. Chewing
tobacco, and noisy eating and spitting during services gradually
came to a halt.

Camp meetings continued to be a world of holy excess, but
by 1840 they had lost some of their wildness. Although sinners
"under conviction" and new converts still shouted, fell and
convulsed their bodies, barking and the jerks were rarer.

Over the first four decades of the nineteenth century the
American people also became more and more likely to be found
at worship on Sunday. The proportion of families affiliated with
a local church or Methodist circuit rose dramatically, particularly after 1820, and there were fewer stretches of wholly
pagan, unchurched territory. "Since 1830," maintained Emerson Davis in his retrospect of America, *The Half Century*,
". . . the friends of the Sabbath have been gaining ground.
. . . In 1800, good men slumbered over the desecration of the
Sabbath. They have since awoke." The number of Sunday mails
declined, and the campaign to eliminate them entirely grew
stronger. "In the smaller cities and towns," thought Frances
Trollope in 1832, worship and "prayer meetings" had come to
"take the place of almost all other amusements." There were
still communities near the edge of settlement where a traveler
would "rarely find either churches or chapels, prayer or

preacher," but increasingly the chief strongholds of "Sunday dissipation" and "Sabbath-breaking" were the working-class neighborhoods of America's larger cities.

The United States did not become a peaceful country, although many of its communities became tamer. In American cities, there was more mob violence in the later 1830s than there had been since the years just before the Revolution. Bands of angry men attacked blacks in Philadelphia, burned down the Catholic Ursuline convent in Boston, rioted over the price of flour in New York and in many places attacked abolitionist speakers and writers. Dueling and no-holds-barred fighting with gouging continued to be the favorite sports of white Southerners at the top and bottom of their society. Match wrestling, family violence and tavern brawling remained popular for different groups of Americans; but a decline in drunkenness did reduce Americans' general propensity to fight, and many public gatherings grew more sober and orderly.

Corporal punishment in American schools first came seriously into question during the 1830s, as Horace Mann and other leaders of the Northern school-reform movement pressed a public campaign against flogging. In Massachusetts and Connecticut, local school districts in the late 1830s began to hire women as teachers in the winter schools; they saved towns money because they were paid less, but where they taught they also created a gentler school regime. There were fewer whippings, and fewer "barrings-out" and confrontations because the older boys, as a town historian recalled, "did not like the idea of laying hands on a woman." Yet even where reform was strongest these changes moved against considerable resistance, and overall the ways of school discipline changed slowly.

For whites, one set of violent public performances waned more dramatically in American public life as the penalties of whipping and the pillory, with their attentive audiences, began to disappear from the statute book, to be replaced by terms of imprisonment in another new American institution, the state penitentiary. Beginning with Pennsylvania's abolition of flogging in 1790, and Massachusetts's elimination of mutilating punishments in 1805, several American states gradually accepted John Hancock's view of 1796 that "mutilating or lacerating the body" was less an effective punishment than "an indignity to human nature." Connecticut's town constables whipped petty criminals for the last time in 1828.

Slaveholding states were far slower to change their provisions for public punishment. The whipping and mutilation of blacks may have become a little less ferocious over the decades, but the whip remained the essential instrument of punishment and discipline. "The secret of our success," thought a slaveowner looking back after Emancipation, had been "the great motive power contained in that little instrument." Delaware achieved notoriety by keeping flogging on the books for whites and blacks alike through most of the twentieth century.

Although there were important stirrings of sentiment against capital punishment, all American states continued to execute convicted murderers before the mid-1840s. Public hangings never lost their drawing power. But a number of American public officials were abandoning the longstanding view of executions as instructive communal rituals. They began to see the crowd's holiday mood and eager participation as sharing too much in the condemned killer's own brutality. Starting with Pennsylvania, New York and Massachusetts in the mid-1830s, several state legislatures voted to take executions away from the crowd, out of the public realm. Sheriffs began to carry out death sentences behind the walls of the jail yard, before a small assembly of representative onlookers. Other states clung much longer to tradition, and continued public executions into the twentieth century.

All in all, there had been "important revolutions in the state of society" since Daniel Drake's boyhood. Those who considered these changes often felt that something had been lost. The webs of visiting and sociability remained, but they were more constrained; as Horace Greeley put it, life was now more "anxious and plodding."

But the Americans who were conscious of living through a sweeping reformation of social ways also saw them as an "advance in civilization," with uncouth and sometimes violent practices giving way to bonds of self-consciousness and discipline. Sewing circles, stricter Sabbaths and more churches, the decline of bear-baiting and horse races, and above all temperance, had partially tamed a people who had once been, a Connecticut local historian observed, "rougher in their ways, more profane, more violent in speech." Much had been gained, they thought, in terms of "improvement," "refinement," order, peace, gentleness of manners and sobriety in enormous numbers of American communities. But the "advance in civilization" had been uneven. In some aspects of their daily lives, North and South were farther apart than ever. New or more sharply defined lines of division appeared among the American people—between drinkers and teetotalers, respectables and disreputables, country folk and city dwellers.

Miriam Green had grown up in rural New Hampshire and then gone to work in the Lowell mills. In the early 1840s she was penning reminiscent sketches of her girlhood in an attempt to recapture "the spirit of agrarianism and hilarity." For much of America it was passing away even as she wrote.

BIBLIOGRAPHY

Primary Sources

These sources are cited or referred to in the text.

Abbott, John. *The Mother at Home: Or Principles of Maternal Duty Familiarly Illustrated.* Boston: 1833.

Addington, Henry Unwin. *Youthful America: Selections from Henry Addington's Residence in the United States of America, 1822, 1823, 1824, 1825.* Edited by Bradford W. Perkins. Berkeley, Calif.: University of California Press, 1960.

Alcott, William. *The Young Man's Guide.* Boston: 1836.

———. *The Young Mother: Or Management of Children in Regard to Health.* Boston: 1836.

Allen, Zachariah. *The Practical Tourist.* Boston: 1832.

American Traveller. Boston: 1828–1830.

The Andrus Bindery: The History of the Shop, 1831–1838. Hartford, Conn.: 1940.

Badger and Porter's Stage Register. Boston, 1825–1839.

Baldwin, Christopher Columbus. *Diary, 1829–1835.* Worcester, Mass.: American Antiquarian Society, 1971.

Ballard, Martha Moore. "Diary, 1785 to 1812." In *The History of Augusta,* by Charles E. Nash, 229–464. Augusta, Maine: 1904.

Barlow, Joel. *The Hasty Pudding: A Poem in Three Cantos.* New Haven: 1796.

Barnum, Phineas T. *The Life of P. T. Barnum, Written by Himself.* New York: 1855.

Barrett, Zeloda. Diary, 1807–1809. Connecticut Historical Society, Hartford, Conn.

Beadle, Harriet. *Reminiscences of My Mother.* Wallingford, Conn.: 1957.

Beecher, Catharine. *A Treatise on Domestic Economy.* Boston: 1841.

Beecher, Henry Ward. *Norwood: Or Village Life in New England.* New York: 1868.

Beecher, Lyman. *Autobiography.* Edited by Barbara M. Cross. Cambridge, Mass.: Harvard University Press, 1961.

Bell, John. *On Regimen and Longevity.* Philadelphia: 1842.

Benjamin, Asher. *The American Builder's Companion.* Boston: 1806 and subsequent editions.

————. *The Country Builder's Assistant.* Greenfield, Mass.: 1797 and subsequent editions.

Blunt, Susan. Reminiscences. Manchester Historic Association, Manchester, N.H.

Boyden, Elbridge. *Reminiscences of Elbridge Boyden, Architect.* Worcester, Mass.: 1890.

Brown, Pamela. "Diary, 1835–38." In *Diaries of Sally and Pamela Brown . . . Plymouth Notch, Vermont.* Edited by Blanche Brown Bryant and Gertrude Baker. Springfield, Vt.: 1970.

Brown, Sally. "Diary, 1832–34." In *Diaries of Sally and Pamela Brown . . . Plymouth Notch, Vermont.* Edited by Blanche Brown Bryant and Gertrude Baker. Springfield, Vt.: William L. Bryant Foundation, 1970.

Brown, William Wells. *Narrative of William Wells Brown, A Former Slave.* Boston: 1847.

Buchan, William. *Domestic Medicine: Or a Treatise on the Prevention and Cure of Diseases by Regimen and Simple Medicines.* New York, Boston, Philadelphia: 1799 and subsequent editions.

Burton, Warren. *The District School As It Was.* Boston: 1833.

Butler, Frances Kemble. *Journal of a Residence on a Georgia Plantation in 1838–39.* Edited by John A. Scott. New York: Knopf, 1961.

Carey, Matthew. *Appeal to the Wealthy of the Land.* Philadelphia: 1833.

————. *A Short Account of the Malignant Fever Lately Prevalent in Philadelphia.* 4th ed. Philadelphia: 1794.

Carpenter, Edward Jenner. Diary, 1844–45. American Antiquarian Society, Worcester, Mass.

Carpenter, Esther Bernon. *South County Neighbors.* Boston: 1887.

Cartwright, Peter. *Autobiography.* New York: 1856.

Child, Lydia Maria. *The American Frugal Housewife.* Boston: 1833.

————. *The Mother's Book.* Boston: 1831.

Clapp, David. Travel Journal, 1831. Library of the Henry Francis Du-Pont Winterthur Museum, Winterthur, Del.

Clarke, Horace. Diary, 1836–37. Old Sturbridge Village Research Library, Sturbridge, Mass.

Cobbett, William. *A Year's Residence in the United States of America.* New York: 1818.

Cocke, Ann. Letter, 1811. In *The Plantation Mistress: Women's World in the Old South,* by Catherine E. Clinton, 26–27. New York: Pantheon Books, 1982.

Coke, Edward. *A Subaltern's Furlough, Descriptive of Scenes in Various Parts of the United States.* New York: 1833.

Currie, William. *A View of the Diseases Most Prevalent in the United States of America at Different Seasons of the Year.* Philadelphia: 1811.

Davis, Emerson. *The Half Century: Or a History of Changes That Have Taken Place . . . Between 1800 and 1850.* Boston: 1851.

Davis, George. *A Historical Sketch of Sturbridge and Southbridge.* West Brookfield, Mass.: 1856.

Dickens, Charles. *American Notes for General Circulation.* New York: 1842.

Dickinson, Timothy. "Extracts from the Journal of Timothy Dickinson." In *Proceedings of the Worcester Society of Antiquity for the Year 1883,* 63–89. Worcester, Mass.: 1884.

Douglass, Frederick. *Narrative of the Life of Frederick Douglass, An American Slave.* Boston: 1845.

Downing, Andrew Jackson. *The Architecture of Country Houses.* New York: 1850.

Drake, Daniel. *Pioneer Life in Kentucky: A Series of Reminiscential Letters from Daniel Drake to His Children.* Edited by Charles D. Drake. Cincinnati: 1870.

Dwight, Timothy. *Travels in New England and New York.* New Haven: 1821.

Emerson, Ralph Waldo. *The Journals and Miscellaneous Notebooks of Ralph Waldo Emerson.* Edited by William H. Gilman et al. Vol. V, *1835–1838.* Edited by Merton M. Sealts, Jr. Cambridge, Mass.: Harvard University Press, 1965.

Farrar, Eliza. *The Young Lady's Friend by a Lady.* Boston: 1853.

Felt, Joseph. *The Customs of New England.* Boston: 1853.

Fisher, Jonathan. Diary entry, October 31, 1811. In *Jonathan Fisher, Maine Parson 1768–1847,* by Mary Ellen Chase, 189–191. New York: Macmillan, 1948.

Fitch, Caroline M. Diary, 1836. Old Sturbridge Village Research Library, Sturbridge, Mass.

Flint, Timothy. *Recollections of the Last Ten Years Passed in Occasional Residences and Journeyings in the Valley of the Mississippi.* Boston: 1826.

Fobes, Edwin. Letters, 1832–39. Old Sturbridge Village Research Library, Sturbridge, Mass.

Fowler, William. *History of Durham, Connecticut.* Hartford: 1866.

Freeman Family Papers. Old Sturbridge Village Research Library, Sturbridge, Mass.

Garrison, William Lloyd. "Tour of the Editor. Letter II." *Liberator* (Boston) 2, no. 41 (Oct. 13, 1832): 162.

Gillespie, William. *A Manual of the Principles and Practices of Road Making.* New York: 1849.

Gilman, Caroline Howard. *Recollections of a Southern Matron.* New York: 1838.

Gilman, Samuel. *Memoirs of a New England Village Choir with Occasional Reflections by a Member.* Boston: 1834.

Goodrich, Charles A. *The Universal Traveller.* Hartford, Conn.: 1836.

Goodrich, Samuel. *Ridgefield in 1800.* Edited by Thompson R. Harlow. Hartford: Acorn Club of Connecticut, 1954.

Goodrich, Samuel G. *Recollections of a Lifetime.* 2 vols. New York: 1857.

———. *A System of Universal Geography.* Boston: 1832.

Gordon, N. B. "Diary, 1829–30." In *The New England Mill Village 1790–1860,* edited by Gary Kulik, Roger Parks, and Theodore Z. Penn, 283–307. Cambridge, Mass.: M.I.T. Press, 1982.

Graham, Sylvester. *The Graham Journal of Health and Longevity.* Boston: 1837–39.

———. *A Lecture to Young Men on Chastity Also Intended for the Serious Consideration of Parents and Guardians.* Boston: 1833.

Greeley, Horace. *Recollections of a Busy Life.* New York: 1868.

Green, Miriam R. "A Country Wedding." *The Lowell Offering* V, no. 12 (December 1845): 268–271.

———. "The Paring (or Apple) Bee." *The Lowell Offering* V, no. 3 (March 1845): 149–152.

Grund, Francis. *The Americans in Their Moral, Social and Political Relations.* Boston: 1837.

Guild, James. "From Tunbridge, Vermont, to London, England—The Journal of James Guild, Peddler, Tinker, School-Master, Portrait Painter, from 1818 to 1824." In *Vermont Historical Society Proceedings* 5, no. 3 (September 1937): 249–313.

Hale, Edward Everett. *A New England Boyhood.* Boston: 1893.
Hall, Francis. *Travels in Canada and the United States.* Boston: 1818.
Hall, Margaret. *The Aristocratic Journey: Being the Outspoken Letters of Mrs. Basil Hall Written During a Fourteen Months Sojourn in America. 1827–1828.* Edited by Una Pope-Hennessey. New York: G. P. Putnam's Sons, 1931.
Hamilton, Thomas. *Men and Manners in America.* Boston: 1833.
Harrison, Fosdick. Sermon, c. 1820. Harrison Family.
Hartwell, James. Letter to Mrs. Jerusha Brown, March 26, 1834. Old Sturbridge Village Research Library, Sturbridge, Mass.
Hawthorne, Nathaniel. *The American Notebooks.* Edited by Randall Stewart. New Haven: Yale University Press, 1932.
Hill, Isaac. *The Farmer's Monthly Visitor.* Concord, N.H.: 1839–1840.
Hood, George. *A History of Music in New England.* Boston: 1846.
Howells, William Dean. *Impressions and Experiences.* New York: 1896.
Howland, Southworth Allen. *Steamboat Disasters and Railroad Accidents in the United States.* Worcester, Mass.: 1840.
Hubbard, Newton S. *The Hubbard Homestead.* Brimfield, Mass.: 1895.
Jennings, Jane Grey. "Memoir of Jane Grey Jennings." *Christian Spectator* (Boston, 1828).
Johnston, David Claypool. *Scraps* (Boston), nos. 1–8, 1828–1849.
Kennedy, John Pendleton. *Swallow Barn: Or a Sojourn in the Old Dominion.* Philadelphia: 1832.
Knowlton, Charles. *The Fruits of Philosophy, or the Private Companion of Young Married People.* Boston: 1833 and subsequent editions.
Krimmel, John Lewis. "Quilting Party." Oil painting, 1813. Henry Francis DuPont Winterthur Museum, Winterthur, Del.
Larcom, Lucy. *A New England Girlhood.* Boston: 1889.
Lesley, Susan Lyman. *Recollections of My Mother, Mrs. Ann Jean Lyman of Northampton.* Boston: 1899.
Lincoln, Asa. The Voluntary Accusation and Examination of Harriet Winter, 1831. Old Sturbridge Village Research Library, Sturbridge, Mass.
Long, Zadoc. *From the Journal of Zadoc Long, 1800–73.* Edited by Pierce Long. Caldwell, Idaho: 1943.
Lovell, Lucy Buffum. "Diary, 1840–44." In *Two Quaker Sisters: From the Original Diaries of Elizabeth Buffum Chace and Lucy Buffum Lovell.* New York: Liveright, 1937, 49–109.
Lung, Peter. *A Brief Account of the Life of Peter Lung.* Hartford, Conn.: 1816.

Mann, Horace. *Fourth Annual Report of the Secretary of the Board of Education.* Boston: 1841.

Marryat, Frederick. *A Diary in America, with Remarks on Its Institutions.* New York: 1839.

Martineau, Harriet. *Retrospect of Western Travel.* London: 1838.

———. *Society in America.* 2 vols. New York: 1837.

Mayo, Minerva. The Life and Writings of Minerva Mayo by Herself 1820–25. Old Sturbridge Village Research Library, Sturbridge, Mass.

Melish, John. *Travels Through the United States of America . . . 1806–1811.* London: 1818.

Merriam, Homer. Annals of the Merriam Family. Merriam-Webster Papers, Beinecke Library, Yale University.

Miller, Lewis. *Sketches and Chronicles: The Reflections of a Nineteenth Century Pennsylvania German Folk Artist.* York, Pa.: York County Historical Society, 1966.

Moore, Clement C. "A Visit from St. Nicholas." In *Poems.* New York: 1844, pp. 128–132. First published in *Troy [New York] Sentinel,* December 23, 1823.

Moreau de St. Mery, Mederic. *Moreau de St. Mery's American Journey 1793–1798.* Edited by Kenneth and Anna M. Roberts. New York: Doubleday & Co., 1947.

Mount Family Correspondence. Library of the Museums at Stony Brook, Stony Brook, New York.

Munger, Hiram. *The Life and Religious Experiences of Hiram Munger.* Chicopee Falls, Mass.: 1856.

Northup, Solomon. *Twelve Years a Slave.* Auburn, N.Y.: 1853.

Owen, Robert Dale. *Moral Physiology, or a Brief and Plain Treatise on the Population Question.* New York: 1831.

Pease, Mary. Letter to Pliny Freeman, February 6, 1840. Freeman Family Papers, Old Sturbridge Village Research Library, Sturbridge, Mass.

Porter, Noah. *An Historical Discourse Delivered at the Celebration of the One Hundredth Anniversary of the Erection of the Congregational Church in Farmington, Conn.* Hartford, Conn.: 1873.

Probate Inventories for Brimfield, Chester, Palmer, Shrewsbury and Sturbridge, Massachusetts, 1790–1850. Worcester County Farmers, Mechanics and Storekeepers Inventory Sample, 1790–1850. Transcriptions at Old Sturbridge Village Research Department. Originals in Hampden County Probate Records,

County Courthouse, Springfield, Mass., and Worcester County Probate Records, County Court House, Worcester, Mass.

Rand, Isaac. "Observations on the Hydrocephalus Internus." In *Medical Papers Communicated to the Massachusetts Medical Society*. Vol. I (Boston, 1790): 75–80.

Robinson, Harriet Hanson. *Loom and Spindle: Or Life Among the Early Mill Girls*. New York: 1898.

Rollins, Ellen E. *New England Bygones*. Philadelphia: 1880.

Rush, Benjamin. "An Account of the Manners of the German Inhabitants of Pennsylvania." *Columbian Magazine* 3 (January 1789): 22–30.

———. *An Inquiry into the Effect of Ardent Spirits...*, 7th ed. Boston: 1812.

Searles Family Letters, 1795–1851. Old Sturbridge Village Research Library, Sturbridge, Mass.

Shattuck, Lemuel. *Report of the Sanitary Commission of Massachusetts, 1850*. Cambridge, Mass.: 1948.

Sheldon, Asa. *Life of Asa Sheldon: Wilmington Farmer*. Woburn, Mass.: 1862.

Shirreff, Patrick. *A Tour Through North America*. Edinburgh: 1835.

Sigourney, Lydia Huntley. *Sketch of Connecticut, Forty Years Since*. Hartford, Conn.: 1824.

Snell, Thomas. *A Sermon Delivered June 27th, 1848: Being the 50th Anniversary of His Ordination*. West Brookfield, Mass.: 1848.

Stowe, Harriet Beecher. *Oldtown Folks*. Boston: 1869.

———. *The Pearl of Orr's Island*. New York: 1862.

———. *Poganuc People*. New York, 1878.

Strickland, William. *Journal of a Tour in the United States of America 1794–1795*. Edited by J. E. Strickland. New York: New-York Historical Society, 1971.

Stuart, James. *Three Years in North America*. 2 vols. Edinburgh: 1833.

Thomas, Isaiah. "Songs, Ballads etc. In Three Volumes. Purchased from a Ballad Printer and Seller in Boston, 1813. Bound Up for Preservation, to shew what articles of this kind are in vogue with the Vulgar at this time, 1814." American Antiquarian Society, Worcester, Mass. Annotated and reorganized photocopy version, Arthur F. Shrader, 1982, Old Sturbridge Village Research Library, Sturbridge, Mass.

Thomas, Robert B. *The Farmer's Almanack*. Boston: 1793–1850.

312   BIBLIOGRAPHY

Thompson, Harold W., ed. *A Pioneer Songster: Texts from the Stevens-Douglass Manuscript of Western New York.* Ithaca, N.Y.: Cornell University Press, 1958.
Tocqueville, Alexis de. *Journey to America.* Edited by J. P. Meyer. New Haven: Yale University Press, 1962.
Torrey, Purley. Letter to Christopher Arms, April 23, 1828. Library, Pocumtuck Valley Memorial Association, Deerfield, Mass.
Trollope, Frances. *Domestic Manners of the Americans.* London and New York: 1832.
Tyler, Mary Palmer. *Grandmother Tyler's Book: The Recollections of Mary Palmer Tyler: 1775–1866.* Edited by Frederick Tupper and Mary Tyler Brown. New York: G. P. Putnam's Sons, 1925.
Underwood, Francis. *Quabbin: The Story of a Small Town with Outlooks on Puritan Life.* Boston and London: 1893; reprinted Boston: Northeastern University Press, 1987, with an introduction by Robert A. Gross.
Upham, Joel. Building Contracts 1827–1839. Worcester Historical Museum, Worcester, Mass.
U.S. Bureau of the Census. *A Century of Population Growth from the First Census of the United States to the Twelfth, 1790–1900.* Washington, D.C., 1909.
———. *Historical Statistics of the United States.* 2 vols. Washington, D.C.: GPO, 1975.
U.S. Census Office. *6th Census, 1840. Compendium of the Enumeration of the Inhabitants and Statistics of the United States.* Washington, D.C., 1841.
———. *7th Census, 1850. Statistical View of the United States... Being a Compendium of the Seventh Census.* Washington, D.C., 1854.
Vigne, Godfrey T. *Six Months in America.* Philadelphia: 1833.
Walker, Amasa. "Manufactures of the Household." Paper delivered before the New England Historical and Genealogical Society, 1875.
Ward Family Papers, American Antiquarian Society, Worcester, Mass.
Webb, Catherine, C. "Diary 1815–1816." In *Chronicles of a Pioneer School from 1792 to 1833,* Emily Vanderpoel, comp., 148–150. Cambridge, Mass.: 1883.
Webster, Noah. *An American Dictionary of the English Language.* New York: 1828.
Weld, Isaac. *Travels Through the States of North America, and the Provinces of Upper and Lower Canada.* 2 vols. London: 1807.

White, Mary. Diary, 1836–1849. Old Sturbridge Village Research Library, Sturbridge, Mass.

Whitney, Peter. *History of the County of Worcester.* Worcester, Mass.: 1793.

Wilkinson, Smith. Letter to George White, 1835. In *Memoir of Samuel Slater,* by George White, 126–128. Philadelphia: 1836.

Wilson, John L. *The Code of Honor.* Charleston, S.C.: 1838.

Woodworth, Samuel. "An Appendix on American Festivals, Games and Amusements." In *Festivals, Games and Amusements, Ancient and Modern,* by Horatio Smith, 313–355. New York: 1831.

Wooten, Henry V. "Diary, 1829." In *Plain Folk of the Old South,* by F. W. Owsley, 126–131. Baton Rouge, La.: Louisiana State University Press, 1949.

Worthington, Erastus. *The History of Dedham* [Massachusetts]. Boston: 1827.

Wyche, Rebecca. "Letter, 1833." In *The Plantation Mistress: Women's World in the Old South,* by Catherine E. Clinton, 24. New York: Pantheon Books, 1982.

Secondary Works

Scholarly works and articles drawn on for evidence and interpretation are listed by chapter. The list for chapter I also includes many wide-ranging studies upon which the book, particularly chapter VII, relies.

CHAPTER 1: *A Busy, Bustling, Industrious Population*

Bidwell, Percy W. "The Agricultural Revolution in New England." *American Historical Review* 26, no. 4 (July 1921): 683–702.

———. "Rural Economy in New England at the Beginning of the 19th Century." *Transactions of the Connecticut Academy of Arts and Sciences* 20 (1916): 241–399.

———, and John I. Falconer. *History of Agriculture in the Northern United States, 1620–1860.* Washington: Carnegie Institution, 1925. Reprint. New York: Peter Smith, 1941.

Blassingame, John. *The Slave Community,* rev. ed. New York: Oxford University Press, 1979.

Boorstin, Daniel M. *The Americans: The Colonial Experience.* New York: Random House, 1958.

————. *The Americans: The National Experience*. New York: Random House, 1964.

Boydston, Jeanne. "To Earn Her Daily Bread: Housework and Antebellum Working-Class Subsistence." *Radical History Review* 35 (April 1986): 7–25.

Brown, Richard D. *Modernization: The Transformation of American Life 1600–1865*. New York: Hill and Wang, 1976.

————. "Afterword: From Cohesion to Competition." In *Printing and Society in Early America*, edited by William L. Joyce et al., 300–308. Worcester, Mass.: 1983.

Bushman, Richard. "Family Security in the Transition from Farm to City 1750–1850." *Journal of Family History* 6, no. 3 (Fall 1981): 238–56.

Chudacoff, Howard R. *The Evolution of American Urban Society*. Englewood Cliffs, N.J.: Prentice-Hall, 1975.

Clark, Christopher. "The Household Economy, Market Exchange and the Rise of Capitalism in the Connecticut Valley 1800–1860." *Journal of Social History* 13, no. 2 (Winter 1979): 169–89.

Clinton, Catherine E. *The Plantation Mistress: Women's World in the Old South*. New York: Pantheon Books, 1982.

Cott, Nancy F. *The Bonds of Womanhood: "Woman's Sphere" in New England, 1780–1835*. New Haven: Yale University Press, 1977.

Cowan, Ruth Schwarz. *More Work for Mother: The Ironies of Household Technology from the Open Hearth to the Microwave*. New York: Basic Books, 1983.

Danhof, Clarence. *Change in Agriculture: The Northern United States, 1820–1870*. Cambridge, Mass.: Harvard University Press, 1969.

Davis, Lance E., et al. *American Economic Growth: An Economist's History of the United States*. New York: Harper & Row, 1972.

Dawley, Allen. *Class and Community: The Industrial Revolution in Lynn*. Cambridge, Mass.: Harvard University Press, 1976.

Deetz, James J. F. *In Small Things Forgotten: The Archaeology of Early American Life*. Garden City, N.Y.: Anchor Press/Doubleday, 1977.

Dublin, Thomas. "Women and Outwork in a Nineteenth-Century New England Town: Fitzwilliam, New Hampshire, 1830–1850." In *The Countryside in the Age of Capitalist Transformation: Essays in the Social History of Rural America*, edited by Steven Hahn and Jonathan Prude, 71–102. Chapel Hill, N.C.: University of North Carolina Press, 1985.

———. *Women at Work: The Transformation of Work and Community in Lowell, Massachusetts, 1826–1860.* New York: Columbia University Press, 1979.

———. "Women's Work and the Family Economy: Textiles and Palm Leaf Hatmaking in New England, 1830–1850." *Tocqueville Review* (1983): 297–316.

Dudden, Faye E. *Serving Women: Household Service in Nineteenth Century America.* Middletown, Conn.: Wesleyan University Press, 1983.

Faler, Paul. *Mechanics and Manufacturers in the Early Industrial Revolution: Lynn, Massachusetts, 1780–1860.* Albany, N.Y.: State University of New York Press, 1981.

Faragher, John Mack. *Sugar Creek: Life on the Illinois Prairie.* New Haven: Yale University Press, 1987.

———. *Women and Men on the Overland Trail.* New Haven: Yale University Press, 1979.

Fischer, David Hackett. *Growing Old in America.* New York: Oxford University Press, 1977.

Fletcher, Stevenson W. *Pennsylvania Agriculture and Country Life.* Harrisburg, Pa.: Pennsylvania Historical and Museum Commission, 1940.

Geib, Susan. "Changing Works: Agriculture and Society in Brookfield, Massachusetts, 1785–1820." Ph.D. diss., Boston University, 1981. Ann Arbor, Mich.: University Microfilms.

Genovese, Eugene D. *Roll, Jordan, Roll: The World the Slaves Made.* New York: Vintage Books, 1972.

Gilmore, William J. "Elementary Literacy on the Eve of the Industrial Revolution: Trends in Rural New England, 1760–1830." *Proceedings of the American Antiquarian Society* 92, no. 1 (April 1982): 87–171.

Grey, Lewis C. *History of Agriculture in the Southern United States to 1860.* Washington: Carnegie Institution, 1933; Reprint. New York: Peter Smith, 1958.

Gross, Robert A. "Agriculture and Society in Thoreau's Concord." *Journal of American History* 69 (1982): 42–61.

———. *The Minutemen and Their World.* New York: Hill and Wang, 1976.

Gutman, Herbert. "Work, Culture and Society in Industrializing America." In *Work, Culture and Society in Industrializing America: Essays in American Working-Class and Social History,* 3–78. New York: Knopf, 1975.

Hall, David D. "The Uses of Literacy in New England, 1600–1850." *Printing and Society in Early America*, edited by William L. Joyce, et al. American Antiquarian Society, 1–47. Worcester, Mass.: 1983.

Hamilton, Milton W. *The Country Printer: New York State 1785–1830.* Reprint. Port Washington, N.Y.: I. J. Friedman, 1964.

Henretta, James A. *The Evolution of American Society 1700–1815: An Interdisciplinary Analysis.* Lexington, Mass.: D. C. Heath, 1973.

————. "Families and Farms: Mentalite in Preindustrial America." *William and Mary Quarterly* 3d series 35, no. 1 (1978): 3–31.

Hirsch, Susan E. *Roots of the American Working Class: The Industrialization of Crafts in Newark 1800–1860.* Philadelphia: University of Pennsylvania Press, 1978.

Hummel, Charles. *With Hammer in Hand: The Dominy Craftsmen of East Hampton, New York.* Charlottesville, Va.: University Press of Virginia, 1968.

Jensen, Joan M. *Loosening the Bonds: Mid-Atlantic Farm Women, 1750–1850.* New Haven: Yale University Press, 1986.

————. " 'You May Depend She Does Not Eat Much Idle Bread': Mid-Atlantic Farm Women and Their Historians." *Agricultural History* 61, no. 1 (Winter 1987): 29–46.

Kaestle, Carl F. *Pillars of the Republic: Common Schools and American Society 1780–1860.* New York: Hill and Wang, 1983.

Kelsey, Darwin, ed. *Farming in the New Nation: Interpreting American Agriculture.* Washington, D.C.: Agricultural History Society, 1972.

Larkin, Jack. *Children Everywhere: Dimensions of Childhood in Rural New England.* Sturbridge, Mass.: Old Sturbridge Village, 1987.

————. "The Merriams of Brookfield: Printing in the Society and Culture of Rural Massachusetts in the Early Nineteenth Century." *Proceedings of the American Antiquarian Society* 96, no. 1 (April 1986): 39–73.

————. "The View from New England: Notes on Everyday Life in Rural America to 1850." *American Quarterly* 34, no. 5 (Winter 1982): 244–61.

Lemon, James T. *The Best Poor Man's Country: A Geographical Study of Early Southeastern Pennsylvania.* Baltimore: Johns Hopkins Press, 1972.

————. "Early Americans and Their Social Environments." *Journal of Historical Geography* 6 (1980): 115–31.

Loehr, Rodney. "Self-Sufficiency on the Farm, 1759–1819." *Agricultural History* 26, pt. 1 (1952): 37–42.

Merrill, Michael. "Cash Is Good to Eat: Self-Sufficiency and Exchange in the Rural Economy of the United States." *Radical History Review* 7 (1977): 42–71.

Norton, Mary Beth. "The Evolution of White Women's Experience in Early America." *American Historical Review* 89, no. 3 (June 1984): 607–54.

———. *Liberty's Daughters: The Revolutionary Experience of American Women, 1750–1850*. Boston: Little, Brown, 1980.

Nugent, Walter T. K. *Structures of American Social History*. Bloomington, Ind.: Indiana University Press, 1981.

Power, Richard Lyle. *Planting Corn Belt Culture: The Impress of the Upland Southerner and the Yankee in the Old Northwest*. Indianapolis: Indiana Historical Society, 1953.

Prude, Jonathan. *The Coming of Industrial Order: Town and Factory Life in Rural Massachusetts, 1810–1860*. New York: Cambridge University Press, 1983.

Rock, Howard. *Artisans of the New Republic: The Tradesmen of New York in the Age of Jefferson*. New York: New York University Press, 1981.

Rorabaugh, William J. *The Craft Apprentice in America: From Franklin to the Machine Age*. New York: Oxford University Press, 1986.

Rothenberg, Winifred. "The Market and Massachusetts Farmers 1750–1855." *Journal of Economic History* 41 (1981): 283–314.

Silver, Rollo P. *The American Printer 1787–1825*. Charlottesville, Va.: University Press of Virginia, 1967.

Stilgoe, John. *The Common Landscape of America, 1580 to 1845*. New York: Yale University Press, 1982.

Wilentz, Sean. *Chants Democratic: New York City and the Rise of the American Working Class, 1788–1850*. New York: Oxford University Press, 1984.

Wolf, Stephanie G. *Urban Village: Population, Community and Family Structure in Germantown, Pennsylvania 1683–1800*. Princeton: Princeton University Press, 1976.

Wood, Joseph P. "Elaboration of a Settlement System: The New England Village in the Federal Period." *Journal of Historical Geography* 10, no. 4 (October 1984): 331–56.

Worrell, John E. "Ceramic Production in the Exchange Network of an Agricultural Neighborhood." In *Domestic Potters in the Northeast, 1625–1850: The Archaeology of a Ceramic Tradition*, edited by Sarah Turnbaugh and William Turnbaugh, 153–69. Orlando, Fla.: Academic Press, 1985.

———. "Recreating Low Technology in a Living History Laboratory." In *Domestic Potters in the Northeast, 1625–1850: The Archaeology of a Ceramic Tradition,* edited by Sarah Turnbaugh and William Turnbaugh, 81–97. Orlando, Fla.: Academic Press, 1985.

CHAPTER 2: *The Rhythms and Limits of Life*

Benes, Peter. *The Masks of Orthodoxy: Folk Gravestone Carving in Plymouth County, Massachusetts 1689–1805.* Amherst, Mass.: University of Massachusetts Press, 1977.

Blake, John B. *Public Health in the Town of Boston 1630–1822.* Cambridge, Mass.: Harvard University Press, 1959.

Carvalho, Joseph III. "Rural Medical Practice in Early 19th Century Rural New England." *Historical Journal of Western Massachusetts* 4, no. 1 (Spring 1975): 1–14.

Cressy, David. "The Seasonality of Marriage in Old and New England." *Journal of Interdisciplinary History* 15, no. 1 (Summer 1985): 1–21.

Duffy, John. *Epidemics in Colonial America.* Baton Rouge, La.: Louisiana State University Press, 1953.

Dye, Nancy Schrom, and Daniel Blake Smith. "Mother Love and Infant Death, 1750–1920." *Journal of American History* 73, no. 2 (September 1986): 329–53.

Easterlin, Richard. "Factors in the Decline of Farm Fertility in the United States. Some Preliminary Research Results." *Journal of American History* 63, no. 3 (December 1976): 600–14.

Estes, J. Worth, Philip Cash and Eric H. Christianson, eds. *Medicine in Colonial Massachusetts, 1620–1820.* Boston: Colonial Society of Massachusetts, 1980.

Habenstein, Robert W., and William M. Lamers. *The History of American Funeral Directing.* Milwaukee, Wis.: Bulfin Printers, 1955.

Jackson, Charles O., ed. *Passing: The Vision of Death in America.* Westport, Conn.: Greenwood Press, 1977.

Leavitt, Judith Walzer. *Brought to Bed: Childbirth in America 1750–1950.* New York: Oxford University Press, 1986.

———. " 'Science' Enters the Birthing Room: Obstetrics in America Since the Eighteenth Century." *Journal of American History* 70, no. 2 (September 1983): 281–304.

———, Gunter Risse, Ronald L. Numbers, and Judith Waltzer Leavitt, eds. *Medicine Without Doctors: Home Health Care in American History.* New York: Science History Publications, 1978.

———, and Ronald L. Numbers, eds. *Sickness and Health in American History: Readings in the History of Medicine and Public Health.* Madison, Wis.: 1978.

Lockwood, Rose Ann. "Birth, Illness and Death in 18th-Century New England." *Journal of Social History* 12, no. 1 (Fall 1978): 111–27.

Ludwig, Allan I. *Graven Images: New England Stone Carving and Its Symbolism 1650–1815.* Middletown, Conn.: Wesleyan University Press, 1977.

McClelland, Peter D., and Richard J. Zeckenhauser. *Demographic Dimensions of the New Republic: American Interregional Migration, Vital Statistics and Manumissions, 1800–1860.* New York: Cambridge University Press, 1982.

Osterud, Nancy, and John Fulton. "Family Limitation and Age at Marriage: Fertility Decline in Sturbridge, Massachusetts 1730–1850." *Population Studies* 30, no. 3 (1977): 481–94.

Riznik, Barnes. *Medicine in New England, 1790–1840.* Sturbridge, Mass.: Old Sturbridge Village, 1965.

Rosenberg, Charles. *The Cholera Years: The United States in 1832, 1849, and 1866.* Chicago: University of Chicago Press, 1962.

Rutman, Darrett B., Charles Wetherell and Anita H. Rutman. "Rhythms of Life: Black and White Seasonality in the Early Chesapeake." *Journal of Interdisciplinary History* 15, no. 1 (Summer 1985): 1–21.

Saum, Lewis O. *The Popular Mood of Pre-Civil War America.* Westport, Conn.: Greenwood Press, 1980.

Scholten, Catherine M. *Childbearing in American Society, 1630–1850.* New York: New York University Press, 1985.

———. " 'On the Importance of the Obstetric Art': Changing Customs of Childbirth in America, 1760 to 1825." *William and Mary Quarterly* 3d series 34, no. 3 (July 1977): 426–45.

Shryock, Richard H. *Medicine and Society in America 1660–1860.* New York: New York University Press, 1960.

Smith, Daniel Scott. "The Demographic History of Colonial New England." *Journal of Economic History* 32, no. 1 (March 1972): 165–83.

———. "Differential Mortality in the United States Before 1900." *Journal of Interdisciplinary History* 13, no. 4 (Spring 1983): 735–59.

Stannard, David E., ed. *Death in America.* Philadelphia: University of Pennsylvania Press, 1975.

———. *The Puritan Way of Death.* New York: Oxford University Press, 1977.

Starr, Paul. *The Social Transformation of American Medicine.* New York: Basic Books, 1982.

Steckel, Richard H. "A Dreadful Childhood: The Excess Mortality of American Slaves." *Social Science History* 10, no. 4 (Winter 1986): 427–66.

Temkin-Greener, Helena, and Alan Swedlund. "Fertility Transition in the Connecticut Valley 1740–1850." *Population Studies* 31, no. 2 (1978): 221–35.

Vinovskis, Maris. "Angels' Heads and Weeping Willows: Death in Early America." *Proceedings of the American Antiquarian Society* 86, no. 2 (October 1976): 275–302.

———. *Fertility in Massachusetts from the Revolution to the Civil War.* New York: Academic Press, 1981.

———. "The Jacobson Life Table of 1850: A Critical Reexamination from a Massachusetts Perspective." *Journal of Interdisciplinary History* 8, no. 4 (Spring 1978): 703–24.

———. "Mortality Rates in Massachusetts to 1860." *Journal of Economic History* 32, no. 1 (March 1972): 184–213.

Warner, John Harley. "Power, Conflict and Identity in Mid-Nineteenth-Century American Medicine; Therapeutic Change in the Commercial Hospital in Cincinnati." *Journal of American History* 73, no. 4 (March 1987): 934–56.

Wells, Robert V. *Uncle Sam's Family: Issues and Perspectives in American Demographic History.* Albany, N.Y.: State University of New York Press, 1986.

CHAPTER 3: *Comfortable Habitations*

Boyett, Tanya. "Thomas Handasyd Perkins: An Essay in Material Culture." *Old Time New England* 70 (1980): 45–62.

Brady, Dorothy. "Consumption and the Style of Life." In *American Economic Growth: An Economist's History of the United States.* Edited by James E. Davis, et al. New York: Harper & Row, 1972.

Brown, Marley. "The Use of Oral and Documentary Sources in Historical Archaeology at Mott Farm." In *Historical Archaeology: A
Guide to Substantive and Theoretical Contributions*, edited
by Robert L. Schuyler, 278–83. Farmingdale, N.Y.: Baywood,
1978.

Bushman, Richard. "American High-Style and Vernacular Cultures."
In *Colonial British America: Essays in the History of the Early
Modern Era*, edited by Jack P. Greene and J. R. Pole, 345–83.
Baltimore: Johns Hopkins Press, 1984.

Cummings, Abbott Lowell. *Architecture in Early New England*. Sturbridge, Mass. Old Sturbridge Village, 1984.

———. "Notes on Furnishing a Small New England Farmhouse." *Old
Time New England* 48, no. 3 (Winter 1958): 65–84.

———. *Rural Household Inventories 1675–1775*. Boston: Society for
the Preservation of New England Antiquities, 1964.

Drucker, Lesley M. "Socioeconomic Patterning at an Undocumented
Late 18th Century Lowcountry Site: Spiers Landing, South
Carolina." *Journal of Historical Archaeology* 15, no. 2 (1981):
58–68.

Flaherty, David. *Privacy in Colonial New England*. Charlottesville,
Va.: University Press of Virginia, 1967.

Glassie, Henry. "Artifact and Culture, Architecture and Society." In
*American Material Culture and Folklife: A Prologue and Dia-
logue*, edited by Simon J. Bronner, 47–62. Ann Arbor, Mich.:
UMI Research Press, 1986.

———. *Folk Housing in Middle Virginia: A Structural Analysis of
Historic Artifacts*. Knoxville, Tenn.: University of Tennessee
Press, 1975.

———. *Pattern in the Material Folk Culture of the Eastern United
States*. Philadelphia: University of Pennsylvania Press, 1968.

Gross, Robert A. "Lonesome in Eden: Dickinson, Thoreau and the
Problem of Community in Nineteenth-Century New En-
gland." *Canadian Review of American Studies* 14, no. 1
(Spring 1983): 1–17.

Haines, Carol L. *"Forms to Sett on": A Social History of Concord
Seating Furniture* Concord, Mass.: Concord Antiquarian Museum, 1984.

Jaffe, David. "One of the Primitive Sort: Portrait Painters of the Rural
North, 1760–1860." In *The Countryside in the Age of Capital-
ist Transformation: Essays in the Social History of Rural
America*, edited by Steven Hahn and Jonathan Prude, 103–

38. Chapel Hill, N.C.: University of North Carolina Press, 1985.

Jobe, Brock. "Urban Craftsmen and Design." In *New England Furniture: The Colonial Era*, edited by Brock Jobe and Myrna Kaye, 3–46. Boston: Houghton Mifflin, 1984.

Kenney, John T. *The Hitchcock Chair: The Story of a Connecticut Yankee—Lambert Hitchcock of Hitchcockville—and an Account of the Restoration of His 19th-Century Manufactory.* New York: C. N. Potter, 1971.

Kniffen, Fred, and Henry Glassie. "Building in Wood in the Eastern United States: A Time-Place Perspective." *The Geographical Review* 56 (1966): 40–66.

Lees, William B., and Kathryn M. Kimery-Lees. "The Function of Colono-Indian Ceramics: Insights from Limerick Plantation, South Carolina." *Journal of Historical Archaeology* 15, no. 2 (1981): 58–68.

Mayhew, Edgar DeN., and Minor Meyers, Jr. *A Documentary History of American Furnishings to 1915.* New York: Scribners, 1980.

Miller, George L. "Marketing Ceramics in North America: An Introduction." *Winterthur Portfolio: A Journal of American Material Culture* 19, pt. 1 (Spring 1984): 1–6.

Noble, Allen G. *Wood, Brick and Stone: The North American Settlement Landscape I: Houses.* Amherst, Mass.: University of Massachusetts Press, 1984.

Nylander, Jane C. "Come, Gather Round the Chimney." *Natural History* 90 (October 1981): 97–104.

Peterson, Harold L. *Americans at Home . . . A Pictorial Source Book of American Interiors.* New York: Scribners, 1971.

Schiffer, Margaret B. *Chester County, Pennsylvania Probate Inventories 1684–1850.* Exton, Pa.: Schiffer, 1974.

Schuyler, Robert L., ed. *Archaeological Perspectives on Ethnicity in America: Afro-American and Asian-American Culture History.* Farmingdale, N.Y.: 1980.

———. "The Spoken Word, the Written Word, Observed Behavior and Preserved Behavior: the Contexts Available to the Archaeologist." In *Historical Archaeology: A Guide to Substantive and Theoretical Contributions*, edited by Robert L. Schyler, 269–77. Farmingdale, N.Y.: Baywood, 1978.

Shammas, Carole. "Consumer Behavior in Colonial America." *Social Science History* 6, no. 1 (Winter 1982): 67–86.

———. "The Domestic Environment in Early Modern England and America." *Journal of Social History* 14, no. 1 (Fall 1980): 3–24.

————. "How Self-Sufficient Was Early America?" *Journal of Interdisciplinary History* 13, no. 2 (Autumn 1982): 247–72.

Skemer, Don C. "David Alling's Chair Manufactory: Craft Industrialization in Newark, New Jersey, 1801–1854." *Winterthur Portfolio: A Journal of American Material Culture* 22, no. 1 (Spring 1987): 1–23.

Soltow, Lee. "Egalitarian America and its Inegalitarian Housing in the Federal Period." *Social Science History* 9, no. 2 (Spring 1985): 199–213.

Stachiw, Myron O. "Impermanent Architecture in the City: Examples from Nineteenth-Century New England." In *Perspectives in Vernacular Architecture*, Vol. 2, edited by Camille Wells, 232. Columbia, Mo.: 1986.

————, and Nora Pat Small. "Tradition and Transformation: Rural Society and Architectural Change in Nineteenth Century Central Massachusetts." In *Perspectives in Vernacular Architecture*, Vol. 3, edited by Thomas Carter and Bernard Herman, Columbia, Mo.: 1988.

Sweeney, Kevin. "Mansion People: Kinship, Class and Architecture in Western Massachusetts in the Mid-Eighteenth Century." *Winterthur Portfolio: A Journal of American Material Culture* 19, no. 4 (Winter 1984): 231–57.

Trent, Robert F. *Hearts and Crowns: Folk Chairs of the Connecticut Coast.* New Haven: New Haven Colony Historical Society, 1978.

Upton, Dell. "Architectural Change in Colonial Rhode Island: The Mott House as a Case Study." *Old Time New England* 69 (1979): 3–4, 18–33.

————. "Pattern Books and Professionalism: Aspects of the Transformation of Domestic Architecture in America, 1800–1860." *Winterthur Portfolio: A Journal of American Material Culture* 19, no. 2/3 (Summer/Autumn 1984): 107–50.

———— "Traditional Timber Framing." In *The Material Culture of the Wooden Age*, edited by Brooke Hindle, 35–91. Tarrytown, N.Y.: Sleepy Hollow Restorations, 1981.

————. "Vernacular Domestic Architecture in Eighteenth-Century Virginia." *Winterthur Portfolio: A Journal of American Material Culture* 17, no. 2/3 (Summer/Autumn 1982): 95–120.

Worrell, John E. "Scars Upon the Earth: Physical Evidence of Dramatic Social Change at the Stratton Tavern." In *Proceedings of the Conference on Northeastern Archaeology*, edited by James A. Moore, 133–45. University of Massachusetts at Amherst, Department of Anthropology *Research Reports* 19 (January 1980).

Zea, Philip. "Rural Craftsmen and Design." In *New England Furniture: The Colonial Era,* edited by Brock Jobe and Myrna Kaye, 47–72. Boston: Houghton Mifflin, 1984.

CHAPTER 4: *The Masks Which Custom Had Prescribed*

Anderson, Larry. "Joseph Palmer's Beard." In *Directions of a Town: A History of Harvard, Massachusetts,* by Robert C. Anderson, 105–8. Harvard, Mass.: Harvard Common Press, 1976.

Apperson, G. L. *The Social History of Smoking.* New York: G. P. Putnam's Sons, 1916.

Banner, Lois C. *American Beauty: A Social History Through Two Centuries of the American Idea, Ideal, and Image of the Beautiful Woman.* Chicago: Knopf, 1983.

Beall, Otho T., Jr. *"Aristotle's Masterpiece* in America: A Landmark in the Folklore of Medicine." *William and Mary Quarterly* 3d series 20, no. 2 (April 1963): 216–20.

Benes, Peter, ed. *American Speech: 1600 to the Present. Annual Proceedings of the Dublin Seminar for New England Folklife.* Vol. 8. Boston: Boston University, 1985.

———. *Foodways in the Northeast Annual Proceedings of the Dublin Seminar for New England Folklife.* Vol. 7. Boston: Boston University, 1984.

Calvert, Karin. "Children in American Family Portraiture, 1670 to 1810." *William and Mary Quarterly* 3d series 39 (January 1982): 57–113.

Cott, Nancy F. "Passionlessness: An Interpretation of Victorian Sexual Ideology, 1790–1850." *Signs* 4, no. 2 (Winter 1978): 219–36.

Cummings, Richard Osborne. *The American and His Food.* Chicago: University of Chicago Press, 1940.

Elias, Norbert. *The Civilizing Process: The History of Manners.* Translated by Edmund Jephcott. New York: Urizen Books, 1978.

Flaherty, David. "Law and the Enforcement of Morals in Early America." *Perspectives in American History* 5 (1971): 203–53.

Fogel, Robert W., et al. "Secular Changes in American and British Stature and Nutrition." *Journal of Interdisciplinary History* 14, no. 2 (Autumn 1983): 445–81.

Haltunen, Karen. *Confidence Men and Painted Women: A Study of Middle-Class Culture in America, 1830–1870.* New Haven: Yale University Press, 1982.

Isaac, Rhys. *The Transformation of Virginia, 1740-1790.* Chapel Hill, N.C.: University of North Carolina Press for the Institute for Early American History and Culture, 1982.

Johnson, Claudia. "That Guilty Third Tier: Prostitution in Nineteenth-Century American Theaters." *American Quarterly* 27, no. 5 (December 1975): 575-84.

Kidwell, Claudia, and Margaret B. Christman. *Suiting Everyone: The Democratization of Clothing in America.* Washington, D.C.: Smithsonian Institution Press, 1974.

Komlos, John. "The Height and Weight of West Point Cadets: Dietary Change in Antebellum America." *Journal of Economic History* 47, no. 4 (December 1987): 897-928.

McClellan, Elisabeth. *History of American Costume 1607-1870.* New York: Tudor Publishing, 1937.

McMahon, Sarah. "A Comfortable Subsistence: The Changing Composition of Diet in Rural New England, 1620-1840." *William and Mary Quarterly* 3d series 42 (January 1985): 26-65.

———. "A Comfortable Subsistence: A History of Diet in New England, 1630-1850." Ph.D. diss., Brandeis University, 1981. Ann Arbor, Mich.: University Microfilms.

Mathews, M. M., ed. *The Beginnings of American English: Essays and Comments.* Chicago: University of Chicago Press, 1931.

Mencken, H. L. *The American Language.* 4th ed. New York: Knopf, 1936.

———. *The American Language: Supplement II.* New York: Knopf, 1948.

Mohr, James C. *Abortion in America: The Origins and Evolution of National Policy 1800-1900.* New York: Oxford University Press, 1978.

Nissenbaum, Stephen. *Sex, Diet and Debility in Jacksonian America: Sylvester Graham and Health Reform.* Westport, Conn.: Greenwood Press, 1980.

Nylander, Jane C. Notes on Clothing. Unpublished ms., 1980. Old Sturbridge Village Research Library, Sturbridge, Mass.

Parr, Albert E. "Heating, Lighting, Plumbing and Human Relations." *Landscape* 19, no. 1 (Winter 1970): 28-29.

Porter, Roy. " 'The Secrets of Generation Display'd': *Aristotle's Masterpiece* in Eighteenth-Century England." *Eighteenth-Century Life* 9, no. 3 (May 1985): 1-16.

Robert, Joseph C. *The Story of Tobacco in America.* New York: Knopf, 1952.

Rothman, Ellen K. *Hands and Hearts: A History of Courtship in America.* New York: Basic Books, 1984.

———. "Sex and Self-Control: Middle-Class Courtship in America, 1770–1870." *Journal of Social History* 18, no. 4 (Spring 1982): 409–25.

Smith, Billy G. "The Material Lives of Laboring Philadelphians, 1750 to 1800." *William and Mary Quarterly* 3d series 38, no. 2 (April 1981): 163–202.

Smith, Daniel Scott, and Michael Hindus. "Premarital Pregnancy in America 1640–1971: An Overview and an Interpretation." *Journal of Interdisciplinary History* 5, no. 4 (Spring 1975): 537–70.

Smith, David C., and Anne E. Bridges. "The Brighton Market: Feeding Nineteenth-Century Boston." *Agricultural History* 56 (January 1982): 87–113.

Stansell, Christine. *City of Women: Sex and Class in New York, 1789–1860.* New York: Knopf, 1986.

Stiles, Henry Reed. *Bundling: Its Origin, Progress and Decline in America.* Albany, N.Y.: 1871.

Warwick, Edward, Henry Pitz, and Alexander Wyckoff. *Early American Dress: The Colonial and Revolutionary Periods. The History of American Dress,* Vol. II. Edited by Alexander Wyckoff. New York: B. Blom, 1965.

CHAPTER 5: *The Population Is All in Motion*

Dunbar, Seymour. *A History of Travel in America.* 4 vols. Indianapolis: Bobbs-Merrill, 1915.

Holmes, Oliver W., and Peter T. Rohrbach. *Stagecoach East: Stagecoach Days in the East from the Colonial Period to the Civil War.* Washington, D.C.: Smithsonian Institution Press, 1983.

Hunter, Louis C. *Steamboats on the Western Rivers: An Economic and Technological History.* Cambridge, Mass.: Harvard University Press, 1949.

Katz, Michael, Michael J. Doucet and Mark J. Stern. "Migration and the Social Order in Erie County, New York: 1855." *Journal of Interdisciplinary History* 8, no. 4 (Spring 1978): 669–701.

Knights, Peter. *The Plain People of Boston.* New York: Oxford University Press, 1971.

———, and Stephan Thernstrom. "Men in Motion: Some Data and Speculations about Urban Population Mobility in the Nineteenth Century." In *Anonymous Americans: Explorations in Nineteenth-Century Social History*, edited by Tamara K. Hareven, 17–47. Englewood Cliffs, N.J.: Prentice-Hall, 1971.

Parkerson, Donald. "How Mobile Were Nineteenth-Century Americans?" *Historical Methods* 15 (1982): 99–109.

Parks, Roger. *Roads and Travel in New England, 1790–1840.* Sturbridge, Mass.: Old Sturbridge Village, 1967.

————. "Roads in New England, 1790–1840." Ph.D. diss., Michigan State University, 1964. Ann Arbor, Mich.: University Microfilms.

Phillips, James Duncan. "Transportation in Essex County." *Essex Institute Historical Collections* 85, no. 3 (July 1949): 248–80.

Pred, Allan. *Urban Growth and the Circulation of Information: The United States System of Cities, 1790–1840.* Cambridge, Mass.: M.I.T. Press, 1973.

Rabinowitz, Richard. The View from the Road: New Englanders at Home. Unpublished paper, 1970. Old Sturbridge Village Research Library, Sturbridge, Mass.

Taylor, George Rogers. *The Transportation Revolution, 1815–1860.* The Economic History of the United States. Vol. 4. New York: Rinehart and Company, 1951.

CHAPTER 6: *The Practice of Music*

Buechner, Alan C. "Introduction and Notes." *The New England Harmony: A Collection of Early American Choral Music.* Folkways Record Album FA 2377, New York, 1964.

Chase, Gilbert. *America's Music from the Pilgrims to the Present.* rev. 2d ed. New York: McGraw-Hill, 1966.

Clarke, Garry E. *Essays on American Music,* Westport, Conn.: Greenwood Press, 1977.

Coffin, Tristram P. *The British Traditional Ballad in North America.* rev. ed. Philadelphia: University of Pennsylvania Press, 1963.

Crawford, Richard J. "A Historian's Introduction to Early American Music." *Proceedings of the American Antiquarian Society* 89, no. 2 (October 1979): 261–98.

Damon, S. Foster. "The History of Square Dancing." *Proceedings of the American Antiquarian Society* 62, no. 1 (April 1952): 63–98.

Epstein, Dena J. *Sinful Tunes and Spirituals: Black Folk Music to the Civil War.* Urbana: University of Illinois Press, 1977.

———. "A White Origin for the Black Spiritual: An Invalid Theory and How It Grew." *American Music* 1, no. 2 (Summer 1983): 53–59.

Flanders, Helen Hartness, ed. and comp. *Ancient Ballads Traditionally Sung in New England.* 4 vols. Philadelphia: American Folklore Society, 1960–65.

Garst, John F. "Mutual Reinforcement and the Origins of Spirituals." *American Music* 4, no. 4 (Winter 1986): 390–406.

Hoover, Cynthia Adams. "Epilogue to Secular Music in Early Massachusetts." In *Music in Colonial Massachusetts II: Music in Homes and in Churches,* edited by Barbara Lambert, 715–867. Boston: Colonial Society of Massachusetts, 1985.

Keller, Kate Van Winkle, and Joy Van Cleef. "Selected American Dances and their English Sources." In *Music in Colonial Massachusetts I: Music in Public Places,* edited by Barbara Lambert, 3–74. Boston: Colonial Society of Massachusetts, 1980.

Laws, G. Malcolm. *American Balladry from British Broadsides.* Philadelphia: American Folklore Society, 1957.

———. *Native American Balladry: A Descriptive Study and a Bibliographic Syllabus.* rev. ed. Philadelphia: American Folklore Society, 1964.

Levine, Lawrence. *Black Culture and Black Consciousness: Afro-American Folk Thought from Slavery to Freedom.* New York: 1977.

Lowens, Irving. *Music and Musicians in Early America.* New York: W. W. Norton, 1964.

Osterhout, Paul R. "Note Reading and Regular Singing in Eighteenth-Century New England." *American Music* 4, no. 2 (Summer 1986): 125–44.

Tawa, Nicholas E. *Sweet Songs for Gentle Americans: The Parlor Song in America 1790–1860.* Bowling Green, Ohio: Bowling Green University Popular Press, 1980.

CHAPTER 7: *Occasions to Meet Together*

Atherton, Lewis S. *The Pioneer Merchant in Mid-America.* repr. New York: Greenwood Press, 1968.

———. *The Southern Country Store, 1800–1860.* Baton Rouge, La.: Louisiana State University Press, 1949.

Boylan, Ann M. "Women in Groups: An Analysis of Women's Benevolent Organizations in New York and Boston, 1797–1840." *Journal of American History* 71, no. 3 (December 1984): 497–523.

Breen, Timothy. "Horses and Gentlemen: The Cultural Significance of Gambling Among the Virginia Gentry." *William and Mary Quarterly* 3d series 39, no. 2 (April 1977): 239–57.

Brown, Richard D. "The Emergence of Urban Society in Rural Massachusetts, 1760–1820." *The Journal of American History* 61, no. 1 (Summer 1974): 29–51.

Bruce, Dickson D. *And They All Sang Hallelujah: Plain-Folk Camp Meeting Religion, 1800–1845*. Knoxville, Tenn.: University of Tennessee Press, 1974.

———. *Violence and Culture in the Antebellum South*. Austin, Tex.: University of Texas Press, 1979.

Davis, David B. "The Movement to Abolish Capital Punishment in America, 1787–1861." *American Historical Review* 63 (January 1957): 23–51.

Glenn, Myra C. "School Discipline and Punishment in Antebellum America." *Journal of the Early Republic* 1, no. 4 (Winter 1981): 395–408.

Gorn, Elliott J. " 'Gouge, Fight, Pull Hair and Scratch': The Significance of Fighting in the Southern Backcountry." *American Historical Review* 90, no. 1 (February 1985): 18–43.

Greenberg, Kenneth S. *Masters and Statesmen: The Political Culture of American Slavery*. Baltimore: Johns Hopkins Press, 1986.

Hampel, Robert L. *Temperance and Prohibition in Massachusetts, 1813–1852*. Ann Arbor, Mich.: UMI Research Press, 1982.

Johnson, Paul E. *A Shopkeeper's Millenium: Society and Revivals in Rochester, New York, 1815–1837*. New York: Hill and Wang, 1978.

Larkin, Jack. "Gathering Places." *Old Sturbridge Visitor* 21, no. 4 (Winter 1981–82): 4–8.

———. "Remembering the Sabbath." *Old Sturbridge Visitor* 20, no. 4 (Winter 1980–81): 4–8.

———. "Zeloda Barrett's World." *Social Education* (November/December 1975): 1–7.

Lender, Mark E., and James Kirby Martin. *Drinking in America: A History*. New York: Free Press, 1976.

McDade, Thomas M. "Introduction: A Note on the Crime, the Trial, and the Execution." In *The Annals of Murder: A Bibliography of Pamphlets on American Murders From Colonial Times to*

1960, edited by Thomas M. McDade. Norman, Okla.: University of Oklahoma Press, 1961.

Matthews, Donald G. "The Second Great Awakening as an Organizing Process: An Hypothesis." *American Quarterly* 21, no. 1 (Spring 1969): 23–43.

Melder, Keith. *The Village and the Nation.* Sturbridge, Mass.: Old Sturbridge Village, 1976.

Nichol, Jessica F. *Quilted for Friends: Delaware Valley Signature Quilts, 1840–1855.* Winterthur, Del.: Henry Fronis DuPont Winterthur Museum, 1986.

Nylander, Jane C. "Toward Comfort and Uniformity in New England Meetinghouses, 1750–1850." In *New England Meetinghouse and Church: 1630–1850,* Vol. 4, *Annual Proceedings of the Dublin Seminar for New England Folklife,* edited by Peter Benes, 86–101. Boston: Boston University Press, 1979.

Owsley, Frank L. *Plain Folk of the Old South.* Baton Rouge, La.: Louisiana State University Press, 1949.

Rabinowitz, Richard. "A Revival of Religion." Unpublished paper, 1969. Old Sturbridge Village Research Library, Sturbridge, Mass.

Rice, Kym S. *Early American Taverns: For the Entertainment of Friends and Strangers.* Chicago: Regnery Gateway, 1983.

Rorabaugh, William J. *The Alcoholic Republic: An American Tradition.* New York: Oxford University Press, 1979.

Rothman, David J. *The Discovery of the Asylum: Social Order and Disorder in the Early Republic.* Boston: Little, Brown, 1971.

Ryan, Mary P. *Cradle of the Middle Class: The Family in Oneida County, New York 1790–1835.* New York: Cambridge University Press, 1981.

Scott, Ann Firor. "On Seeing and Not Seeing: A Case of Historical Invisibility." *Journal of American History* 71, no. 1 (June 1984): 7–21.

Tyrell, Ian R. *Sobering Up: From Temperance to Prohibition in Antebellum America, 1800–1860.* Westport, Conn.: Greenwood Press, 1979.

West, Mark Irwin. "A Spectrum of Spectators: Circus Audiences in Nineteenth-Century America." *Journal of Social History* 15, no. 2 (Winter 1981): 265–70.